Allegiance, Opposition, and Misunderstanding

Allegiance, Opposition, and Misunderstanding

A Narrative Critical Approach to Mark's Christology

BY DEVEN K. MACDONALD

Foreword by Ernest van Eck

◆PICKWICK *Publications* · Eugene, Oregon

ALLEGIANCE, OPPOSITION, AND MISUNDERSTANDING
A Narrative Critical Approach to Mark's Christology

Copyright © 2018 Deven K. MacDonald. All rights reserved. Except for brief quotations in critical publications or reviews, no part of this book may be reproduced in any manner without prior written permission from the publisher. Write: Permissions, Wipf and Stock Publishers, 199 W. 8th Ave., Suite 3, Eugene, OR 97401.

Pickwick Publications
An Imprint of Wipf and Stock Publishers
199 W. 8th Ave., Suite 3
Eugene, OR 97401

www.wipfandstock.com

PAPERBACK ISBN: 978-1-5326-1129-2
HARDCOVER ISBN: 978-1-5326-1131-5
EBOOK ISBN: 978-1-5326-1130-8

Cataloging-in-Publication data:

Names: MacDonald, Deven K. | van Eck, Ernest (foreword).

Title: Allegiance, opposition, and misunderstanding : a narrative critical approach to Mark's christology / by Deven K. MacDonald, foreword by Ernest van Eck.

Description: Eugene, OR : Pickwick Publications, 2018 | Includes bibliographical references and index.

Identifiers: ISBN 978-1-5326-1129-2 (paperback) | ISBN 978-1-5326-1131-5 (hardcover) | ISBN 978-1-5326-1130-8 (ebook)

Subjects: LCSH: Bible. Mark—Criticism, interpretation, etc. | Jesus Christ—History of doctrines—Early church, ca. 30-600.

Classification: LCC BT198 M2 2018 (print) | LCC BT198 (ebook)

Manufactured in the U.S.A.   03/06/18

To Patrick and Evelyn. May you see the revelation of the Son of God and offer him your allegiance.

Contents

Foreword by Ernest van Eck | ix
Acknowledgments | xiii
Abbreviations | xiv

1 Introducing a Narrative Critical Approach to "Son of God" in Mark | 1
2 Legitimacy of a Narratological Approach to Mark | 21
3 Placing "Son of God" in History, Research, and Context | 49
4 Son of God in Mark | 80
5 A Synchronic Approach to Son of God Theology in Mark | 137
6 Concluding Thoughts and Reflections | 175

Appendix | 183
Bibliography | 185
Ancient Documents Index | 201

Foreword

By Ernest van Eck

Since the seminal work of Rhoads and Michie on Mark as a story, narrative criticism, also known as narratology, has come a long way.[1] As a result of Rhoads and Michie's publication, several publications saw the light that took Mark's narrative structure seriously. The reading of Mark, as a story, also became interdisciplinary. The works of literary theorists, such as Boris Uspensky (*A poetics of composition: The structure of the artistic text and typology of a compositional form*; 1973), Mieke Bal (*De theorie van vertellen en verhalen: Inleiding in de narratologie*; 1978), Gerard Genette (*Narrative discourse*; 1980), and Franz Stanzel (*The theory of narrative*; 1986), now were part of the reading of Mark from a narrative point of view. Using the main tenets of literary theory, concepts such as narrator, implied author and implied reader, real author and real reader, narrative point of view, and narrative world, now were the tools of the trade.[2] Also in focus came several studies on the development of characters in a narrative (as round or flat characters), the way in which a narrator uses time (as story time or narrative time), and the role space, as focal space, plays in a narrative. Narrative criticism, as a synchronic reading of a text, was on the map.

As narrative criticism as exegetical method developed, so did the understanding of the titles used for Jesus in the gospels. Previously the titles used in the gospels to describe Jesus in the gospels were studied in terms what is known as "titular Christology." Now the focus shifted from a "high Christology" to what is now known as narrative Christology, that is, the

---

1. This seminal work on Mark read as a story was initially published by Rhoads and Michie. For the most recent edition of this work, see Rhoads, Dewey, and Michie, *Mark As Story*.

2. See, for example, Peterson, "Point of View in Mark."

study of the meaning of the titles used for Jesus as they develop in a gospel narrative. Contributions to this new approach are many, but the name of Robert Tannehill stands out, especially with regards to Mark.[3] His work on the narrative Christology in Mark surely was the impetus for many studies with the same focus, of which the most recent is the work of Malbon (2009), titled *Mark's Jesus: Characterization as narrative Christology*.

In this publication, the author builds on previous work done on Mark as narrative, and narrative Christology, with an insightful reading of the meaning of Jesus as Son of God in Mark. After introducing the narrative-critical approach to understand the title Son of God in Mark, focusing mainly on the so-called "secrecy in Mark," framing it as misunderstanding, MacDonald focus on Mark's genre, describing it as *bioi*, a genre that seems to best fit the data which is especially interested in revealing Jesus as Son of God in Mark, a choice, he believes, strengthens the revelatory dimension of the misunderstanding theme in Mark.

To set the scene for his interpretation of the Son of God title in Mark, MacDonald first attends to the question on what, in the ancient world, it meant to be the "Son of God." Attention is given to the Old Testament concept of Son of God, the manner it is used in the Dead Sea Scrolls, its use for divine men in Greaco-Roman mythology, in the hero myths on Heracles and Perseus, and the possibility that the Roman imperial worship should be seen as the context in which the title in Mark should be understood. In this discussion, the usage of Son of God in the Synoptics and in the Pauline writings is also examined. He concludes that the most fitting hermeneutical context to approach Son of God in Mark's gospel is the Old Testament and its twin themes of royal Messiah and Son of God.

In his own narrative-critical reading of the Son of God title in Mark, MacDonald concludes that Mark's Christology serves a definitive goal of evoking his readers to consider closely aligning themselves with Jesus and adopting the motif of allegiance that is present throughout the narrative. Mark as narrator, by using specific chosen literary devices, presents Jesus as the Son of God, especially as climaxed in the centurion's words in Mark 15:39. Through the literary devices used, the implied reader of the narrative is invited to identify with Jesus as Son of God. One could argue that this is not new. But this is not where MacDonald's contribution lies. He also convincingly argues that the themes of allegiance, understanding, and misunderstanding are germane to understand Mark's presentation of Jesus as Son of God. By developing the tension in his narrative around these themes, Mark leads the reader to a point of anxiousness where one asks,

---

3. See also Kingsbury, *Christology of Mark's Gospel*.

"when and who will see that Jesus is the Son of God"? It is only in the unlikeliest of characters, the centurion, that this misunderstanding is resolved. By shaping his narrative in such a way, Mark opens the call of discipleship to whoever will switch allegiance from Caesar son of god, to Jesus, the true Son of God (discipleship). The motif of misunderstanding is resolved at the crucifixion with Jesus because the "secret" is out. The reader, then, is faced with two options: allegiance or opposition to Mark's Jesus.

MacDonald's narrative-critical reading of Mark truly stands in the tradition of a narrative-critical approach to Mark, and his presentation of Mark's understand of Jesus as Son of God in Mark is insightful and new. It will be interesting to see, in future, how scholars with the same interest engage with his proposed understand of Jesus as Son of God in Mark's narrative.

Acknowledgments

THERE ARE A NUMBER of people I'd like to mention. First, I'd like to thank the University of Pretoria for allowing me the privilege to study, research, and write at their institution. To my supervisor, Ernest van Eck, I am beyond thankful for your tireless help. Your attention to detail, careful consideration of my work, and helpful suggestions have made this project a success.

To the innumerable scholars and theologians who have helped me, I wish to express my gratitude. To Keith Bodner who first taught me the subtly of narrative criticism; to Stephen Dempster, who always modeled the very best of gospel-informed scholarship; and to Craig Evans, who opened my eyes to literature of the Ancient World, to these men, I say thank you.

To the family at Summerside Community Church, thank you for allowing me the freedom to delve into the Gospel of Mark and complete this work. Your encouragement and prayers have been a blessing. It is my pleasure to share with you each week the revelation of the Son of God. To those who helped me in the editing process, Liz Fildey, Kat Dimoff, and Chris Lear, I say thank you.

Finally, thank you to my parents, Keith and Lucille, from whom I first came to hear of the great narratives and story of the Bible. To my dear wife Heather, for a thousand reasons, this being but one, I say thank you. Your support, help, and love over the years have made this possible. I love you.

Abbreviations

Apollod	Apollodorus
Arrian, *Anab*	Arrian, *Anabasis of Alexander*
Athenaeus *Deipn.*	Athenaeus, *Deipnosophistae*
BCE	Before the Common Era
BGU	*Aegyptische Urkunden aus den Königlichen Staatlichen Museen zu Berlin, Griechische Urkunden.* 15 vols. Berlin, 1895–1983
CIA	*Corpus inscriptionum atticarum.* Edited by W. Dittenberger et al. 4 vols. Berlin: G. Reimer, 1873–1902
CIG	*Corpus inscriptionum graecarum*
CE	Common Era
Col.	Column
1–2 Cor	1–2 Corinthians
Dan	Daniel
Deut	Deuteronomy
Dio Cassius *Hist. rom*	Dio Cassius, *Historia romana*
DSS	Dead Sea Scrolls
Exod	Exodus
FGH	*Die fragmente der griechischen historiker*
Gal	Galatians
Gen	Genesis
Heb	Hebrews

ABBREVIATIONS

Homer *Il.*	Homer, *The Illiad*
Hos	Hosea
IG	*Inscriptiones graecae.* Editio minor. Berlin, 1924–
IGR	*Inscriptions graecae ad res romanas pertinentes.* Edited R. Cagnat et al. 4 vols. Paris: Leroux, 1911–1927
ILS	*Inscriptiones latinae selectee.* Edited H. Dessau. 3 vols. Dublin: Weidmann, 1974
Isa	Isaiah
Jas	James
Jer	Jeremiah
Josh	Joshua
Judg	Judges
LXX	Septuagint
Mal	Malachi
Matt	Matthew
MS(S)	Manuscript(s)
NT	New Testament
Num	Numbers
OGIS	Orientis graeci inscriptiones selectae. Edited by W. Dittenberger. 2 vols. Leipzig, 1903–1905
OT	Old Testament
Ovid *Metam.*	*Ovid, Metamorphasis*
1–2 Pet	1–2 Peter
Phil	Philippians
Philo *Eternity*	Philo, *On the Eternity of the World*
Pliny *Nat.*	Pliny, *Naturalis Historia*
Plutarch *Alex*	Plutarch, *On the Fortune of the Virtue of Alexander*
P.Oxy	Oxyrhynchus Papyrus
Ps/Pss	Psalms
Pss. Sol	*Psalms of Solomon*

Rev	Revelation
Rom	Romans
1–2 Sam	1–2 Samuel
SB	*Sammelbuch griechischer Urkunde aus* Ägypten. Edited by F. Preisigke, et al. 5 vols. 1915–1955
Strabo *Geogr*	Strabo, *Geographica*
SIG	*Sylloge inscriptionum graecarum*
TDNT	*Theologcal Dictionary of the New Testament.* Edited by Gerhard Kittel and Gerhard Friedrich. Translated by Geofferey W. Bromiley. 10 vols. Grand Rapids, MI: Eerdmans, 1964–1976
1–2 Thess	1–2 Thessalonians
1–2 Tim	1–2 Timothy
Vol.	Volume
Wis	*Wisdom of Solomon*
Zech	Zechariah

1

Introducing a Narrative Critical Approach to "Son of God" in Mark

SETTING THE STAGE: INTRODUCTION

FOR NUMEROUS CHRISTIANS THROUGHOUT the ages the assertion that Jesus is the "Son of God" has been understood as a simple proposition, one that possess ontological and cosmic dimensions. After all, orthodox, trinitarian theology is something that the Church affirmed, and something that the Holy Scriptures seems to clearly teach.

In the Gospel of Mark, for example, the locale to which the majority of our time and attention will be given, Jesus is called the Son of God in the opening line (textual issue not withstanding). He is next named "Son" by a voice from heaven at the baptismal scene (Mark 1:11). The demonic world seems to clearly understand this reality based on the narrative of Mark (Mark 1:24; 3:11; 5:7). At yet another significant juncture, the transfiguration (Mark 9:7), Jesus is again called "Son" by a voice from heaven. The reality that Jesus is the Son of God is hinted at, implied, and referenced a number of times (Mark 12:1–2; 13:32; 14:36; 15:39), the final time by the most unlikely of voices, a Roman centurion. Obviously, then, the divine sonship of Jesus is a significant theme in Mark's Gospel.

For many, it is an axiom that does not require much defense or explanation. However, the application of higher criticism to the Synoptic Gospels has yielded a host of interpretation about Jesus' identity and the manner in which the Evangelists understood the title. In the twentieth century, opinions about how this title is to be understood abounded—with some arguing that the Gospel writers were drawing from Divine Man mythology in the Greco-Roman world, and others proposing that it primarily refers to Jesus as "Son of David Messiah."

One of the reasons for the diverse manner in which the title is understood is that the various disciplines used to approach the primary documents seemed to function in relative isolation. For example, a classic historical critic of the New Testament may ignore the literary dimensions of the text and arrive at an understanding of Jesus that is somewhat, if not entirely, at odds with the Jesus in the actual story. Or, to put the example in reverse, the narrative critic that ignores that historical dimension of the primary documents may arrive at a conclusion that is primarily subjective in nature because it is not anchored to anything in the first century. This impasse can be bridged by taking a comprehensive approach to the question. Any answer to what it means to be the "Son of God," and how Mark understood this reality, and how he intended his audience to both appropriate and respond to this truth, must take into account all the data that is available. Such a significant and complex question cannot be treated from a singular vantage point. Any approach to this question must engage deeply with the author (implied and, to a lesser degree, historical); text (from a historical critical and narratival perspective); and the reader (implied and historic). This is the task at hand.

Although this study is firmly committed to a narrative critical approach, subjectivity must be avoided at all costs. Thus, the manner in which form, redaction, and social-scientific criticism will come into play must be explained. In this chapter, the foundation for the present study is laid out. After examining what roles the various disciplines will fill, and how the ever-important "secrecy" theme in Mark is to be understood, the central thesis of the study will be stated and explained.

FORM CRITICISM AND THE EVANGELIST AS "AUTHOR"

There is little doubt that, originally, the tradition about Jesus was spread, not through written documents, but through oral traditions. This is hinted at in Luke 1:2. Individual told individual, and the story spread. To make the telling and remembering process more effective, and to communicate certain points and expectations, certain devices or forms were used. This is where the discipline of form criticism comes into play.

The term "form criticism" is taken from the German word "*Formgeschichte*." Form criticism was first applied to the Old Testament by Hermann Gunkel in the early twentieth century. His two major works on Genesis and the Psalms demonstrate a preoccupation with uncovering the oral traditions that underlie the various passages that make up these books. The first New Testament scholar to use the word as part of a title was Martin Dibelius in 1919. Other scholars that applied it to the New Testament included Bultmann and Schmidt. Following Bultmann were his students, Ernst Käsemann and Günther Bornkamm.[1] These individuals understood the Gospels to be the result of a community, rather than one particular author.[2] Aside from these German authors, Vincent Taylor in Britain adopted it as well in 1933, though with many modifications.[3] In the first half of the twentieth century, form criticism was highly touted as a significant breakthrough in biblical studies and was almost beyond challenge.[4]

Form criticism, which had its zenith of influence in the twentieth century, has roots that go back to century earlier. Much of the approaches found in form critical studies of the Gospels come from the early work done on the life of Jesus. When the church's dogma was challenged, and the relationship between history, faith, and literature was studied in depth, questions began to emerge. These questions included: In what way can the Gospels be described as history? Or, how did myth and legend shape and form the oral traditions that were eventually codified in what we call the New Testament? Once it was accepted by scholars that the Gospels were made up of sources rather than a single witness or source, the interest of these scholars extended into extrapolating what kinds of sources were present in the texts, and, additionally, how they came to be shaped and molded by the mythologization process (e.g., Bultmann).

As a goal, form criticism seeks to uncover the various forms or units and their original historical context. The answers for where the events described/narrated in the Gospels actually originated may, according to the form critic, be the historical Jesus, the Gospel writers, or the Christian community and its *Sitz im Leben*. In many respects, the process of investigation was not actually such that its central goal was uncovering the historical Jesus. This, it was thought, was almost entirely impossible to accomplish. It

---

1. Blevins, *Messianic Secret*, 157.
2. A helpful introduction to the discipline, history, and practice of form criticism is McKnight, "Form and Redaction Criticism"; McKnight, *What Is Form Criticism?* 1997; Taylor, *Formation of the Gospel Tradition*; Grant, "Where Form Criticism and Textual Criticism Overlap," 11–21.
3. Taylor, *Formation of the Gospel Tradition*.
4. Kline, "Redaction Criticism of the Gospels," 177.

was not the historical Jesus that held the key to the present day application and significance for the Christian faith, but, rather, primitive Christianity; thus uncovering it became central. Along this line, Wright explains,

> Form-criticism, the tool usually associated with Bultmann, was not, at its heart, designed to find out about Jesus. It was part of the other great "Quest," which still goes on despite being in principle even harder than the Quest for Jesus: the Quest for the Kerygmatic Church, the attempt to reconstruct movements of thought and belief in the first century, and in particular to recapture (in both senses) the early Christian faith.[5]

Likewise, Dibelius himself viewed the origin of the text as being found most likely in the *Sitz im Leben* of the church; specifically in the preaching and teaching of the early Christians (*kerygma* and *didache*).[6]

The approach of form criticism is to subdivide the various pericopes and accounts in the Gospels to their individual literary homes. Before these accounts where written, it is argued, they circulated orally and would likely have a similar origin to others that fall into the same camp, and would likely have been redacted by the respective Evangelist in similar ways.[7] Yet, one of the charges that form critics have faced from their critics has been the lack of precision in the forms themselves. A few forms are generally accepted: *logia, parables, speeches, miracle accounts, pronouncements,* and *narratives.* Apart from these, other, less-agreed upon forms have been put forward, but are often unique to individual scholars. An example of this would be Bultmann who argued for four forms.[8] These groups are often subdivided even more, such as the various forms of the form miracle story (exorcisms, healings, epiphanies, etc.). No authoritative list of forms is agreed on, though, in broad strokes, there does exist a number that are generally accepted.[9] Moreover, as form criticism evolved as a discipline, and new insights about ancient literature were uncovered, it was continually refined.

It is explained, quite functionally, by Bock,

---

5. Wright, *Jesus and the Victory of God*, 22.

6. For a recent overview and assessment on form criticism's hundred-year history and the interplay between form and community, see: Byrskog, "Century with the Sitz Im Leben."

7. For a differing view on the manner in which oral tradition functioned in the early church, see Riesner, "Jesus as Preacher and Teacher," 185–210; Dunn, *Oral Gospel Tradition*; and Dewey, *Disciples of the Way*.

8. Concerns about these categories are noted by Bock, "Form Criticism," 173–96.

9. McKnight, *What Is Form Criticism?* 21–33.

> When I was a child, there was a special moment when the teacher said, "Once upon a time." I knew it was time to hear a fairy tale. I also could count on the last words bringing joy and something like, "And they lived happily ever after." Such is the nature of form. In a set format, stories or events are told in certain ways, with certain stylistic or programmatic indicators that let the reader know the type of account that is present.[10]

Bock's simple, straightforward explanation captures a quintessential aspect of form: expectation. If forms as unique as those referred to by Bock existed in Biblical literature—as we have cause to suspect—then recovering and categorizing these forms would prove most helpful in the task of exegesis and interpretation.

The two most dominant voices in the form critical conversation, both in advancing the case for the discipline and in applying it to the New Testament, are, as mentioned before, Dibelius and Bultmann. Though, as it stands today, the most pertinent and longest lasting impact of form criticism on Synoptic studies has been that which was applied to the parable. Scholars such as C. H. Dodd and Joachim Jeremias both used the insights of form criticism on the parables with significant results.[11]

One of the most important oversights that form criticism left itself open to was the minimization of the role of the Evangelists themselves.[12] Were they simply compilers of tradition, or, as the redaction critics sought to argue, theological writers who used, edited, and modified their sources to shape their didactic aims? In the end, form criticism left alone, without the help of other disciplines, stripped the Gospels of the input of their respective authors.[13] More than loosely connected pearls on a string, the Gospels, the redaction critics believed, betrayed a fairly sophisticated arrangement and shaping of the form to communicate their worldview. It became less about seeing through the text, than seeing the finished text.

Although the form critical approach has led scholars to approach the text with more awareness and sensitivity to the manner in which conventional oral forms solidified and were eventually codified, that lasting detrimental charge against a narrow approach such as this, is that the *Sitz im Leben* overshadowed the Evangelist. With advances in narrative criticism, literary theory, and social-scientific criticism, returning to a predominantly

---

10. Bock, "Form Criticism," 106.

11. McKnight, in his assessment of the most recent results form criticism has yielded, highlights the work of Dodd and Jeremias. McKnight, *What Is Form Criticism?* 50–55.

12. Meagher, "Die Form," 459–60.

13. Kline, "Redaction Criticism of the Gospels," 178.

form critical approach seems unwise. Thus, for this present study, while attention will be given to the various forms, the bulk of energy will be devoted to looking at the text and uncovering the point of view and Christology of the implied author, rather than seeking to uncover the community that gave it birth and the host of varying forms that could be used to see "through" the text.

REDACTION CRITICISM AND WREDE'S MESSIANIC SECRET

Once some of the short falls of form criticism became apparent, scholars turned again to approach the texts with the biblical authors more involved in the conversation. The Evangelists, according to the redaction critics, cannot be viewed solely as compilers; they must be viewed as authors and theologians in some sense as well. While, for form critics, attention is primarily given to the community that gave it birth through its oral traditions, the redactions critics place their attention on the historical author of the Gospels. What is sought is insight into the theological aims of the authors. This is found through noting how the authors of the Gospels edit, combine, omit, augment, and insert their sources. This was accomplished, primarily, through examining how Matthew and Luke make use of Mark and Q. What compositional techniques do they employ? How do they shape their sources? These are some of the questions that the redaction critic is after.

The discipline of redaction criticism, from the German *Redaktionsgeschichte,* came to the forefront of New Testament studies in the second half of the twentieth century. The term *Redaktionsgeshichte* originated with Willi Marxen's *Mark the Evangelist,* originally published in German in 1954. His area of emphasis was the opposition between Galilee and Jerusalem in Mark.[14] Additional scholars that were influential in the field include Bornkamm (who focused on Matthew) and Hans Conzelmann (who focused on Luke).

One of the most significant works applying this method to Mark's Gospel is William Wrede's 1901 *Das Messiasgeheimnis in den Evangelien.* Wrede's was a pioneering work. He argued that the Messianic secret motif in Mark is central to understanding the Gospel, the Evangelist's Christology, and the manner in which the written account was shaped in order to explain why Jesus' Messiahship was misunderstood by his original audience. Wrede argued that since the early church came to view Jesus as the Messiah only after the resurrection, they had to explain why this is not explicitly clear

---

14. Van Eck, *Galilee and Jerusalem,* 14–15.

during Jesus' life and ministry. This, he went on, meant that it is unlikely that Jesus made this claim during his life. Wrede pointed to the injunctions for silence in Mark as being a literary device which Mark used to make this tension intelligible. His view of the inner inconsistency in Mark is made,

> If Jesus repeatedly commands sick people (I leave the cases of possession out of account here) to keep the fact of their healing secret, he nevertheless frequently performs his miracles in the full glare of publicity. Here there lies an inner contradiction in Mark's presentation, if there is otherwise a unity of thought behind these injunctions.[15]

Wrede contests that the commands to silence by Jesus must be explained in such a way that does justice to the oddness of such a request, and to the overall christological dimensions of the Gospel.[16] He argues that the Messianic secret not only extends to Jesus' identity (the who) but also to the works of Jesus (the what).[17] To state it plainly, for Wrede, the motif of secrecy was much more central to Mark than the motif of revelation.[18]

Further, Wrede's contention is that, somehow, the interpreter must explain the two ends of the spectrum that are seen in the New Testament. On one side of the spectrum, we have the Gospel of John with its robust and developed Christology and, on the other side of the spectrum, one sees verses such as Acts 2:36; Rom 1:4; and Phil 2:6–11, which some say seem to indicate that Jesus "became" the Messiah after his resurrection.[19] In his chapter entitled "The Self-Concealment of the Messiah" he concludes,

> We now summarize the results of our observation. Exegetes have been unable to explain Jesus' command, which was repeated again and again up to the very last, to keep silent about his messianic dignity. For they have not been able to find a likely *motivation* which is conceivable for this historical Jesus and which can be applied to all the individual situations.[20]

---

15. Wrede, *Messianic Secret*, 17.

16. Illustrative of these commands to silence is Mark 1:43–45; 3:12; 4:34; 7:17–23; 8:29–31; 9:28, 31; 10:32–34; 13:3, and the parabolic nature of much of Jesus' teachings (i.e., Mark 4:11).

17. Cf. Kingsbury, *Christology of Mark's Gospel*, 3.

18. Blevins, *Messianic Secret*, 5.

19. A helpful explanation of these two "poles" is given by Kingsbury. His assessment of Wrede's work is worth noting. Kingsbury, *Christology of Mark's Gospel*, 2.

20. Wrede, *Messianic Secret*, 48.

Eventually, Wrede's thesis was adopted and, in some instances, adapted by form critic proponents such as Dibelius and Bultmann. Blevins notes the irony of Dibelius' advocating for Wrede's view,

> For Dibelius, the Messianic secret was key to understanding of Mark's Gospel. In contrast to his usual low evaluation of the Gospel writer's creative role, here he contended that the Messianic secret stemmed from the writer, Mark himself.[21]

Blevins continues and explains that Bultmann "in toto" adopted and applied Wrede's thesis in this work.[22]

Although Wrede's thesis was, at first, touted as a significant step forward in New Testament Gospel interpretation, voices began to cry out against it. Albert Schweitzer who wrote during the same period, opposed Wrede's skeptical view of the historical foundation that undergirded Mark's narrative.[23] By engaging the Evangelist's work from a position sensitive to the eschatological dimension of Jesus' life and teaching, Schweitzer was able to retain an underlying historical foundation that Wrede rejected.[24] Schweitzer's negative assessment of Wrede's work was especially influential in British scholarship.[25] Later, in 1967, Heikki Räisänen published a monograph entitled, *Messiasgeheimnis* in which he argues that Wrede's thesis was entirely too simplistic and lacks explanatory scope.[26] A few years after Räisänen, Dunn offered a helpful assessment of Wrede's thesis in an article. After examining the nature and manner in which Wrede explained the secrecy motif, Dunn offered a number of criticisms. One of which is that "it [Wrede's thesis] fails to do sufficient justice to the full scope of the secrecy motif in Mark."[27]

One of the issues that Wrede failed to properly factor in is the number of times in Mark that Jesus' notoriety and fame spread throughout the surrounding region. These situations display the opposite of secrecy. In fact, they display that, according to the narrative, Jesus' fame spread out rather quickly (Mark 1:27, 28, 32–34, 45; 2:2, 12; 3:7; 4:1). Dunn summarizes the essence of this point,

---

21. Blevins, *Messianic Secret*, 85.
22. Ibid., 90.
23. Schweitzer, *Von Reimarus Zu Wrede*.
24. Schweitzer, *Quest for the Historical Jesus*, 296–314. Additional assessment is offered by Blevins, *Messianic Secret*, 27.
25. Kingsbury, *Christology of Mark's Gospel*, 5.
26. Räisänen, *Das "Messiasgeheimnis" Im Markusevnagelium*, 145–48.
27. Dunn, "Messianic Secret in Mark," 98.

> This publicity motif may not simply be dismissed as though it left the theory of Messianic secret unaffected. On the contrary, it shows that at most we can speak of Messianic *misunderstanding*, but hardly of Messianic *secret*.[28]

There is something to be valued in what Dunn expressed. The term "misunderstanding" seems to fit the data better and will be used from here on out. Misunderstanding in Mark is a well-known and well-tested motif, but Wrede's approach to it is insufficient. The real question at hand is, first, what is the misunderstanding about? Then, what is the purpose of it? Is it designed to demonstrate predestination's role in the narrative and in community life[29] or, is it primarily about revelation?[30] To put it another way, what it the misunderstanding about, and what does it do for the implied audience and the characters in the story?

Secrecy and the Son of God: A Matter of Revelation

Before approaching the question of whether the misunderstanding motif has a revelatory core or something else, the question that must be answered is what the "misunderstanding" is about. What is this motif in Mark revealing about Jesus? Do the characters in the story misunderstand that Jesus is the Messiah, or that he is the Son of God. The argument here is that it is the latter.

Following Räisänen, Dunn, and others, Kingsbury understands the secrecy motif in Mark as being primarily anchored around the issue of divine sonship, rather than his Messiahship.[31] One of the foundations of this study is that Kingsbury is correct and the theme of misunderstanding is most connected with Jesus' divine sonship. This, it will be argued, does better justice to the narratival dimensions of the text than Wrede's thesis. This study will utilize the insights and contributions of redaction criticism whilst anchoring the study in realm of narrative criticism that engage the text as a whole. A brief summary of Kingsbury's argumentation and the various views that are used to explain and understand the Messianic "secret" is needed at this point.[32]

---

28. Ibid., 100.
29. Watson, "Social Function of Mark's Secrecy Theme."
30. Dunn, "Messianic Secret in Mark"; Kingsbury, *Christology of Mark's Gospel*.
31. Kingsbury, *Christology of Mark's Gospel*, 1–33.
32. The argument that the secret in Mark is more to do with his divine sonship than his messiahship is not unique to Kingsbury. See also: Moule, "On Defining the Messianic Secret in Mark"; Luz, "Das Geheimnismotiv Und Die Markinische Christologie."

Thus far, it has been argued that there does exist a phenomenon of secrecy (or, to put it better, misunderstanding) in Mark. Wrede contested that it was about the Messiahship of Jesus. Kingsbury argues against this, and points to the often-found link in Mark between "identity" and "Son of God" as opposed to "identity" and "Messiah."[33] He also notes how, in Mark, "Christ" can be used as a name (Mark 9:41), as a title in a name (Mark 1:1), or as a title (Mark 8:29; 12:35; 13:21; 14:61; 15:32).[34] He writes,

> And as for its need for definition, of the seven times Mark ascribes "Messiah" to Jesus, five times he explains how it is to be understood. Four times Mark defines "Messiah" in terms of either "Son of David" (12:35), or "King of Israel" (15:32), or "Son of God (the Blessed)" (1:1; 14:61), and one time he defines it ... by means of the context with which he associated it (8:29).[35]

Kingsbury goes to lengths to discredit much of Räisänen's work on the Messianic secret in Mark. Räisänen's contention is that there is essentially no secrecy theme in Mark at all. Kingsbury, however, argues against Räisänen's thesis. This, he does, by systematically responding to a number of criticisms that Räisänen presents in his 1976 *Messiasgeheimnis*. Kingsbury both deconstructs and presents a different interpretation of the passages that deal with the theme of secrecy. In the end, Kingsbury concludes that Wrede was wrong in what he understood to be the secret's theme. He likewise argues against Räisänen and posits that the secrecy theme (or "misunderstanding" to continue the distinction) is in play in the narrative.

More interaction with Kingsbury's central thesis will be offered in chapter 5. For now, suffice it to say that the misunderstanding motif in Mark is present. The number of injunctions to silence, the gross misunderstanding of Jesus' identity and mission by both "insiders" and "outsiders" must be dealt with. In, contrast to Räisänen, it cannot be explained away, and, similar to Kingsbury, the thesis presented here is that the motif is connected with Jesus' divine sonship and, only by extension, to his Messiahship. But what role does the motif of misunderstanding play in Mark? With that question, attention will now be given to a few theories seeking to offer an answer. One such answer is offered by Watson.

---

33. Kingsbury, *Christology of Mark's Gospel*, 14.
34. Ibid., 15.
35. Ibid.

Francis Watson: Secrecy and "Predestination"

Wrede's thesis concerning the Messianic secret in Mark, and the subsequent adoption or rejection of his propositions, was highlighted above. For the purpose of the present study, a greater interaction with alternative theories of the secrecy motif is in order. One such view is that the secrecy motif in Mark has, at its core, the issue of predestination, rather than revelation. This view is proposed by Watson.[36] Watson, writing just after the release of *The Messianic Secret*[37] understands the secret in Mark as being, first of all, thoroughly coherent, and, secondly, as being entwined with the theme of predestination. By "coherent," he seems to be saying that there exists in Mark a level of deliberateness and intentionality regarding the secrecy motif. It is not, in Watson's view, an afterthought. Further, he believes that there is no distinction between the "miracle secret" (which he explains as an injunction to silence stemming from a miracle) and the "messianic secret."[38] He summarizes his understanding of the predestination rational for secrecy as "saving knowledge is granted to the chosen few but withheld from the rest."[39] In Mark 9:9 the injunction for silence is given to those on the "inside," or, to use Watson's language, those who are "predestined" (the disciples). What is happening in this instance is not a reversal of the predestination theme, but, rather, the passage is a post-Easter tradition that is inserted in the life of Jesus.[40] He argues that this is so because of three reasons. First, it appears that 2 Pet 1:17–21 understands the transfiguration as a post-Easter reality.[41] Second, Watson believes that the insertion of post-resurrection accounts into the pre-resurrection narrative occurs elsewhere in the Gospels. For example, he offers similar accounts in Luke 5:1–11 and John 21:1–8 (miraculous catch of fish) and Matt 14:28–31 and John 21:7 (Peter's walking on water).[42] The third reason why the transfiguration ought to be viewed as a post-Easter account, according to Watson, is that there are several parallels with the ascension story in Acts 1:9–12.[43] In the end, Watson notes that Mark 9:9 is a "special case" and does not negate the predestination motif surrounding the secrecy theme in Mark.[44]

36. Watson, "Social Function of Mark's Secrecy Theme."
37. Tuckett, *Messianic Secret*.
38. Watson, "Social Function of Mark's Secrecy Theme," 54.
39. Ibid., 55.
40. Ibid., 55–56.
41. Ibid., 55.
42. Ibid.
43. Ibid.
44. Ibid., 56.

Watson goes on to argue that the centurion's confession in Mark 15:39 does not, as others have argued, serve the motif of revelation. Instead, he understands it this way because of the events at the temple. He writes, "It [the confession] follows the tearing of the veil in the temple (15.38), which signifies God's abandonment of the Jewish system of worship and, by implication, Israel as a whole."[45] Watson then goes on to explain that the revelation of Jesus as the "Son of God" is not a reality that only comes to the forefront of the story after Jesus is crucified (revelation motif of secrecy). Rather, it is also on the cross that Jesus' identity is revealed. He writes,

> 15.39 is not claiming that Jesus' identity is revealed *only* in his death on the cross, but *even* in his death on the cross. The crucifixion appears to be an overwhelming obstacle to Mark's claim that Jesus is the Son of God, and he must therefore show that here too Jesus sonship is revealed—and not only in baptism, miracles, and Transfiguration. ... His presentation of Jesus' death is occasioned not by the *theologia crucis* of dialectical theology, but by apologetic needs. The view that Mark's secrecy theme stressed the centrality of the cross as the place of revelation is therefore unwarranted.[46]

Watson's theory about the Messianic secret is linked to the social function of the motif in Mark's community. For Watson, the issue of predestination is not a theological question *per se*, about man's relationship to God, but rather is a sociological question about "sect and society."[47] He explains that, since suffering is such a dominant theme in Mark, and since the disciples in the narrative never actually do experience suffering, then Mark must be motivated by sociological or community suffering issues rather than historical questions.[48] Since suffering was expected by Jesus and whoever would follow him in discipleship, then so, too, must those who follow in the disciples' footsteps be prepared to suffer. Additionally, according to Watson, two primary functions stem from the doctrine of predestination and the secrecy motif. They are, first, that it strengthens the feel of "eliteness" of a specific community and encourages resolve and, secondly, that it explains to a community why it is suffering such hardship.[49] These, he argues, are the same two functions that predestination plays in the rest of the New Testament.[50]

---

45. Ibid.
46. Ibid., 57. Italics original.
47. Ibid., 60.
48. Ibid., 66.
49. Ibid., 62.
50. Ibid., 63–64.

He concludes: "this theme is the expression of a belief in predestination, according to which saving knowledge is bestowed on the few and hidden from the majority."[51] Additionally, there are a number of times that the "crowds" or "countryside" come to view Jesus as an authoritative teacher and marvel at him (examples include Mark 1:27, 28, 32–34, 45; 2:2, 12; 3:7; 4:1). In these instances, the revelatory dimensions of Jesus' miracle and healing work seems to be directly related to the breaking of the secrecy motif.

Watson is commended for the comprehensiveness with which he formulates his theory. Yet, there are a number of difficulties with his view. First of all, his argument that the transfiguration is a post-Easter tradition inserted into the narrative, and the subsequent examples that he offers of other instances in which this occurs, is unlikely. A number of similarities are present in the two accounts. A number of aspects of the transfiguration theme are linked to the broader context of Mark, and a number of differences exist in the account from the ascension story in Acts 1. For example, the mention of "Moses" and "Elijah" as being with Jesus in Mark 9, as opposed to "two men" (Acts 1:10) cannot be explained away. Where Moses and Elijah are silent and do not factor into the account other than to be, in some sense, minimized in relation to Jesus, the two men in white (Acts 1:10) speak and give direction to the disciples. In Mark, there are three disciples present at the transfiguration, in Acts, it appears to be all "the apostles he had chosen" (Acts 1:2). Additionally, the voice from heaven in Mark 9 has no parallel in Acts. The central component of the transfiguration is the voice from heaven. In Acts, it is completely different. The same type of differences can be found in the other "examples" that Watson offers.

Moreover, understanding the tearing of the veil as God's rejection of Israel seems hard to see. Mark bases his narrative on the framework of understanding that is seen in the Old Testament and Second Temple literature and culture. He begins his Gospel with reference to "the good news" about the "Christ" (Mark 1:1). One would be hard pressed to understand his account as good news when it culminates in the complete rejection of Israel. Watson fails to take into consideration Jesus' words about the temple's destruction in Mark 13:2 (cf. Mark 15:29). The point here is not that Jesus is pronouncing a curse on all Israel's worship, but rather, he is casting a new vision for where and what the temple is to be. This means that the events described in Mark 15:39 must be understood differently than Watson proposes. Finally, one of the weaknesses of Watson's proposal that needs addressing is in the manner in which he constructs a theory of the identity of Mark's intended audience. Other than referencing the motif of suffering

---

51. Ibid., 64.

for those who would follow Jesus, Watson does not explain how he arrives at his conclusion about what exactly the community was wrestling with. What was their *Sitz*? Why this *Sitz* and not another?

In summation, the theme of predestination, although helpful to keep in mind for interpreting Mark, is insufficient as a comprehensive explanation for the secrecy theme in Mark. Perhaps Watson would have benefited from a more thorough narrative critical engagement with Mark. Notes on how a pericope is functioning in Mark's story, and how the Evangelist is developing and communicating his Christology, are not as frequent in the article as one would hope. Although this study rejects the predestination theme as the motif's *raison d'etre*, the sociological question about audience is one that will be revisited. Although the *Sitz* that Watson formulated is built from the exegetical data in Mark, he nevertheless would have benefited from adding to this the narrative contours of the Gospel.

Misunderstanding and Revelation

Running alongside the commands for silence is the theme of Jesus' true identity slowly, but surely, being revealed in various ways. From a narrative perspective, the implied reader is well informed about the character of Jesus. From the beginning of the story through to the end it is clear that Jesus is the Christ, the Son of God. The implied reader and, likely, the indefinite audience filter the characters who interact with Jesus in the first half of the book with what is revealed in Mark 1:1. To put it another way, the characters in the story do not need to proclaim "Messiah Son of God!" every time Jesus passes by for the reader to assume this is in some way what is implied. For example, after Mark 1:1, the reader sees a number of instances in Mark where people are amazed and marvel at Jesus, spread his fame, where great crowds follow Jesus around, and where he publicly heals and teaches (e.g., Mark 1:23, 24, 27, 28, 32, 37, 39; 2:2, 12, 13, 15). The narratival point of these is to reveal what Jesus does in light of who he is. The cumulative impact of the themes of "understanding" and "misunderstanding" will be examined in chapter 5. For now, the point to be noted is that the theme of "revelation" has captured accurately the motif of misunderstanding in Mark.

Misunderstanding: Framing the Question

Two questions that address the foundational approach of this study must be considered before the methodological approach can be explained in full. First, what exactly is the nature of the truth that the characters in the story seem unable to grasp? What is the misunderstanding about? This question addresses the manner in which the disciplines of form, redaction, and narrative criticism are used in order to frame the discussion at hand. It was argued, following Kingsbury, that the motif of misunderstanding is primarily related to the divine sonship of Jesus.

The second question that must be answered is What role in the narrative does this misunderstanding play? Is the secret being used by Mark to correct Christology, as Weeden has argued? Is it being used to teach about the nature of predestination? Or something else? The view taken here is that it is designed to do something else. It has been argued that the purpose of the misunderstanding is to heighten the revelatory impact of tension of misunderstanding in Mark. It will be argued that Mark has rhetorical intentions that he is concerned about communicating.

SOCIAL-SCIENTIFIC CRITICISM

Although social-scientific criticism does not function in the forefront of this study, any attention given to the implied author will need to be anchored to some reality. It seems best to have that anchor spot be the agrarian society that was a historical reality in first century Israel. The use of the social sciences in biblical interpretation is explained by Van Eck:

> While historical-critical analysis tends to focus on individual actors, extraordinary actions, distinctive properties, person rather than societal relationships, and on the diachronic change of these aspects, sociological analysis tends to focus on social groupings, regular, recurrent and routinized behaviors common properties systemic relations and structured patterns of behavior.[52]

The impetus of this is not to simply interpret the document that one has in front of oneself (in this case a biblical Gospel), but, rather, to make sense of and uncover the world which gave rise to it. Doing this allows one to "analyze the text and context of a biblical document."[53] The intention or impact of a particular passage cannot be properly understood unless the world from which it came is kept in view. What social systems, relationships, symbols, groups, or class gave birth to it? To illustrate the real world application and significance of this approach, Elliott in his book, *What is social-scientific criticism,* presents a hypothetical situation in which an

---

52. Van Eck, *Galilee and Jerusalem,* 83.
53. Ibid., 85.

individual from Moscow is visiting his friend in California and, together, they go to a baseball game.[54] Elliott's analogy demonstrates the incredible amount of questions, clarifications, and assumptions by his Russian friend that the American may not even be aware of, but that, nevertheless, shape the event, give it meaning to the crowd, and that would, no doubt, confuse someone completely unfamiliar with the game, its rules and regulations, and its place in American culture. Information that the historical audience and characters take for granted is often not expressly communicated in the literature that an author pens because these assumptions are generally shared by an audience and, thus, left unstated. After his analogy, Elliott offers a definition:

> Social-scientific criticism of the Bible is that phase of the exegetical task which analyzes the social and cultural dimensions of the text and of its environmental context through the utilization of the perspectives, theory, models, and research of the social sciences.[55]

After the scholar has offered an exegetical assessment of a text and offered some form of interpretation about what it means and meant, the questions, according to Elliott, must be asked: "Did people really think and act that way and, if so, why? Do these exegetical conclusions square with ancient patterns of belief and behavior?"[56] This is the reason that a narratological approach to a Gospel must not be done from a purely subjective manner. What is possible, when evaluated from a social-scientific perspective, may be found to be less than probable. This is often done through the study of what anthropologists often classified as *emic* and *etic*. *Emic* refers to the interstation and explanation offered by the historical (and literary) characters, and, specifically, the author. On the other hand, *etic* is the interpretation of why these individuals explained reality in this way—why they "thought and behaved" in such a way.[57] This, however, does not simply mean that the approach is completed from a posture of pride, or from an ethnocentric perspective. Since all knowledge is socially conditioned in some form, it is simply seeking to draw attention to the vastly different point of view that exists between—in our case—the world of the Gospels and twenty-first century.

This approach will function in two ways for a narratological study such as this. First, the world of story, as a self-contained reality, must be

---

54. Elliott, *What Is Social Scientific Criticism?*, 2–3.
55. Ibid., 7.
56. Ibid., 11.
57. Ibid., 39.

examined from a social-scientific vantage point. This will be done through the tripartite "author," "text," "reader" paradigm. Second, moving away from the self-contained world in the narrative, what sociological world gave birth to such a story? This question, as well, will be addressed with this three-headed interpretative framework.[58] This is not, primarily, a social-scientific study of "Son of God" in Mark. That being said, attention will be given to insights from the field as they pertain to the thesis being set forward.

NEW LITERARY CRITICISM AND THE NEW TESTAMENT

Perhaps as a response to form criticism's near neglect of the finished text and, in keeping with broader literary trends in the twentieth and twenty-first centuries, the emergence of the New Literary Criticism, with its myopic approach to the text itself, is worth noting. These "New Critics" advocated for an approach to the text that is almost resistance to any historical questions about the author, audience, or the world in which it arose. The text is viewed as autonomous and, it is argued, must be understood almost singularly in this way. Questions about the historical author, what he thought, meant, or believed are secondary. Questions about the historical context from which it is written are also relegated to the sidelines. The approach proposes that the text is a self-referential body and everything that is needed for interpretation is provided by the contents of the text.

One of the primary goals of New Literary Criticism is that of a "close reading" and attention is given to this endeavor, not to the historical and social-scientific concerns that have dominated biblical (and literary) studies in the past.[59] For this study, the argument will be that a close reading and concern for the historical questions that the texts present to the interpreter are not mutually exclusive. Thus, the approach will incorporate elements of both.

METHODOLOGICAL APPROACH

Thus far it has been proposed that, in Mark, the motif of misunderstanding relates primarily to Jesus' divine sonship, and that the result of this motif is the tension being developed surrounding the revelation of Jesus' true

---

58. For an explanation and investigation of these two dimensions, see Van Eck, *Galilee and Jerusalem*, 72–125.

59. McKnight and Malbon, *New Literary Criticism and the New Testament*, 18–19.

identity. The task at hand now is to continue from this preliminary consideration of foundations (there is in Mark a motif of misunderstanding and it related to Jesus' divine sonship and plays a revelatory role in the narrative) to considerations of methodology. Through the contexts of author, text, and reader, the title "Son of God" will be examined. When this tripartite grid is combined with a historically plausible and probable anchor, we come to understand Mark's Christology in a much fuller way.

The methodological approach of this thesis is to begin by examining of the legitimacy of a narratival approach. In chapter 2, after a preliminary consideration of the history and reception of narrative criticism, it will be argued that, due to the genre of Mark, and the audience to which the book was written, there is warrant for approaching the book with a sensitivity to the literary dimension of the work. The genre that seems to best fit the data is *bioi*, which is especially interested in revealing the central character in view. This, in turn, further strengthens the revelatory dimension of the misunderstanding theme in Mark. The question of audience, it will be argued, is best addressed by taking a broad view of audience in the sense that an indefinite audience is historically plausible, and, that it forces attention to be given to the finished text, rather than the community that may or may not have given birth to it or given reason for its creation.

Chapter 3 will place the question about what it means to be the "Son of God" in context. Here, we are answering the historical questions about "Son of God." This is the basis from which we will build our tripartite interpretative framework. After all, there were numerous "sons of god" in the Ancient World. What contextual horizon is best for interpreting this title? Is the most probable parallel Divine Men from Greaco-Roman mythology? Is it hero myths such as Heracles and Perseus? What role does Imperial worship play in Mark's story world? Some of these views were passionately advocated for by biblical scholars in the first half of the twentieth century and, so, attention must be given to them. This chapter will begin with the Old Testament concept of Son of God. Here, attention is given to Israel as "God's Son" and the promises made to David in 2 Sam 7. After examine the Old Testament usage of the title, the manner in which the Dead Sea Scrolls used, understood, and interpreted this title, is addressed. Next, the study will examine the Greaco-Roman and Hellenistic background of the title. Finally, the usage in the New Testament is presented. Both the usage of "Son of God" in the Synoptics and in the Pauline writings is examined. The central argument of this chapter is that the most fitting hermeneutical context to approach "Son of God" in Mark's Gospel is the Old Testament and its twin themes of royal Messiah and Son of God.

Chapter 4 is the exegetical engagement with the instances in which Jesus' divine sonship is mentioned, either directly or indirectly, in Mark. This is where the "text" component of the tripartite framework is engaged. Each of these are examined. The desire in doing this is to twin the insights of a narrative criticism with the historical critical approach. Throughout this chapter, the case that the locale of origin and best hermeneutical context for understanding the title "Son of God" is, in fact, the Old Testament. Although each instance is examined textually, historically, and narratively, special attention is given to Mark 1:1, 9:7, and 15:39.

Chapter 5 is where the exegetical data that is evaluated from a narratively sensitive vantage point. Here, through the two remaining pieces of the tripartite interpretive framework, "author" and "reader," it will be argued that Mark's Christology serves a definitive goal of evoking his readers to consider closely aligning themselves with Jesus and adopting the motif of allegiance that is sprinkled throughout the narrative. Through the point of view of the implied author, and lesson from a reader-response approach, we will arrive at this conclusion.

The closing chapter reviews the ground that has been traversed in the study, and reviews the original research that was offered. A few points of further research are given, as well as some suggestions for hermeneutical cooperation in New Testament studies such as the cooperation that is needed between narrative critical experts and traditional historical critics. This, coupled with a hermeneutic that demands that explanations and interpretations of the New Testament be both possible and plausible is offered as a final point of consideration.

THESIS STATED AND EXPLAINED

A lot of ground is soon to be covered. A bird's eye view of the thesis to be set forward is needed at this point. Thus, the primary thesis that is being argued in the study is this: After examining the author, text, and reader of the second Gospel, it becomes evident that, through rather sophisticated literary devices, Mark presents Jesus as the Son of God. This he does in such a way that climaxes in the centurion's words in Mark 15:39. This, in turn, is designed to present the implied reader with a character in the story to identify with, and model. The themes of allegiance, understanding, and misunderstanding are germane to this. By developing the tension in his narrative around these themes, Mark leads the reader to a point of anxiousness where one asks, "when and who will see that Jesus is the Son of God?" It is only in the unlikeliest of characters, the centurion, that this misunderstanding is resolved. By shaping his narrative in such a way, Mark opens the call of discipleship to whoever will switch allegiance from Caesar son of god, to Jesus, the true Son of God (discipleship). The motif of misunderstanding is resolved at the crucifixion with Jesus because the "secret" is out. The reader, then, is faced with two options: allegiance or opposition to Mark's Jesus.

How will this thesis be approached? The framework and interrelationship between three important contexts will be examined: author, text, and reader. The epithet "Son of God" will be studied in relation to these horizons.

2

Legitimacy of a Narratological Approach to Mark

INTRODUCTION

THE DISCIPLINE OF BIBLICAL studies now known commonly as "narrative criticism" is a relatively new approach that has gained notable traction in the past four decades. Before the publication of *Mark as Story*,[1] relatively little attention was given in scholarly circles to the narrative dynamics of the Gospels, and such things as setting, narration, space, scene, and character were typically only treated as secondary to more historical concerns. This can be demonstrated through examining the 1960 New Testament Series publication *Literary Criticism of the New Testament*.[2] Students or scholars thinking anachronistically may unwittingly select this book from the shelf, expecting it to follow suit with more recent approaches to the literary dimensions of the New Testament, but such is not the case. Instead of focusing on elements essential to a story such as plot, narration, and characterization, this literary critical book is concerned more with the historical critical method's form, source and redaction criticism.[3] Such an example serves to demonstrate how the term "literary

---

1. Rhoads, Dewey, and Michie, *Mark as Story*.
2. Beardslee, *Literary Criticism of the New Testament*.
3. It should be noted that Beardslee did in fact call for greater attention to be given to the genre of the Gospels. Beardslee was ahead of his time in a number of respects,

criticism" has morphed to encompass more than just issues of authorship and ancient literary sources. When one picks up the book *What is Narrative Criticism?*[4] itself part of the same series as Beardslee's book) by Mark Allen Powell, written just thirty years later, a significant difference can be noted. Powell is primarily interested in the Gospels as *story*—a literary product that has some sense of cohesion, and which warrants a close reading.

Narrative criticism has garnered attention in the past few decades because, in some regards, it is a push back against the limits of a strictly historical critical (diachronic) method of interpretation, which for almost one hundred years had taken the lion's share of attention in scholarly circles. For more than a century, this was the dominant approach for Gospel studies and, although the results it promised and the results it produced were not commensurate by any stretch, the value of the historical critical method should not be minimized. This study will be firmly rooted in a narrative critical approach, yet it will not dispose of the historical questions, nor ignore data such as authorship, source or redaction critical insights, and will include some overall horizontal readings of certain passages. Nevertheless, it will remain committed to the moorings of its narrative critical harbor. By paying special attention to the finished text, this study will examine the Gospel of Mark and investigate the manner in which the author uses the title "Son of God." Each occurrence of this title in reference to Jesus of Nazareth will be examined individually, and the narrative of plot flow and development highlighted. When this data is brought into view with the historical realities of authorship, context, and the theology implicit in the Gospel itself, it will be demonstrated that the author of Mark is a sophisticated author (narrator) who offers his readers not only a complete narrative filled with tension and climax, but also as an author possess a didactic aim that the readers are invited to adopt and model.

NARRATIVE CRITICISM HISTORY

For over a century, the dominant approach to New Testament studies has been that of a historical-critical (diachronic) nature. The disciplines of tradition, source, form, redaction, and to a lesser extent, literary criticism, ruled the day. The past few decades have seen a host of different approaches rise up and attempt to shoulder their way in to the conversation. One can now

---

but the discipline of narrative criticism had not yet been developed, as it soon would be.

4. Powell, *What Is Narrative Criticism?*

find commentaries and articles written from a number of varying perspectives such as rhetorical criticism, social-scientific criticism, feminist criticism, not to mention such approaches as structuralism, deconstructionism and a number of reader-oriented approaches (i.e., synchronic approaches).

Amid this competition, the discipline known commonly as narrative criticism has found a place at the table and shows no sign of leaving. Although many are quick to point out the dangers or shortcomings of this particular approach,[5] its proponents are equally anxious to hear all that it has to say. An approach such as this does not simply fall out of the sky, but is the product of a long development and, in many respects, is the logical progression in New Testament studies rather than a novel, uninvited guest. We shall begin our study of narrative criticism by examining its predecessors. Our attention will be given to source, form and redaction criticism. They will be studied in that order.

SOURCE CRITICISM AND LITERARY RELATIONSHIP

We have four Gospels in our New Testament. Matthew, Mark and Luke form what is known as the Synoptics, John being the fourth. Nearly every introduction to the New Testament or commentary on the Gospels will devote significant time to a discussion of the various theories about the literary and compositional relationship between the Gospels. Did Matthew use Mark or did Mark use Matthew? Did Luke refer to Mark and Matthew or was it some combination of extant sources we no longer possess? It has been called the "Synoptic Problem."[6] The literary relationship between the Synoptic Gospels has been perhaps the most hotly contested literary question in human history. Even from the early years of the Church, the desire for an explanation has been evident.[7] This section will investigate the data from the Gospels that illustrate the need for a source critical explanation of the literary relationships between the Gospels. After surveying the different proposals for dealing with this phenomenon, the priority of Mark will be argued as being the most sufficient theory currently available to scholars.

---

5. Broadhead, "Narrativity and Naiveté"; Evans, "Source, Form and Redaction Criticism."

6. Matthew, Mark, and Luke were named the Synoptic Gospels by J. J. Griesbach at the close of the eighteenth century: Griesbach, *Synopsis Evangeliroum*. The word "Synoptic" is from the Greek συνόψις meaning "seen together." For a helpful introduction to the debate, see Dungan, *History of the Synoptic Problem*.

7. See, for example, Tatian's *Diatessaron* (c. 165), and Augustine of Hippo's *Harmony of the Gospels* (fifth century).

First of all, what is the justification for the necessity of a literary relationship between the Synoptics? Could they not simply be drawing from the same oral tradition, and so overlap in some capacity is to be expected? Such an explanation is not sufficient. The need for a literary explanation for the relationship between the Synoptics can be demonstrated in three areas: first, the order of their events; second, their content; third, their specific language. Each of these three will now be examined.

Order of Events in the Synoptics Demonstrates a Literary Relationship

The sequence of events in the Synoptic Gospels overlap to some degree because whether they are drawing from some source of common knowledge or are a result of literary dependence, they are essentially covering the same material. Their attention is given to covering the life of Jesus. Jesus was Jewish, he had a relatively short ministry, he taught, he healed, and he had disciples. He was crucified and resurrected. All four Gospels agree upon these facts. However, more than just a vague outline, there are significant portions of the Synoptics that share the same order. Take, for example, Matt 16:32—20:34, Mark 8:27—10:52, and Luke 9:18–51 and 18:15–43. All three sections begin with the micro-narrative of Peter's confession and Jesus' charge for secrecy concerning his Messianic identity, followed by predictions of his death and a call to selfless discipleship. In all three Synoptics, the healing of an epileptic boy appears next, which is followed by yet another prediction by Jesus of his forthcoming death.

The similarities in order cannot be explained away on the basis of coincidence. A form critical approach clearly demonstrates that the various pericopes found in these (and the other) parallel sections of the Synoptics are different and would have functioned differently in their respective *Sitz im Lebens*. The arrangement of these different forms into the same order shows that there must be a literary relationship between the Synoptics.[8]

Triple Tradition: A Case for Literary Relationship

The so-called "triple tradition" is material found in all three Gospels. For instance, 97.2 percent of Mark is found in Matthew, and 88.4 percent of

---

8. For additional parallels, see Matt 12:46—13:58; Mark 3:31—6:6; Luke 8:19–56. A helpful chart is given in Carson and Moo, *Introduction to the New Testament*, 89.

Mark is found in Luke.[9] The sheer amount of material that the Synoptics share lends credence to the view that some form of literary interdependence of the Gospels is present. When the Synoptic Gospels are compared with the Gospel of John, one can note almost right away that, although the focus is primarily the same, an incredible amount of diversity is apparent. One of these three is "not like the others" and the odd one out is John.

Specific Wording

Not only do the Synoptics overlap in order of events and content, but the similarities continue and extend to the actual words used. For example, when one compares Matt 19:13–15, Mark 10:13–16 and Luke 18:15–17, a number of lines exist that exhibit exact agreement, not only of order, but also vocabulary and wording. Any Gospel synopsis, especially in Greek, alerts the reader of the high level of similarities that exist between these three texts.[10] The agreements are such that any hypothesis that ignores the obvious literary relationship between the texts must be scrutinized and most likely abandoned. Oral tradition, although likely playing a role in the formation of the Gospels, is not a sufficient explanation.[11]

This short introduction into the so-called "Synoptic Problem" is by no means exhaustive. Nearly every New Testament introduction or commentary on the Gospels will engage with this type of argumentation so a prolonged treatment is not necessary. Having established that a literary relationship of necessity must exist between the Synoptics, we must now turn our attention to the various explanations that have been offered to account for this phenomenon. Again, this aspect of our present study will not be exhaustive, but will offer enough to justify the view of Markan priority in Gospel studies, a premise that this study will build on.

There are generally four theories offered to explain the literary relationship between the Synoptic Gospels.

- Matthew composed first; Mark and Luke used Matthew (Augustine).
- Matthew composed first; Luke used Matthew; Mark used both (Griesbach-hypothesis).

---

9. Figures taken from Stein, "Syoptic Problem," in Green, McKnight, and Marshall, *Dictionary of Jesus and the Gospels*, 787.

10. For an excellent example of a synopsis, see Farmer, *Synopticon*. See also: Stein, *Studying the Synoptic Gospels*, 30.

11. Bauckham, *Jesus and the Eyewitnesses*. For an investigation into the oral tradition and Gospel formation see Wansbrough, *Jesus and the Oral Gospel Tradition*.

- Mark composed first; Matthew and Luke used Mark and another common source known as "Q" (German *Quelle*) (two-source hypothesis).
- Mark composed first; Matthew and Luke used Mark and Q and "M" and "L": material unique to them respectively (four-source hypothesis).

For a number of reasons, the view offered by Augustine is tenuous at best. Few hold this view today and, for this reason, the remaining three options will be the center of our study. In 1797, J. J. Griesbach published his influential treatment of the Synoptic Gospels.[12] His theory—that Matthew wrote first and was used by both Mark and Luke—had the value of not only being well argued and explained, but also kept with Church tradition. It was convincing and demonstrated a high degree of explanatory scope. For almost one century it was the dominant theory in Gospel studies. As Gospel studies progressed, and the Synoptic Problem continued to receive attention, a new view was proposed by the German H. J. Holtzmann (1863),[13] and the British B. H. Streeter (1926).[14] Both Holtzmann and Streeter argued that Mark was written first, and that Matthew and Luke made independent use of Mark, along with document called "Q" (from the German *Quelle*, meaning "source"). Streeter went even further, suggesting a Four-Source theory.[15] In Streeter's view, Matthew and Luke used additional sources respectively called "M" and "L" which is commonly designated *Sondergut* (German: "special material"). For many Gospel critics, the view that M and L were written documents is difficult to prove. Some scholars use M and L for material that is simply unique to Matthew and Luke respectively and do not assume that these were necessarily written sources.[16] The nature of "M" and "L" are debated[17] and it is impossible to know for sure if they were written sources, oral tradition, or a collection of written documents. Luke's *Sondergut* composes between one-third and one-half of his Gospel.[18] Matthew's unique material features a rather large portion of his discourse material.[19]

Today, most scholars agree that Mark was written first, and that Matthew and Luke made independent use of Mark and Q. Additionally, they would agree that Matthew and Luke possess M and L—contents unique

---

12. Greisbach, *Synopsis Evangeliroum*.
13. Holtzmann, *Die synoptischen Evangelien*.
14. Streeter, *Four Gospels*.
15. Ibid.
16. Carson and Moo, *Introduction to the New Testament*, 94.
17. Giles, "'L' Tradition," 431.
18. Ibid.
19. Burnett, "M," 511–12.

LEGITIMACY OF A NARRATOLOGICAL APPROACH TO MARK

to them. What is debated, however, is the nature of this *Sondergut*.[20] The consensus thinking justifies itself when one considers the following three points. First, of all the Gospels, Mark has the crudest Greek writing; this is an argument from style. Second, Mark often features the hardest reading and/or embarrassing readings. Third, an argument from redaction demonstrates the likelihood of Markan priority. A few brief examples of the above points will demonstrate the thesis.

First, Mark often lacks the literary finesse or style of the other Gospels. It would be difficult to explain why Mark, in possession of Matthew and Luke, would choose to make his Greek more difficult and less polished. For example, in Mark 10:20, we read, "I have observed" which is an aorist middle verb and is rather awkward and stylistically ugly. In the parallels, Matt 19:20 and Luke 18:21, the Greek has been smoothed out and the verb is rendered in the aorist active. It is easier to understand Matthew and Luke preferring to smooth the Greek of Mark, than it is to suppose that Mark, in possession of Matthew or Luke, chose the other. Or again, in Mark 4:41, "obeys" is a singular verb, while the subject, "winds and sea" is plural. Matthew 8:27 and Luke 8:25 rightly use the plural verb form here. This is just a sampling of the instances in which the Greek in Mark is notably inferior to the writing in Matthew and Luke.[21]

Second, Mark features the harder, or more embarrassing, readings. The most famous of this type of reading is found in Mark 1:12, where the Spirit "drove" Jesus into the wilderness. The Greek verb used in verse 12 is ἐκβάλλειν. This same word is used a little later by Mark in 1:34, where Jesus is exorcising demons by "casting them out." This potentially confusing and embarrassing language is cleared up by both Matthew (Matt 4:1, Jesus is "led"), and Luke (Luke 4:1, Jesus is "led"). In Mark, Jesus and his disciples are often portrayed in a light that may be construed as negative or undignified. For example, in the narrative of the calming of the sea, Mark's Jesus asks the frightened disciples, "have you no faith?" This is quite the rebuke from Jesus toward the disciples. Matthew records Jesus' words as, "O men of small faith" (Matt 8:26), and Luke, as "where is your faith?" (Luke 8:25). A number of instances of this type of apparent smoothing out of Mark by

20. This view may or may not argue that M and L were written sources. For a bibliophagy demonstrating the near consensus in biblical studies on the two-source hypothesis, see Evans, "Source, Form, and Redaction Criticism," 23, n. 15; Goodacre, *Synoptic Problem*, 21; and the extensive endnote tracing the scholarly literature from the beginning to end of the twentieth century by Wenham, *Redating Matthew, Mark and Luke*, 245. Recently, the very existence of Q document has come under fire. See Goodacre, *Case against Q*.

21. Additional arguments from style are found in Stein, *Studying the Synoptic Gospels*, 56–59; Evans, "Source, Form, and Redaction Criticism," 23.

Matthew and Luke abound. Summing up the argument about the potentially embarrassing elements of Mark being altered by Matthew and Luke, Craig Evans writes, "Has Mark rewritten the essentially positive portraits of the disciples, as he finds them in Matthew and Luke, or have Matthew and Luke improved upon the negative portrait that they found in Mark."[22] The answer seems evident.

An additional argument—though one from silence—is what Mark omits. If Mark had both Matthew and Luke at his disposal, why would he then omit so many powerful and significant portions of the Gospels? Certainly, some of this can be explained by an appeal to the redactorial aims of the author of Mark; perhaps he deliberately omitted some of the material at his disposal. What is left out, however, of Mark, is hard to explain away through this appeal. Absent from Mark is the Sermon on the Mount and the Lord's Prayer. It is easier to assume that Matthew and Luke added this material than it is to think that Mark chose not to put it in for whatever reason. Again, this is only an overview. Space and time do not permit a full treatment of the Synoptic Problem. The bulk of our attention is being placed on Mark as a narrative, not the literary relationship between Matthew, Mark, and Luke. That being said, it is still important for this present study to engage with the problems of source criticism. This study will begin its line of argumentation from a premise of Markan priority, and thus be somewhat limited in the ability to approach Mark from a redaction-critical view point, though some work has been done on the Gospel of Mark from a redaction critical approach.[23] Regardless of the view one takes on the authorship, and priority of Mark, the value of a narrative critical approach remains. Rather than looking "outside" the Gospel of Mark by reading the Synoptics horizontally, this thesis will look "in" to the literary work and confine the bulk of the study to this one locale.

AUDIENCE OF A GOSPEL: NARROW COMMUNITY, ALL CHRISTIANS, OR BOTH?

The question of the intended audience of a Gospel must now be considered. If the Gospels were, in the case of form criticism, simply unrelated tradition put together, anything even approaching narrative criticism would be impossible. The texts would not be designed to be coherent or a have any sense of unity. If, on the other hand, we follow the redaction critics and assume

22. Evans, "Source, Form, and Redaction Criticism," 23.

23. See, for example, Marxsen, *Mark the Evangelist*; Black, *Disciples according to Mark*; Pryke, *Redactional Style in the Marcan Gospel*.

that the Gospels were written for one particular audience or community that faced a very specific issue in their group then, without being confident as to what that particular issue was, a narrative approach to the Gospels could not begin without first uncovering the issues that led to its composition. Or, what if Bauckham's hypothesis (which we will turn to shortly) is correct, and the original intended audience was indefinite, or general? Issues with Bauckham's work have been noted[24] but it still demands attention and is not easily dismissed in totality. Redaction critics are concerned with Mark as theologian; narrative critics with Mark as author. This present study is concerned with both. It will be argued here that the expectation (if not intention) of the author of Mark was that his Gospel would be read widely; not just in the community to which he wrote. This expectation indicates an intelligibility of Mark to those outside the original directly intended audience. Although it appears that the original audience was a Roman one, the Gospel was expected to read more widely than that. If the Gospels were written, at least partially, for a general audience, the implied reader is no longer some hypothetical person or group placed in history, but is instead one and the same with an indefinite readership—a general audience.[25] With that, we turn our attention now to a discussion on audience. Here, it will be argued that the Gospels were written to be understood by a broad audience. It is not necessary to follow Bauckham in totality to find his hypothesis helpful. Using Bauckham's work as a starting point, it will be argued that the Gospels were written for a specific audience, but were expected to be read widely. The bulk of the investigation will focus on Bauckham's work. The reason for this is that the specific audience that Mark was supposed to have been writing to has been highly debated and a significant amount of literature written to argue in favor of either a Roman, Syrian, or Galilean provenance for Mark's Gospel.[26]

Richard Bauckham, in his influential *The Gospels for All Christians*, sought to challenge the scholarly consensus that the Gospels were written to address issues germane to the respective authors' own communities. This he does with finesse and a level of comprehensiveness that demands close attention. The question of audience, whether it be a localized community under siege by some specific heresy or challenge or a general audience predominately Christian, is important for our present study. One of the chief hesitations that scholars offer for embracing a narrative critical reading is

24. Van Eck, "Sitz for the Gospel of Mark?"

25. The term "indefinite readership" is not the author's own. See Bauckham, *Gospels for All Christians*, 45.

26. For a helpful overview of the debate surrounding provenance, see Van Eck, "Sitz for the Gospel of Mark?" 969–82.

the lack of attention given to the historical critical method. This caution is warranted because the Gospels were written in a specific context, at a specific time in history—one which is not our own. Neglecting the historical dimension seems akin to living in the time of the judges, where "all did (or interpreted) what was right in their own eyes." Or, to put it another way, a narrative critical approach divorced from the historical horizon of interpretation is a faulty approach prone to anachronism and errors of all kind. To properly merge the disciplines of narrative criticism and the historical-critical method is not impossible, but does require a starting point that has been carefully evaluated. This is why the present study will invest space and time to exploring the genre of the Gospels. Are they simply a string of pearls of oral traditions spliced together by a compiler? Were they written in response to a specific community's needs? Or are they of such a genre that they are carefully written and carefully arranged to form a cohesive whole which warrants a close reading—in other words are they intelligible to readers from outside of the author's own community, or the community to which he wrote? To this, Bauckham answers yes. Building on Bauckham's thesis that the Gospels were intelligible and meant to be understood by to those outside of the author's own community, and establishing the genre of the Gospels will allow this present study to progress through the Gospel of Mark from a narrative critical perspective, and provide justification for doing so. If the Gospels are broad in their implied readership, and if the genre is one that is prone to well thought-out and cohesive plot line, a narrative critical approach will not violate the text, nor will it divorce it from its historical moorings. Rather, it will be a natural response to those two realities.

This discussion obviously involves a further consideration of source, form, and redaction criticism, but it is also a question of *kind*—a question of genre. This study will argue that the implied reader is represented best when a general approach to audience is accepted rather than giving the most of attention to the reconstruction of the community that gave birth to the Gospel. Now in saying this, is does not indicate that one should gloss over the internal data within Mark that indicates he was writing to a specific group.[27] That data is important and must factor in to the hermeneutical scheme that one approaches the text with. However, what this Section is seeking to offer is a marriage of these two realities. Yes, it is argued, the book of Mark was written for a specific audience, but was expected to be read widely and as such although there is value in uncovering to whom the Gospel was written, there is also value is realizing that the indefinite readership is also a factor.

---

27. Van Eck, "Sitz for the Gospel of Mark?"

Mark was written to be understood by a specific audience and a general audience.

It is axiomatic that, for well over a century, nearly every commentary on a Gospel would spend time reconstructing that Gospel's community that prompted the formation of the writing. This was done for all the canonical Gospels (not to mention Thomas and Q). Bauckham surveys the history of interpretation of this approach and, although his survey is not exhaustive, it nevertheless demonstrates that this was (and is) the consensus view.[28] He highlights the work of such notable scholars as W. D. Davies and D. C. Allison, along with Joseph Fitzmyer, and notes how they "discuss the introductory questions about the Gospels, simply assuming that the question about the context in which a Gospel was written and the question about the audience for which a Gospel was written are the same questions."[29] What Bauckham sets out to do is to challenge this type of thinking by arguing that the Gospels were written for a general circulation or an indefinite readership. The points he offers are worth noting here.

First, Bauckham notes that mobility and transportation in the first century Roman world were remarkably high. Travel was generally safe, featured many established routes, and was a rather common occurrence by all levels of society. He extrapolates the significance of this reality as follows: "So the context in which the early Christian movement developed was not conducive to parochialism; quite the opposite."[30] The early Christian movement did not flourish in extreme isolation or independence. Instead, through frequent travel, interaction, and communication, the movement most likely had some sense of overlap or, at the least, featured a high degree of interaction.

Second, Bauckham refers to the distinct nature of the early Christian movement as being based around literature. Paul's letters are frequently referring to other churches and encouraging one congregation to be aware and involved in what other churches are doing or facing (1 Cor 1:2; 9:5; 16:3; 1 Thess 2:14).

The third point made by Bauckham complements the previous two. Since the churches were aware and involved in what each other were facing, and since travel was relatively safe, the first century Christian leaders moved around from location to location. Extensive citations from the New Testament are given by Bauckham for the following Christians leaders, demonstrating that they were itinerate in some respects in their ministry:

28. Bauckham, *Gospels for All Christians*, 13–22.
29. Ibid., 16.
30. Ibid., 32.

Peter, Barnabas, Mark, Silas, Apollos, Phillip the evangelist and his prophet daughters, Aquila and Priscilla, Andronicus and Junia, Agabus, and the brothers of the Lord.[31]

Fourth, attention is given to yet another dimension of the early Christian communities: churches often sent letters to one another. Examples of this include the church in Rome writing to the churches in Asia Minor (1 Peter), and another letter written to the church in Corinth (1 Clement). Bauckham also points out the obvious implication that letters imply messengers. These messengers would have to be housed, greeted as guests, welcomed into the community and be expected to convey information verbally as well.[32]

As a fifth point, Bauckham offers the concrete evidence that we do have for close contacts between churches in different regions from around the period just after the writings of the Gospels. Here, he offers three examples. (1) The now extant fragment of Papias' prologue surviving in Eusebius' work; (2) The letters of Ignatius, which were written only a few decades after the Gospels; and (3) Hermas *Shepherd of Hermas*. These letters were written just a few decades after the Gospels and demonstrate a high degree of cooperation and shared interest.

For point number six, Bauckham explains how diversity and conflict in the early church demonstrates that communities did not function in stringent autonomy or independence. They interacted, they met one another, they argued! He explains, "None of this evidence for conflict and disagreement suggests that any version of Christianity formed a homogeneous little enclave of churches, out of communication with other churches."[33]

Bauckham's hypothesis utilizes the data from the New Testament and early church well. In discussing the task of reconstructing the communities to which the Gospels were written, he notes, "As a matter of fact, it seems very doubtful whether we can know anything worth knowing about them."[34] So, once again, the point must be made. By focusing on the finished text as we have it, instead of devoting unnecessary time to the historical unknown, a valid argument can be made in favor of a hermeneutic that relies and draws on narrative criticism, which itself demands attention to the whole of the text.

At this point, one may ask what the value of moving from the concept of a narrow community to an indefinite reader has for the discipline of

---

31. For references, see, Bauckham, *Gospels for All Christians*, 34.
32. Ibid., 38.
33. Ibid., 43.
34. Ibid., 44.

narrative criticism. Two of the dominant approaches in the typical historical critical method offer a drastically different understanding of the finished text than does narrative criticism. The cry of all scholars employing a narrative sensitive hermeneutic is simple: "View it as a complete text. Remember, it's a story!" The form critic sees the text as being of a very different nature. Instead of a coherent story, it is seen as a series of traditions put together and, as such, by nature cannot be taken seriously as a literary composition. The redaction critic sees the final text not as a simple cocktail of traditions, but as a carefully crafted work in which attention is given to combating certain teaching in the communities from which they were birthed. There is value in the redaction critical approach that will be addressed in chapter 4 and 5. The argument here, however, is that Mark (or any Gospel writer, for that matter) very well may have shaped and utilized the material he had available to address certain needs within a specific community, but that it was still done with the expectation of a wider readership. It was not written to a hermetically sealed group living in isolation and thus unintelligible without a full reconstruction of the community. So, to answer our initial question regarding the value of moving from the primary concept of intended audience to indefinite audience, the answer is clear. If the intended audience was in fact an indefinite audience, only a narrative critical approach does justice to the author's original intentions: telling the story of Jesus in a coherent manner which is comprehensible to a general audience.

All this talk about indefinite readership is not intended to propagate the view that Mark wrote his Gospel for an endless audience, as if he wrote in the heading "Dear Christians of the world. . ." Rather, it is intended to demonstrate that the Gospel is such that those who do not compose the original audience can understand it. Now, as mentioned earlier, there is debate surrounding who that original audience was. Common proposals for Mark's audience include Roman, Syrian, and Galilean communities. It will be argued here that the Roman context best fits the data that we have.

The discussion surrounding the original audience for Mark's Gospel is extensive. Space does not permit an exhaustive study of the data, but an overview will suffice to illustrate the strength of the argument being set forward. Internal evidence present in Mark seems to suggest that the audience was a group of Greek-speaking believers who possessed a foundational knowledge of the Old Testament. Additionally, the audience appears to have been unfamiliar with Aramaic, since Mark takes the opportunity to explain Aramaic expressions at every instance (Mark 3:17–22; 5:42; 7:11, 34; 9:43; 10:46; 14:36; 15:22, 34).

The early church tradition links Mark to Rome.[35] The majority of commentators hold to the view that Mark wrote primarily to the believers in Rome, but this view has been challenged in recent years.[36] The presence and extensive use of "Latinisms" in Mark supports the Roman audience view.[37] A number of technical Latin terms such as: mat, basket, legion, soldier of the guard, denarius, fist, pitcher, tax, penny, centurion, to satisfy, scourge, and praetorian, are transliterated into Greek.[38] Although Matthew and Luke possess some "Latinisms," the amount and extent of usage in Mark indicate a Roman audience.

Mark does not explain a number of christological titles, but rather assumes the reader is aware of their connotations (Son of God, Son of Man, Son of David). Further, the introduction of John the Baptist is not as forthcoming with background information as Matthew and Luke, and he is introduced simply as "John." Cities, rulers, characters, and the disciples are all introduced and talked about in a manner that assumes the audience's knowledge of them. If the audience were composed of believers, they would have been familiar with these places, people, and events from the oral messages they had heard up until this point.

Mark's description of the woman in 7:26 also shed light on to audience he was writing to. There, he calls the woman "Syrophoenician." This description or phrase would likely not have made sense to those from the East. This description is used, however, in Roman sources as a way to identify or distinguish people based on geography.[39] This is yet more evidence for a Roman provenance. Additional points are summarized by Van Eck.[40] The foundation moving forward will be that Mark wrote for a Roman audience (which has exegetical and interpretive value) with the expectation that it would be read more widely than just one Roman community of Christians (which permits a literary approach and lends itself to keeping one eye on the finished text and one eye on redaction critical questions).

Narrative criticism is not a replacement to traditional historical critical approaches. It is an addition to the tool-box, not the multi-tool that meets every need. The justification for a narrative critical approach is based on the data that is gleaned from redaction critic and the conclusion that the

---

35. Cunningham, *Mark*.

36. Marcus, *Mark 1–8*, 33–37; Boring, *Mark*, 18–20. Boring opts for Syria or Galilee.

37. Winn, *Purpose of Mark's Gospel*, 80–82; Witherington, *Gospel of Mark*, 20.

38. For a list, see, Stein, *Mark*, 11. Additionally, See Hooker, *Gospel according to St. Mark*, 16, who argues that Latinism can be explained by noting that both Greek and Hebrew had Latin words in various parts of the Empire.

39. Gundry, *Mark*, 318.

40. Van Eck, "Sitz for the Gospel of Mark?" 970–73.

Gospel is intelligible and comprehensible to those outside of the Roman community that Mark wrote. The importance of genre comes into play once narrative criticism has done its work. Once a scholar has noted significant literary devices and techniques in a work, the classification of the text then guides the interpretative dimension that naturally follows. Since the goal of this thesis is to offer an assessment of Mark's Son of God theology, the question of genre governs the way we approach the data we find in the Gospel.

GENRE

A reader approaches a text in a certain way depending on its genre. We would expect to read a historical biography written in the twenty-first century to be very differently than we would read a cookbook. Or, to make the point in a more refined way, a careful reader would read a historical novel differently from a history text book. At its most basic level, genre creates a foundation upon which an author builds, and upon which a reader understands. The reader knows, to some degree, what to expect and how to interpret what he or she is reading. In the same way, the author, whether knowingly or not, naturally assumes certain literary features or characteristics native to the genre in which he or she is writing. Collins is right when she remarks that, from a traditional Christian viewpoint, genre matters little in a study of the Gospels. They are "Gospels" and interpreted, understood and followed as such.[41] Collins explains, however, that from a historical perspective, the question of genre is significant. For example, she notes that the *Gospel of Thomas* is quite different in feel and content from the canonical Gospels. Clearly, there is some difference here in genre, and the simple title, "Gospel" is not sufficient for the historian.

For historians and scholars, the question of genre directly impacts the hermeneutical approach that they take with the text. At its most germane, genre affects all communication, whether the recipient is aware of it or not. Pennington describes the importance of genre well:

> readers or hearers in any culture naturally develop a "literary competence" by which they are able to discern what to expect from a communicative event. For the person embedded in his or her own culture, this literary competence may not be something he or she is aware of or able to articulate, but it is influential nonetheless. A foundational element in such literary

---

41. Collins, *Mark*, 15.

competence is the ability to discern genre, or what type of literature or communicative event is occurring.[42]

For our present study, understanding the genre of Mark is essential for ensuring that we approach the text properly. Should the genre of Mark be proven to be a *sui generis* (unique genre), then we have no real foundation upon which we could suppose that the Gospel warrants being interpreted as a whole text. For example, if the Gospel of Mark was formed through various traditions being randomly combined to form a text, then expecting literary elements, continuing motifs, or patterns of repetition becomes a mere fantasy. If, however, the genre is thought to be that of a Greco-Roman biography, then we can expect to find these same elements in the text. Under the reign of form criticism, the Gospels are seen as a window to the early church traditions and kerygma. Under the reign of source criticism, the Gospels are a window to the varying Christian communities that gave them birth. In narrative criticism, however, the Gospels are not something we look *through*, but something we look *at*. They are an end in themselves and warrant a close study. Marcus rightly notes, "[Genre] is a potentially important issue, since reader" conception about what sort of book they are reading can shape their experience of the book; we pick up a historical novel, for example with different sorts of expectations from those with which we pick up a biography or a history.[43]

It is true that every literary work or communicative event is flexible and that there are no unpardonable variations within genres. There are no rules that cannot be broken. That being said, there are within genres certain reoccurring identifiable features that help shed light on the nature and purpose of the communicative event. Pennington again engages the genre question with the analogy of "family resemblance."[44] By this he means that, although there is often a great deal of difference between family members, there are nevertheless certain common characteristics that identify them as being of the same family.

A brief survey of the genre debate in Gospel studies is warranted and so follows. An extensive historical survey is beyond the scope of the present study, so for expediency, five significant scholars that factored in the genre debate will be noted.[45] The five scholars that will be reviewed at his

---

42. Pennington, *Reading the Gospels Wisely*, 18–19.

43. Marcus, *Mark 1–8*, 64.

44. Pennington, *Reading the Gospels Wisely*, 19.

45. For a longer examination of the history of the genre debate, see, Burridge, *What Are the Gospels?* 3–24; Talbert, *What Is a Gospel?* 1–23; Shuler, "Synoptic Gospels and the Problem of Genre"; Shuler, *Genre for the Gospels*, 1–23; Baird, *Comparative Analysis*

point are: C. W. Votaw, K. L. Schmidt, C. H. Talbert, Phillip L. Schuler, and Richard Burridge. These five individuals are noted here not because they are the only individuals to have reflected or written on the question of genre, but because their views typify the history of the genre debate. With that in mind, we turn our attention to the first.

C. W. Votaw

Clyde Weber Votaw published an article in the *American Journal of Theology* in 1915 that gave special attention to the question of genre for the Gospels. After a brief survey of the Greco-Roman literature of the day and the differences that it has with the Gospels, he remarks,

> The Gospels are to be viewed, not as historical writings produced by a historical impulse and method, but as propagandist writings of this early Christian movement. They contain historical reminiscences, or memorabilia, of Jesus' ministry; but for the practical use these may serve in the evangelistic mission.[46]

Votaw seems to believe that the Gospels themselves are not primarily about Jesus, *per se*, but about the early Christian movement's view of Jesus. Votaw continues in his essay and argues that, at no point between the events of the first century surrounding Jesus and the penning of the Gospels was the Jesus tradition subjected to any form of historical verification or review. Again, the primary concern of the Gospels is not to record the life and teachings of their protagonist, Jesus, but to communicate the faith of the early church; In Votaw's words, they serve "propagandist" purposes and are primarily "popular" in their focus. Votaw argues that there are two approaches to biography in the Greco-Roman world: historical-biography and, what he calls, popular-biography. The difference between the two is that, whereas historical-biography is concerned with accurately conveying dates, locations, and facts, popular-biography is concerned with introducing the reader to the dynamic individual under consideration. Although there is undoubtedly, according to Votaw, overlap between these two approaches, they can be distinguished if the primary concern of the work under consideration is determined. For example, a historical-biography can be identified by its concern for the *historical* dimensions of its story. A popular-biography can be identified by its concern for the memorabilia, disconnected from history.

---

of the Gospel Genre; Longenecker and Tenney, *New Dimensions in New Testament Study*, 97–114.

46. Votaw, "Gospels and Contemporary Biographies," 47.

In the end, Votaw arrives at the conclusion that the Gospels are, in fact, biographies, but not of the historical kind. He argues that the Gospels are popular biography, concerned more with the goal of promoting the person of Jesus, than reflecting back on the historical realities of his life and ministry. After arriving at this conclusion, he then turns his attention to Greco-Roman literature that shares features with the Gospels and seeks to highlight the parallels between the two genres. The three ancient works with which the Gospels can most readily be compared, according to Votaw, are the works that report the lives of Epictetus, Apollonius, and Socrates. Regarding the similarities between these and the Gospels, Votaw writes,

> It was the purpose of these writings to make known the personality and the message of these three great moral-religious teachers. The authors wrote with a practical, not with a chronicling intent. They did not make historical investigation, or give a systematic accurate account of the life (though the Life of Apollonius is in general chronological order, like the accounts of the Life of Jesus in the Synoptic Gospels), but gave memorabilia of the teaching, with more or less incident in conjunction (the Life of Apollonius has much incident material, the writings about Socrates have but a small amount of incident, the Discourses of Epictetus have none).[47]

According to Votaw, the closest parallel to the recounting of the Jesus story is that of Socrates. Not only are they both written to vindicate one recently executed by the state, but they are also written with the same interval between the events themselves and their being set to the page. For Votaw, the fact that both the Gospels and the life of Socrates share similar aims and content, indicate that they can assuredly be of the same kind of genre. It must be remembered that Votaw wrote before form criticism had been discovered, and as such, he often neglects the forms found in the Gospels. He is primarily concerned with the content of the Gospels, rather than arriving at any type of refined literary definition of genre or form. Votaw does not define genre at any point, nor does he interact with literary theory in a meaningful way. Schuler remarks on Votaw's approach, "This shortcoming will continue to plague the genre debate for some time. It is not until much later that a more refined literary theory of genre is applied to the debate surrounding the Gospel's genre."[48]

---

47. Ibid., 55.
48. Shuler, *Genre for the Gospels*, 22.

Karl Ludwig Schmidt

Where Votaw saw a popular level biography, Schmidt saw a series of pericopes or units that once circulated orally, now put to text in the New Testament Gospels.[49] According to Schmidt, these oral units were strung together like pearls on a piece of string by the Gospel writers. Unlike Votaw (who wrote only a few years prior to Schmidt), Schmidt's proposal was rooted in the new discipline of form criticism that was becoming increasingly popular in New Testament studies, especially in Germany at that time.

Schmidt proposed that the Gospels were completely void of any literary personality of their writers. This was due to their being a collection of oral traditions set side by side in the text rather than a popular biography designed to convince the reader of the merit of the story's protagonist, as Votaw believed.

The general approach of Schmidt to the question of genre was to group literary works into one of two possible classifications: *Hochliteratur* and *Kleinliteratur*. For Schmidt, *Hochliteratur* was any literature where the author's personality was discoverable within the text. In this type of literature, the author's creativity shines through and is available for study. The other category, *Kleinliteratur*, is akin to folk literature. Shuler articulates Schmidt's view of *Kleinliteratur* like this: "that vast, loosely defined body of material consisting of small and often incoherently joined literary units."[50] Because this is so, to speak of an "author" in the traditional sense is a misnomer. As such, to speak of a Gospel genre is likewise inaccurate. One may speak of the genre of specific pericopes or units, but not of a Gospel as a whole. This means that the Gospels were unable to be compared with any ancient work of literature, and that any parallels between them and Greco-Roman *bios* were superficial and irrelevant; the Gospels, according to this viewpoint, are *sui generis*. This is a point that the great New Testament scholar Rudolf Bultmann agreed with. He, following suit with Schmidt's line of reasoning, argued that, within the "Greek Tradition," no analogies could be found for the Gospels.[51]

---

49. Schmidt, *Der Rahmen der Geschichte Jesu*.

50. Shuler, *Genre for the Gospels*, 6.

51. Bultmann, *History of the Synoptic Tradition*, 371–72. In explaining how unique he views the genre of the biblical Gospels, Bultmann goes so far as to say, "What analogies can be suggested? There are none in the *Greek Tradition*. . . . There is no historical-biographical interest in the Gospels, and that is why they have nothing to say about Jesus' personality, his appearance and character, his origin, education, development; quite apart from the fact that they do not command the cultivated techniques of composition necessary for grand literature, nor let the personalities of their author appear" (372).

The issue that scholars in present day have found with Schmidt's proposal is that his literary terms, although quite vague and undefined, are rather rigid in their application. Additionally, as Burridge, and Kelber before him, noted that the very act of the locating, arranging and putting down in writing of these disparate traditions would no doubt affect the manner in which they are to be understood.[52] This step seems to be a consideration that the staunch form critics have neglected. With the introduction of redaction criticism, the role of the author is returned to a place of prominence.

Charles Talbert

Up until the 1970s, the debate surrounding the genre of the Gospels seemed somewhat fixed. They were thought to be a unique genre that defied literary categories. Two influential books and a conference at Tübingen, however, offered a different perspective. With their suggestions, scholars began to accept the classification of the genre *bios* with varying qualifications.

The first book that led in this was Charles Talbert's *What is a Gospel?*[53] His arguments will be examined first. Talbert, writing just a few years before Philip Shuler, argued that the Gospels were in keeping with much Greco-Roman literature, specifically those of a biographical nature. Talbert was rather pointed in his criticism of Bultmann's narrow approach to the question of genre. He rejected Bultmann's three objections to understanding the Gospels as biography. Talbert argued that there were a number of distinct types of ancient biography. Type "A" centered around an individual who functioned as a copy for the reader to emulate (e.g., Lucian's *Life of Demonax*). Type "B" were biographies written to deal with false views of the teacher and correct the interpretation that was current at the time. Examples of this subsection of biography include Xenophon's *Memorabilia*, Philodemus' *Life of Epicurus*, and Philostratus' *Life of Apollonius of Tyana*. For example, according to Talbert, Xenophon wrote to "preserve the figure of Socrates from distortion, to present him properly so that his deeds and words might serve as a model for other men."[54] Type "C" were biographies that intended to discredit a certain teacher. This, Talbert explained, was often used as a weapon against different schools of philosophy by those antagonistic towards them. Type "D" was designed to bolster one specific tradition or school that developed in the teacher's wake. This type of biography

---

52. Burridge, *What Are the Gospels?* 13–14; Kelber, *Oral and the Written Gospel*, 16–20.

53. Talbert, *What Is a Gospel?*

54. Ibid., 94.

was used to highlight where the teacher's "living voice" was presently found in the world. An example of this would include the *Life of Aristotle*. Talbert was not done there, but continued to include a final type of biography: Type "E" served as the "hermeneutical key" for understanding and interpreting a teacher's words and legacy. Talbert offered a number of examples in this subsection including Porphyryss *Life of Aristotle,* and Secundus' *Life of Secundus the Silent Philosopher.*

After claiming that "this new method of classification of ancient biographies according to their social function ... yielded substantial results."[55] Talbert applied this framework to the Gospels. He believed Mark and John were Type "B" because they were written to correct erroneous views of Jesus that existed at the time. He argued that Luke-Acts was Type "D," written to solidify a certain group within the early church. Matthew, however, was Type "E" serving to unlock the teachings and life of the founder of Christianity. Despite the claims of "substantial results," this method of classification has not gained a hearing in scholarship. In fact, David Aune, writing about Talbert, went so far as to describe him as a "blindfolded man staggering across a mine-field."[56] Although Talbert was instrumental in bringing about a resurgence of interest in viewing the Gospels as biography, his narrowly defined "Types" are problematic. Talbert has, however, furthered this discussion of genre by highlighting the mythic and cultic aspects of ancient biography.

Those who follow what Talbert helped pioneer, have tended to pay more attention to literary theory and, more specifically, questions about what exactly constitute a "genre." Regardless, Talbert's work is significant and deserves to be remembered as the pioneering work in the field of Gospel studies that defended and propagated the view that the Gospels were biography.

Philip Shuler

Shuler's 1975 PhD dissertation at McMaster University, in Hamilton, Canada was eventually shortened and published in 1982. Shuler should be commended for advancing the discussion concerning literary theory and genre studies. Nevertheless, the section devoted to literary theory remained quite brief, serving primarily as a precursor to the comparison of ancient biographies to the Gospels, instead of as foundational for establishing the

55. Ibid., 97.
56 Aune, "Problem of the Genre of the Gospels," 85; See also, Burridge, *What Are the Gospels?* 85.

basis of the conversation surrounding the nature of genre.[57] Whereas Talbert distinguished between mythic and cultic, Shuler divided ancient biography into two categories: historical biography and laudatory biography (what he comes to call *encomium*). Of primary interest to Shuler is the classification and identification of the *encomium*. He argues that this particular genre features three important aspects that distinguish it from historical biography: first, the goal of praising or celebrating the individual being considered; second, the literary technique of comparison and amplification; and third, Shuler explains that to distinguish *encomium*, one must, "identify more precisely the particular occasions, subjects, and *topoi* with which the encomium is primarily *concerned*."[58] This final point is pertinent due to the common usage of this genre for public oration and display. Collins captures Shuler's views by saying,

> [He] defined a subtype of biography that he called "encomium" or laudatory biography. The members of this subgroup are characterized as impressionistic portrait, rather than detailed critical reports, exhibiting the presentation of the pattern of a life from birth to death; the use of the rhetorical techniques of amplification and comparison; and the aim of praising the central character.[59]

Shuler's work has been significant in Gospel studies and the genre debate. Issues with his work have been addressed by scholars[60] but his impact on the genre debate and the increasing identification with biography has been significant.

Richard Burridge

Although both Talbert and Shuler argued for the classification of the Gospels as "biography," by and large, they neglected serious engagement with literary theory surrounding the nature and function of genre. Burridge, in his landmark *What are the Gospels? A Comparison with Greco-Roman Biography*, sought to address these deficiencies and present a compelling case for the genre title "biography" of the Gospels. Burridge's book, now in its second edition, is largely considered the definitive English work on the question of genre for the Gospels. In recent years there have been a number

---

57. Shuler, *Genre for the Gospels*, 24–34.
58. Ibid., 51.
59. Collins, *Mark*, 26.
60. Burridge, *What Are the Gospels?*, 86–89; Collins, *Mark*, 26.

of scholars who have sought to build upon or sharpen some of the ideas that Burridge proposed, and his work continues to endure as a significant milestone in the field.[61] Put simply, Burridge argued that a Gospel is a "life" of Jesus. He offered parallels form Greco-Roman antiquity of similar size, focus, and verb usage (with the protagonist being the one who acts) to demonstrate that the Gospels fit within the biography genre that was present in Greek and Roman literature.

Burridge began his study with a detailed study of genre theory. Burridge sided with Alastair Fowler, arguing that genre was not so much about precise classification, but about meaning.[62] Burridge, after highlighting the debate surrounding the genre question relating to the Gospels, proposed first that the generic features of any genre ought to be the first area of attention. These generic features of genre include:

1. *Opening Features*: This would include the title, opening formulae/prologue/preface.

2. *Subject*: Obviously, the importance of the subject under consideration cannot be overestimated for the question of genre. One would hardly classify a computer repair manual as a biography! Burridge analyzes the relationship between verbs and their subjects, asking "who" is doing "what"? His argument being that the one most often functioning as the "who" would likely be the work's protagonist. Here, Burridge offers statistical analysis of *The Iliad*. Secondly, along with the verbs subject, which can help the reader ascertain the overall subject of a work, the allocation of space is another statistic that Burridge considers helpful in locating the primary subject of a work. Again, one would hardly assume that the subject for that same computer repair manual was the Queen of Sweden even if the Queen was mentioned once or twice.

3. *External Features*: External features would include mode of representation. The question here is "was the work originally designed to be performed, acted, read, or preached?" Secondly, the meter of the work is important for the question of genre. Certain works required certain meters. Here, Burridge points the reader to Aristophanes, the ancient writer who often changed meter when writing a joke or poking fun at an individual. An additional external feature important for genre consideration is that of overall length. Works by Herodotus, Thucydides, Pausanias, and others are compared by their size. A

---

61. See, for example, Pennington, *Reading the Gospels Wisely*, 25–31; Collins, *Mark*, 27–30; Alexander "What Is a Gospel?" 13–37.

62. Fowler, *Kinds of Literature*.

current-day example of this would be the common sense realization that a children's picture book would hardly be classified as a fantasy novel in the vein of Tolkien, or George R. R. Martin. Yet another generic feature within a genre is the structure or sequence. In essence, works of a similar genre will share a similar structure. Additionally, what is omitted is also important to consider. What does the author choose to leave unspoken, inferred, or mysterious? Works of a common genre share common habits in what they choose not to include. Additionally, Burridge argues that the scale of the work is significant. For example, rarely would someone confuse the Oxford Encyclopedia for a children's book; the length of the work is an indicator of the genre to which it belongs. Next, when considering literary units, works in the same genre will demonstrate similar "selections and patterns."[63] While the use of a source cannot determine the genre of a work (since different genres may use the same source), the patterns and types of sources being used form an external feature that links works from the same genre. The final external feature that Burridge offers is that of characterization. Here he argues that the methods of ancient characterization often avoided the psychological approach, and instead focused on the actions and words of the individual under consideration. The manner in which the character of the protagonist is unveiled in a work depends largely on the genre the work reflects.

4. *Internal Features*: Burridge argues that for the genre of *bios*, the setting is a clear "mediator" for the work.[64] In contrast to historical works which, for obvious reasons, lack a unifying use of particular settings, *bios* often draw from certain narrative constructs such as particular settings native to works within the field. Next, Burridge offers that topics/motifs are a common thread which unify works in the same genre. He gives a number of examples from New Comedy, a genre that includes works by Menander and Euripides. Although much has been made in the past of the significance of motifs and topics, Burridge cautions against a reductionist view on this particular internal feature. Because of the manner in which these motifs become culturally significant and generic, they often span genres and, as such, cannot be used in isolation to determine the genre of a particular text. The style and tone of the work are the next two internal features that Burridge discusses. Style refers to a work's intended audience (high-brow, educated, or popular), and tone is the atmosphere the work commu-

---

63. Burridge, *What Are the Gospels?*, 120.
64. Ibid., 122

nicates. The fifth internal identifier of genre that Burridge presents is that of characterization. While he cautions that modern approaches to characterization, such as overt psychologicalizing, cannot be applied to ancient works, the manner and form in which characterization happens in these works is an important aspect of the genre question. He argues that works which share a genre will describe and present their characters in similar ways. The sixth consideration, social setting and occasion, along with the seventh, authorial intent and purpose, are offered last. These are fairly self-explanatory and represent a narrowing of the understanding of genre. Although the authors of ancient works may have had any number of intentions or goals in their writing, being sensitive to this dimension of a work serves to aid in the genre question.

Using these four features, Burridge offers a method of genre analysis. His criticism that the literary dimension of genre investigation has not been adequately explored is addressed in a more sufficient manner in his work. By using these parameters of generic features, and applying them to the Gospels, Burridge arrives at the conclusion that the Gospels are in fact, biographies. These generic features are first applied to Greco-Roman works, then to the Gospels. In the end, Burridge concludes,

> Thus, there is a high degree of correlation between the generic features of Greco-Roman βίοι and those of the synoptic gospels; in fact, they exhibit more of the features than are shown by works at the edges of the genre, such as those of Isocrates, Xenophon, and Philostratus. This is surely a sufficient number of shared features for the genre of the synoptic to be clear: while they may well form their own subgenre because of their shared account, *the synoptic gospels belong within the overall genre of βίοι.*[65]

Burridge's work on the genre of the Gospels is perhaps the most significant in the last fifty years. Although his work has served to bolster the belief that the Gospels are *bios*, it is not without some difficulties. Whereas Talbert was rather creative with his Type A to Type E subgenres, the simplicity of Burridge's proposal, that the Gospels are primarily exemplary, is perhaps overstated. Burridge defines the genre of the Gospels as biography but does not demonstrate the variances within that title. Collins is right in her assessment of Burridge's thesis that the Gospels are primarily exemplary: "In spite of Burridge's attempt to find something analogous in the Gospels, it is

65. Burridge, *What Are the Gospels?*, 218 (emphasis original).

clear that their portrayal of Jesus' so-called character and virtues belongs to a different cultural context and has a purpose beyond exemplary."[66]

A second issue with Burridge's work that has drawn criticism is the lack of engagement with Jewish sources as a possible precursor to the Gospels. As was indicative of much German and, to a lesser extent, American scholarship in the early to mid-twentieth century, the dominant landscape that scholars sought to settle Gospel studies in was primarily a Greco-Roman one. Little real attention was given to the second-temple context that gave birth to the early church, and shaped its theology and identity. This is perhaps one of the most significant areas of weakness in Burridge's work. The Hebrew Bible offers a number of life stories that center around one prominent individual, chronicling the individual's virtue, deeds and character from life until death. Loveday Alexander, who offers a helpful assessment of the importance of Hebrew sources to the genre question, writes,

> The Hebrew Bible itself is much more deeply prone to "bio-structuring" than is classical Greek historiography. Much of the narrative of the Hebrew Bible is built around biographical "story cycles" like those of Samson or Elijah, cycles in which individual tales of the hero's prowess "are so arranged to encompass his entire life, from birth to death."[67]

Alexander's words deserve our attention. Arriving at an understanding of the genre question requires that we engage with the actual historical realities under which the Gospels were written. It is well and good to highlight the similarities that exist between Greco-Roman biographies and the Gospels, but we must also consider the parallels that exist in Jewish literature, especially the Hebrew Scriptures; knowing that the early church was birthed out of Jewish soil requires this of us.

A BROAD VIEW OF GENRE

Burridge's arguments (along with Shuler and Talbert's), that the Gospels cannot be *sui generis*, is persuasive. On methodological grounds, this premise of a *sui generis* labeling of the Gospels is indefensible. Their collective reconstruction and categories, however, require addition. Yes, the Gospels share similarities with Greco-Roman biography in subject, content, motifs, verb usage, and length, but there is more to be considered. The hero of the Gospels is categorically different from the heroes of Greco-Roman

66. Collins, *Mark*, 28.
67. Alexander, "What Is a Gospel?" 36.

biographies. Unlike Alexander the Great, or Aristotle, Jesus is not presented by the Gospel writers as simply a great leader or influential teacher—he is none other than the Son of God, the Messiah who has come to bring to fulfillment Israel's history. Pennington summarizes this reality as such, "[He is] the epicentric [sic] and climactic point of the grand story of what God is doing in the world."[68] Further, the Gospels build upon the history of God's people as revealed in the Hebrew Bible. Additionally, Pennington notes that the Gospels are not only concerned with Jesus' character and virtue, but also his very nature.[69] Jesus not only says words, he *is* the Word (John 1). Jesus is wisdom, life, and love personified. The Hebrew Bible, Second Temple Judaism, and the Talmud do not have anything in them that provides a close parallel to the form of the Gospels.[70]

CONCLUDING THOUGHTS

A brief summary of where we have come thus far is in order at this point. We began by establishing that the Gospels were written to a Roman audience with the expectation that they would be shared, traded, and read in a wider context than one community. This means that our focus of interpretation should be the finished text we have, rather than solely on the reconstructed historical context of Gospel communities. This area of investigation relied heavily on Richard Bauckham's work on Gospel audiences. From there, we progressed to an investigation into the genre of the Gospels. If, as the form critics suggest, the Gospels are a unique genre that was essentially oral tradition codified, then our approach to interpretation will differ drastically than if the text is a careful and sophisticated literary work. The problem with the form critical view—other than the methodological issue and the impossibility of an author creating a totally "new" genre—is that it constantly seeks to strip away the finished text we have in order to reconstruct the oral tradition that supposedly underpins it. This approach focuses on the *Sitz im Leben* of the Gospels, but can forget the other "life setting": that of the authors themselves. This approach cannot offer much assessment on the work, or theology of the "author" since, in this view, the author is little more than a compiler. If, however, it can be demonstrated (and this is now becoming the dominant view) that the genre that best describes the Gospels is that of *bios* (in one form or another) then it stands to reason that the central

---

68. Pennington, *Reading the Gospels Wisely*, 27.

69. Ibid., 28.

70. See, for example, the work done on the Talmud: Neusner, *Why No Gospels in Talmudic Judaism?*

figure or hero of the story is developed and written about with intention and originality that warrant a close reading of the final product. This reality is explained by Rhoads, Dewey, and Michie:

> Our study reveals Mark's narrative to be of remarkably whole cloth. The narrator's point of view is consistent. The plot is coherent: Events that are anticipated come to pass; conflicts are resolved; prophecies are fulfilled. The characters are consistent from one scene to the next. Oral techniques of storytelling such as recurring designs, overlapping patterns, and interwoven motifs interconnect the narrative throughout. There is also a consistent thematic depiction of the human condition, faith, God's rule, ethical choices, and the possibilities for human change. The unity of this Gospel is apparent in the integrity of the story it tells, which gives a powerful overall rhetorical impact.[71]

This chapter has demonstrated that rather than seeking to uncover specific, myopic issue(s) that the Gospels were written to counter, the most logical interpretation of the facts is that they were written to an indefinite audience and offer a biography of sorts of the central character Jesus of Nazareth. In the end, Burridge's comments may be offered as a summary: "The gospel is Christology in narrative form."[72] The premise rests on the previous two lines of argument. First, the implication of a general audience or indefinite audience is that the Gospel is concerned with its message and its audience; its message being "the gospel of Jesus Christ, God's Son." Second the implication from the genre investigation is that as *bioi*, the gospel is primarily concerned with revealing the person and works of Jesus as the protagonist and central figure not just in covering his "virtues." These two lines of argument form the basis from which we will proceed. The Gospel of Mark will be approached from this vantage point. Since Jesus, in Mark's Gospel, is called the Son of God, we now turn our attention to the title Son of God and its historical and literary significance.

---

71. Rhoads, Dewey, and Michie, *Mark as Story*, 3.
72. Burridge, *What Are the Gospels?* 123.

3

Placing "Son of God" in History, Research, and Context

INTRODUCTION

THE STRENGTH OF NARRATIVE criticism—its focus on the finished text—can also become its weakness. Because the New Testament Gospels are so focused on the life and death of Jesus of Nazareth—a historical person—they are inherently historical. In studying the narrative usage of the Son of God, historical questions must be answered. What does Mark mean when he uses the term Son of God? How is he using it? How would the general indefinite readership interpret this title? How would his readers, an assorted lot likely composed of Jewish and Greco-Roman individuals, understand this title? These are all important questions. By taking a narrative critical approach to studying the Son of God motif in Mark, the intention is not to neglect the historical concerns, but rather to answer the aforementioned questions in a way that does justice to the finished text that we have, and that can rest on a historical foundation that likewise "fits" within the historical context in which the book was written. In summation, this study does not use the finished text as a window to see *through* into the historical situation that gave birth to the text. Instead, this study seeks to bring together an esteem and appreciation for the text we do have with the broader historical context that we know. This is a study that moves from what we know and have to interpretation.

It seeks to avoid the error of fragmenting and isolating texts of a Gospel, and subsequently losing the Gospel in the process. It also seeks to avoid the error of breaking the text free from of its historical moorings and interpreting it in a vacuum. This approach is obviously prone to some serious deficiencies.

The application of a subjective hermeneutic that can take the Gospel and "run" with it in whatever direction one so chooses is most certainly in need of scrutiny. We must at once prioritize the finished text we do have, and also evaluate the historical context in which the work was composed. However, far from seeking to uncover the pressures that one particular community was facing, this study will take a much broader approach to the historical questions. We cannot know what a specific community was facing at the time in which they received Mark's Gospel, because, to put it simply, first, we do not have any information about that community (other than internal clues from the text), and second, the idea of a Gospel writer writing to one specific audience is tentative at best, and, as was established in chapter 2, we must maintain the expectation that the Gospel can be interpreted and meaningfully engaged by those who are outside of the original community. Here, we would do well to investigate the trends and events in the broader historical context of the Greco-Roman world, Second Temple Judaism, the Hebrew Bible, and the Qumran Community. These broad trends would no doubt influence the writing and reception of the book of Mark, and will therefore be our focal point for this next section.

For many modern Christians, it is axiomatic that Jesus is the Son of God. What many may find surprising is that in the Ancient World there were a number of individuals that were recognized, at least in some respects, as being the son of the gods as well. In this chapter, we will study a number of those individuals. However, before examining Greco-Roman mythology and comparing those "sons of gods" to the early church articulation of Jesus' divine nature, there are a few problems that must be avoided at all costs: specifically, reductionism and unfounded revisionism.

By reductionism, I mean that that any attempt to understand the theological, and even doxological, import of the title "son of God" must take all sources and contextual horizons into account. For example, any historical investigation that lifts Jesus from his Jewish life and times, and simply equates him with historical figures such as Perseus, Heracles, or Alexander the Great, is guilty of this error. A responsible scholar approaching the text from either a strictly historical, or even a narrative critical approach, must take into account all the factors. One cannot flat line Jesus or cut away all the trappings that come with the investigation of a historical figure. We think of the importance cultural, religious, sociological, and economic factors play in our own day-to-day lives. If we were so fortunate to be the subject of a biography in the distant future, we would expect the writer of such a work to properly investigate all these dimensions. A study of our own life must take into account the complex matrix in which we live. The same can be said for Jesus.

Second, in regard to the unfounded revisionism error, we assert that one cannot paint a historical figure however he or she sees fit. Each fact that a study such as this builds upon must not only be plausible, but also logical, and able to be demonstrated with examples from the primary sources. An example of this error in practice can be seen in the History of Religions approach that we will come to shortly. The question of what the author of Mark means when he uses the title Son of God in relation to Jesus and how his audience would likely interpret it must be answered in a way that does not base its findings on leaps in logical, or in oddly contrived, imaginative ways that remain unfounded. Simply put, it must fit with what we *do* know and not be built on what we *do not* know.

It has been argued thus far in this chapter that attention and priority must be given to the historical context in which Jesus lived, and in which the writers of the New Testament lived. We must take all the facts into account and not ignore significant areas of study. Thus, this chapter will begin with an investigation of the Old Testament's usage of the title Son of God. Next, the usage of this title in Second Temple Judaism and the Dead Sea Scrolls community will be noted. After that, attention will be given to the New Testament's frequent usage of the title. Finally, we will end our study by looking at how the title functioned in cult worship, and in the religious and social life of the broader Greco-Roman world. This chapter takes serious the notion of an indefinite or general readership and audience for Mark's Gospel. Since, as Bauckham has hypothesized, the Gospels were most likely written for an assorted lot of peoples from diverse backgrounds, exploring the dominant trends and beliefs which were present in the first century is important. Since this is so, the current section will be quite diverse.[1]

---

1. An earlier and simplified form of this chapter can be found in MacDonald, "Son of God in Mark." Here, MacDonald engages the question of the meaning of "Son of God" from a more historical critical locale. The Greco-Roman background and usage of the title "Son of God" featured more prominently than in this study, with special attention being given to the concept of Divine Men and History of Religions approach.

SON OF GOD IN THE OLD TESTAMENT

The Old Testament uses the title "Son of God" a number of times in a number of ways. The phrase "Son of God" is found in:

- Gen 6:2
- Exod 4:22–23
- 2 Sam 7:14
- Job 1:6
- Ps 2:7
- Ps 89:26–27
- Dan 3:35
- Hos 11:1
- Mal 2:10

Although the title is used more than a few times, it is used in distinct ways to refer to different groups or individuals.[2] For example, it is used of angels (Gen 6:2; Job 1:6; Deut 3:25), of Israel (Exod 4:22–23; Hos 11:1; Mal 2:10), and of the king (2 Sam 7:14; Ps 2:2, 7; 89:26–27). Of particular interest for our present study is the link between kingship and divine sonship.

Psalm 2, one of the "Royal Psalms,"[3] refers not only to the "Lord's anointed" (v. 2) (LXX: χριστοῦ; Hebrew: מְשִׁיחוֹ),[4] but also to the "Son" (v. 7). Psalm 2:7 in the LXX reads, "διαγγέλλων τὸ πρόσταγμα κυρίου κύριος εἶπεν πρός με υἱός μου εἶ σύ ἐγὼ σήμερον γεγέννηκά σε." The writers of the New Testament made frequent use of Ps 2.[5] What it originally meant, however, is still highly debated by scholars. Many have argued that Ps 2 relied heavily on Egyptian and Assyrian sources.[6] Psalm 2, coupled with Ps 45, in which the king is addressed as "God" (Hebrew: אֱלֹהִים), demonstrate that,

---

2. There are obvious differences between the Hebrew understanding and usage of the word "son" and the Greek usage and understanding. For an overview of these differences, see Collins and Collins, *King and Messiah as Son of God*, 10; Hengel, *Son of God*, 21–23.

3. Eaton, *Kingship and the Psalms*; Ross, *Commentary on the Psalms*, 157.

4. The LXX renders "anointed" in this way forty-five times.

5. Broyles, "Psalm 72's contribution to Messianic Ideal," 25, follows United Bible Societies' *Greek New Testament*, and proposes eighteen New Testament quotations of Ps 2, and twenty-five quotations of Ps 110.

6. See note by Collins and Collins on German scholarship and the influence Assyrian and Egyptian thinking had on Ps 2. Collins and Collins, *King and Messiah as Son of God*, 10.

in some sense or another, the idea of divine sonship of the king was present even in the early traditions of the Hebrew Bible.

As well, Ps 89:26–27 refers to a person who is "highest of the kings of the earth" (LXX: βασιλεῦσιν; Hebrew: מַלְכֵי) and who calls God his "father" (LXX: πατήρ, Hebrew: אבי). It also states that he is made God's "firstborn" (LXX: πρωτότοκον, Hebrew בְּכוֹר). The allusion in this Psalm to God's everlasting covenant with this king provides another link to 2 Sam 7:14 and Ps 2. Here again, the divine sonship of the king is apparent.

This idea of divine sonship is also found in the writings of *Ben Sira* and the *Wisdom of Solomon*. Sirach 4:10 reads, "Be like a father to the fatherless and help a widow as a husband would; and God will call you 'son,' show you his favor, and save you from the pit" (Hebrew: משחת ויצילך ויחנך בד יקְאָד יאל: and the LXX: καὶ ἔσῃ ὡς υἱὸς ὑψίστου).[7] The *Wisdom of Solomon* states, "For if the righteous (one) is God's son (υἱὸς θεοῦ), He will help him" (*Wis.* 2:18). Fourth Ezra 2:28 refers to "my son"[8] and "Christ" in this way, with this particular usage being repeated again in chapters 7, 13, and 14. Collins claims that the context of 4 Ezra fits into a transcendent-Messianic paradigm as it draws upon Dan 7 and Isa 11:4.[9]

Whether or not one is able to determine the precise meaning of these texts or come to an understanding of what being "God's son" ontologically entailed, establishing that the phrase "God's son" occurred numerous times in Old Testament literature benefits our study by confirming that the idea of being "God's son" was present in the respected Hebrew texts of first century Israel.[10] Further, the Old Testament demonstrates that divine sonship was reserved for those within the Davidic covenant.[11] Kings from the line of David related to God as "father" and God to them, as a "sons." Texts such as 2 Sam 7:14–15; 1 Chr 17:13–14; 22:10 make this evident. Central to the Old Testament concept of divine sonship of the king are the ideas of covenant and authority. It is worth noting that Israel is called "God's son" in Exod 4:22. About this particular reference, Schreiner makes this connection:

> Considering the OT as a canonical unit, we observe that Israel occupies a special position as God's son. And yet, the Davidic

---

7. Fitzmyer, *Dead Sea Scrolls and Christian Origins*, 66.

8. For a discussion on the Syriac and Latin rendering of these verses, see Collins, "Scepter and the Star," 165. Here, Collins states that even if the reading "servant" be preferred as original, it still can retain its messianic nature through the alternating usage of "son" and "servant" in the *Wisdom of Solomon* (2:13; 2:16).

9. Collins, *Scepter and the Star*, 168.

10. See MacDonald, *Son of God in Mark*, for a summarization of Collins' view of the link between the Son of God and Messianic figures in the OT and Dead Sea Scrolls.

11. MacDonald, *Son of God in Mark*, 16.

king also functions as God's unique son. The king receives the same covenantal promises that Israel receives. Ultimately he will rule the world as God's viceregent.[12]

At this point, we will turn to the Dead Sea Scrolls to investigate its usage of this important title. The concept of Messianism in Jesus' time, as it relates to this title, will subsequently be explored and explained. The pure volume of academic work that has been produced in the last ten years on this topic reveals that the study of Messianism is still very much a current scope of study.[13] And so, we consider this question: In what sense was the Messiah thought of as divine?

SON OF GOD AND THE DEAD SEA SCROLLS

Prior to the 1950s, scholars often criticized those who pursued the origin of Jesus' title "Son of God" in the Old Testament. Even after the discovery and publication of the Dead Scrolls in the late 1960s, some believed it was pointless to search for the New Testament origins of this title in Jewish thought.[14]

It has been argued by many scholars that the Dead Sea Scrolls offer a link between the Son of God and the Messiah/kingly figure.[15] C. F. D. Moule commented, "It is certainly demonstrable that to be God's son was ... recognized to be one of the Messiah's characteristics."[16] The reasoning here is that there are thematic similarities between these two titles but not that the two are in any way synonymous. Perhaps Collins offers the clearest explanation of the relationship in the Dead Sea Scrolls between the titles "Son of God" and "Messiah." In evaluating the nature of the "Son of God" figure in the Dead Sea Scrolls, he writes,

> The designation "Son of God" reflects the status rather than the nature of the messiah. He is the son of God in the same sense that the King of Israel was begotten by God according to Psalm 2. There is no implication of virgin birth and no metaphysical speculation is presupposed. He may still be regarded as a human

---

12. Schreiner, *New Testament Theology*, 235.

13. See, for example, Evans and Flint, *Eschatology, Messianism, and the Dead Sea Scrolls*; Bird, *Jesus Is the Christ*; Collins and Collins, *King and Messiah as Son of God*; Porter, *Messiah in the Old and New Testaments*; Zetterholm, *Messiah*; Fitzmyer, *One Who Is to Come*; Bryan, *Resurrection of the Messiah*; Collins, *Scepter and the Star*.

14. Kummel, *Theology of the New Testament*, 76.

15. See Collins, *Scepter and the Star*, 154–63; For an opposing view, see Fitzmyer, "4Q246," 153–74.

16. Moule, *Origin of Christology*, 28.

being, born of human beings, but one who stands in special relationship to God.[17]

A significant amount of writing has been done on the nature and nuances of Messianism in the Dead Sea Scrolls.[18] Addressing the contentious nature of Messianic studies related to the Scrolls, Al Wolters referred to it is a "minefield of contested claims."[19] It is difficult to ascertain what the exact parameters should be for an investigation on this topic.[20] Although this is a difficult area of study, there is evidence of a fusion of Messianic expectation and the title "Son of God" within the Messianism of the Dead Sea community. Since there are a number of scrolls that use this precise title, it would be helpful for us to now turn our attention to a few significant texts.[21]

The Qumran's *Florilegium* (4Q174) sheds some light on the 2 Samuel passage that existed at that time:

> The Lord declared to you that He will build you a House. I will raise up your seed after you. I will establish the throne of his Kingdom [forever]. I [will be] his father and he shall be my son. He is the Branch of David who shall arise with the interpreter of the Law [to rule] in Zion.[22]

The association in 4Q174 between the Branch of David and the Son of God is significant, for, as noted by John Collins, the *Patriarchal Blessings* (4Q252=4QpGen) explicitly called the "Branch" the "Messiah of Righteousness."[23] Furthermore, 4Q369 refers to one "made ... a firstborn son," and someone who was "a prince and ruler in all your earthly land." Although this text exists only in fragments, it is clear from the text that a ruler, who is the firstborn son, is most likely connected to the Davidic line.[24]

---

17. Collins, *Scepter and the Star*, 168.

18. For a brief survey of the debate see Evans and Flint, *Eschatology, Messianism, and the Dead Sea Scrolls*, 1–9. A more detailed survey is, Charlesworth, Lichtenberger, and Oegema, *Qumran-Messianism*.

19. Wolters, "Messiah in the Qumran Documents," 75.

20. For example, Evans, "Are the Son of God texts at Qumran Messianic?" 135–36, offers nine possible messianic terms in the Dead Sea Scrolls.

21. See also Collins, who offers a number of possible, fragmentary texts that speaks of "Son of God" at Qumran. Collins, *Scepter and the Star*, 64

22. See also the NASB's rendering: "I will be a father to him and he will be a son to Me."

23. 4Q252. Col 5 reads, "[And] the one who sits on the throne of David [shall never] be cut off, because the 'ruler's staff' is the covenant of the kingdom, and the thousands of Israel are 'the feet,' until the Righteous Messiah, the Branch of David, has come."

24. Collins, *Scepter and the Start*, 165.

4Q246: "Son of God Text"

An important document for the discussion about what exactly "Son of God" means is *4Q246*. The exact meaning of this scroll's text has garnered significant review and discussion in recent years. The question is primarily about who exactly this "Son of God" character is. One possibility is that the figure is a future Jewish king; another is that the "Son of God" figure is an evil earthly king (most likely Syrian). Column 1:7b—2:1, 5, 6 of the text reads,

> [But your son] shall be great upon the earth, 8 [and all people sh]all make [peace with him], and they all shall serve 9 [him.] (For) he shall be called [Son of] the [gr]eat [God], and by his name shall he be named. He shall be hailed Son of God [אל די ברה], and they shall call him Son of the Most High [עליון בר] . . . his kingdom [shall be] an everlasting kingdom, and all his ways [shall be] in truth. He shall jud[ge] 6 the land with truth, and everyone shall make peace.[25]

On significant contribution that the discovery of this Scroll makes is that it demonstrated that the title "Son of God" was used outside of the Greco-Roman world and that the writers of the New Testament (specifically Gospels) had at their disposal these concepts and ideas, and that they may not have just borrowed their concepts of "Son of God" from Greco-Roman sources. Since the Messiah was to come from David's line and be the king,[26] and since the king was, in some respects, "God's Son," it is not difficult to see how the idea of the Messiah as God's son developed. Tom Schreiner, in linking the Qumran documents to the New Testament, even ventures to say:

> "Son of God" seems to have been a messianic title in Second Temple Judaism as well. Several texts from Qumran are most naturally understood to refer to the Messiah as the Son of God . . . the conjunction between "Messiah" and "Son of God" in the NT is scarcely surprising. Indeed, in Jewish circles "Son of God" did not designate one as deity, though in the NT it becomes clear that Jesus is the Son of God in an even more profound way than anticipated at Qumran.[27]

---

25. This translation is taken from *Scrolls*, 94. For critical study of this important Aramaic text, see: Fitzmyer, "4Q246: The 'Son of God' Document from Qumran," 153–74; Collins, *Scepter and the Star*, 154–72; Evans, "Jesus and the Dead Sea Scrolls," 94.

26. See, for example, the introduction Matthew's Gospel, "The genealogies of Jesus Christ Son of David," (Matt 1:1). See also Wolters, "Messiah in the Qumran Documents," 77. He lists the following documents: *4QpIsa^a*, *4Q285*, *1QSB*, *4Q174*, *4Q2552*, and *CD*.

27. Schreiner, *New Testament Theology*, 235.

However, following this line of thought, Wright cautions,

> But we must stress that in the first century the regular Jewish meaning of this title has nothing to do with an incipient trinitarianism; it referred to the king as *Israel's representative*. Israel was the son of YHWH: the king who would come to take her destiny on himself would share this title.[28]

Again, the basic tenet that our current study rests on is that, to properly understand the Markan usage of the title "Son of God," our approach must be one that is both logical and plausible. This part of our study seeks to demonstrate that it is reductionist to argue that the title "Son of God" was lifted from Hellenistic cult worship. It seeks to demonstrate that it is possible, even probable, that the meaning of this important title rests more in the field of Jewish history and sacred texts than in the Hellenistic world. With that being said, our study will now bring some attention to the infamous parallels that were present and popular in the broader Greco-Roman world in the first century. Though these are important for developing an understanding of the way Mark would be interpreted by its original indefinite audience, it will be argued that the dissimilarities between Jesus, God's son, and the infamous Hellenistic Rulers and Divine Men are as significant, if not more, than their similarities. We will begin with an examination of Divine Men in Hellenistic culture and cult worship.

SON OF GOD IN HELLENISM

In Greco-Roman thinking, Zeus was the supreme deity that ruled from Mount Olympus. One can find examples of his power, strength, and authority throughout the literature and mythology of the day.[29] Although almighty Zeus ruled supreme in the cosmos, he was known to have an affinity for human women. He was said to have fathered a number of children with a number of mortal women. The children that came as a result of these encounters were endowed with incredible powers and abilities.[30] Even after these individuals had died, to have their remains resting in a city or town was considered good fortunate.[31] One such figure was Heracles (often known as Hercules).[32] Heracles inherited superhuman strength, courage

28. Wright, *Jesus and the Victory of God*, 485–86.

29. See for example, *The Odyssey* and *The Iliad* by Homer.

30. A detailed treatment of Heracles is offered by MacDonald, *Son of God in Mark*, 37.

31. Momligliano, "How Roman Emperors Became Gods," 181.

32. Homer Il., 14.319.

and wisdom from his father. The amazing exploits of Heracles are more than can be detailed here, but there are a select few which deserve attention. Apollodorus records *The Twelve Great Labours of Heracles*, which were an attempt by Heracles to atone for his past errors.[33] Heracles also assists in the conquering of Troy[34] and saves Prometheus from his punishment at the hands of Zeus and defeats a number of giants.[35] Heracles, whose name is later changed to Hercules in the Roman Empire, reveals both the best and worst of humanity and the gods. There is no question that he possesses divine attributes. Additionally, his status with the gods of Olympia is higher than that of a mere mortal. Homer records that, upon Heracles's death, his divine self is taken to Mount Olympus and he is declared a god.

Another of Zeus's demi-god offspring is Perseus. The writing of Apollodorus, in Library 2, contains the most complete account of the myth of Perseus. Apollodorus records that Perseus's mother, Danae, is the daughter of Acrisius, the king of Argos. Fearing a prophecy that claims the son of Danae will kill him, King Acrisius imprisons his daughter to keep her from any man. Apollodorus claims that Zeus is taken by Danae's beauty and impregnates her.[36] Perseus is the offspring. King Acrisius, infuriated by the situation, locks Danae and the child in a chest and throws them into the sea. The boy and his mother survive, however, and are taken in by a local fisherman. Later, Perseus is sent on a mission to bring back the head of Medusa in order to protect his mother. For any mortal, this mission would be fatal, but Perseus, because of his divine abilities and the help of the gods, succeeds and returns with Medusa's head.

Perseus accomplishes other great feats, such as saving Princess Andromeda from a sea monster, defeating the jealous Phineas and becoming the forefather of a large, stable family line.[37] Perseus is a typical example of a Divine Man and a son of god—fathered by Zeus, he receives a divine nature, allowing him to possess characteristics that differentiate him from "mere" humanity. The fact that he is the "son of a god" both destines him for greatness and allows him to fulfill that destiny.[38]

The concept of divine sonship in the Hellenistic world continued to change and develop as time went on. Eventually, Hellenistic rulers

33. Apollod., *Library V.*, 1–2.5.12.
34. Ibid., 2.7.2.
35. Ibid., 2.5.11.
36. Apollod., *Library II.*, 2.4.1; see also Ovid *Metam.*, 5.149–99.
37. Ovid *Metam.* V., 1–238.
38. In addition to Heracles and Perseus, one may note the similar mythology surrounding Theseus. MacDonald examines the account of Theseus in relation to Divine Men mythology in "Son of God in Mark," 38.

PLACING "SON OF GOD" IN HISTORY, RESEARCH, AND CONTEXT 59

appropriated it as well. One such example of this is Alexander the Great. The process of deification has been studied by scholars with reference to the minting of coin and the images found therein.[39] Alexander III of Macedon, better known as Alexander the Great, perhaps the most well-known general and leader of the Ancient World, claimed divine sonship and was the object of cult veneration in his lifetime. Born in Pella in 352 BCE, Alexander succeeded his father and took the throne at the age of 16. In a short time, he established an extensive empire that stretched from Greece to Egypt to what is modern day Pakistan. The Greek essayist Plutarch records that a series of supernatural events surrounded Alexander's birth, even quoting one individual who believed that the reason Artemis' temple burned down the day Alexander was born was that the goddess was busy "bringing Alexander into the world."[40] In 332 BCE, after a successful campaign, which included the siege of Tyre and Gaza, Alexander turned his attention to Egypt. After conquering Egypt, he was led through a series of miraculous events to the oracle of Zeus-Ammon.[41] One source recounts the events:

> On arriving at the shrine and finding out there was an oracle in it, Alexander wished to consult it. The priest and the prophet said that it was impossible for them to give out an oracle on that day. Alexander insisted. To his pressing demand the seer replied: "Lad, you are irresistible." At this Alexander was delighted. Then the seer at once told him that he was not Philip's son but the son of Zeus Ammon himself. Alexander recalled the account of his mother Olympias that a dragon once prevailed over her just about the birth of Alexander. So he trusted the oracles all the more.[42]

Apparently these words had an impact on Alexander because, from this point on, his divine lineage became more central to his image than it had before. Soon after these events, on the eve of the battle of Gauguamel in 331 BCE, Alexander gave a rallying speech that reminded his soldiers of his illustrious, divine heritage.[43] And it was not just his words that reflected this newfound identity; it was also his manner of dress. Athenaeus, a second century Roman historian, said,

---

39. Grant, *From Alexander to Cleopatra*, 91–104.
40. Plutarch *Alex.*, 3.5–9.
41. Ibid., 37.3–4; Strabo *Geogr.*, 17.1.43.
42. *Pseudo-Callisthenes; FGH*, 151 F 10; For additional accounts of his meeting with the "oracle," see *FGH* (138 F 8), and Strabo (*Geogr.* 17.1.43).
43. Plutarch *Alex.*, 331.

> And Ephippus tells us that Alexander used even the sacred vestments at his entertainment; and sometimes he would wear the purple robe, and cloven sandals, and horns of Ammon, as if he had been a god; and sometimes he would imitate Artemis, whose dress he often wore while driving his chariot.... Sometimes he would appear in the guise of Hermes.... Often, he wore a lion's skin, and carried a club like Heracles.[44]

The claim of divine sonship, according to W. W. Tarn, offered Alexander the "right" in the eyes of the Greek world to wield the power that he had secured for himself.[45] Alexander, who had demonstrated near miraculous powers on the battlefield, now, with the ability to claim a level of divinity from his lineage, called for even greater levels of devotion by implementing *prokynesis* and cult practices. Although this mandate had a number of setbacks,[46] the act was highly significant in establishing Alexander's divine status. To this end, Taylor remarked,

> The attempt to introduce *proskynesis* is very important for the development of Alexander's position as divine monarch, for whatever the attitude of the Persians toward their king, the Greeks and doubtless the Macedonians interpreted the *proskynesis* as an act of worship, and Alexander's desire to have the ceremony observed before him was equivalent to a request for worship.[47]

Although this was an audacious request on the part of Alexander, his claims to divinity were accepted in some cities, even if tentatively. Some Greek cities even continued to hold festivals and celebrations in his honor long after his death.[48] Pliny records that Alexander was honored as a god in Ephesus with the public display of a portrait of him wielding a thunderbolt[49]—a scene that references both the events of his birth[50] and his link with Zeus.[51] However, despite Alexander's request for worship, the majority of cities remained

---

44. Athenaeus *Deipn.* XII., 537–38
45. Tarn, *Hellenistic Civilization*, 35.
46. For an account of the crisis that unfolded when Alexander made this request, see Arrian, *Anab.*, 4.11.
47. Taylor, *Divinity of the Roman Emperor*, 18–20.
48. Dreyer, "Heroes, Cults, and Divinity," 218–34.
49. Pliny *Nat.* XXXV, 92.
50. Plutarch *Alex.*, 2.
51. Ibid.

unconvinced.[52] Nevertheless, to some extent, he was recognized as being the "son of Zeus" and did receive cultic attention in different forms.[53]

SON OF GOD AND ROMAN IMPERIAL CULT

The Roman Imperial cult has been the subject of much academic writing in the last century.[54] That there existed a sharp distinction between the public and private, or perhaps the political and religious realms of life was once a commonly held view. However, this view has now been challenged and the general understanding is that members of the Imperial cult were not only religiously motivated, but also personally invested.[55] Additionally, it is clear that for many individuals in the Roman World, the cultic aspects of the Roman Imperial cult were significant in everyday life and in burial practices.[56] Without a doubt, there are both political and religious aspects to cult worship, but as Pleket argues, for the man in the street, there is really not a significant difference.[57] Many scholars, however, contend that the Imperial cult was really an empty "shell" and that few if any truly worshiped the emperors in the way they would other, established "old-guard" gods.[58] Even still, scholars maintain that it is difficult, at most points, to tell the difference between homage and worship.[59] Part of this is due to the diversity that existed in the Roman provinces. Ancestral gods played significant role in the life of the people, and often the Imperial cult was absorbed into locally held beliefs. Simon Price, is his influential *Rituals and Power: The Roman Imperial Cult in Asia Minor* even goes so far as to argue that many of the scholarly approaches to the question of how the Imperial cult functioned in day-to-day life in the Roman World is unfortunately inherently "Christianized" and that the idea of "belief" as a religious term is missing the point.[60]

---

52. For an overview of the development and resistance to his divinity, see Taylor, *Divinity of the Roman Emperor*, 242–62; Sweet, *Roman Emperor Worship*; Weinstock, *Divus Julius*; For additional sources, see MacDonald, *Son of God in Mark*, 48–56.

53. See also Arrian, *Anab.* VII, 23.2; Collins and Collins, *King and Messiah as Son of God*, 49; and Taylor, *Divinity of the Roman Emperor*, 24–27.

54. For a brief synthesis of literature written on the Imperial cult, see Taylor, *Divinity of the Romans Emperor*, vii–x.

55. Gradel, *Emperor Worship and Roman Religion*, 1–27.

56. Pleket, "An Aspect of the Emperor Cult," 332.

57. Ibid., 333.

58. Nock, "Place of Religion," 45.

59. Momligliano, "How Roman Emperors Became Gods," 181.

60. Price, *Rituals and Power*, 10.

A thorough examination of the exact nature, confines, and intricacies of the Imperial cult is beyond the scope of this Study, the primary data is still such that it must be engaged with. Thus, at this point attention will be given to Roman Emperors that made claims to divine sonship.

The tradition of Imperial worship began early in Rome's history. Drawing from the tradition of the Greeks, it was not long before Roman leaders adopted the concept of deification and began to present themselves in the likeness of gods.[61] Since the practice of apotheosis was largely frowned upon in Rome proper, the eventual adoption of this process by city and its leaders likely indicate that it had long be a part of religious practice in the East.[62] Once such example is Julius Caesar. Born in 100 BCE, Gaius Julius Caesar was instrumental in bringing about Rome's transition from a republic to an empire. The Roman historian Suetonius, in *Divus Ivlivs*, portrays him in a positive light. While the exact chronology and series of events surrounding the declaration of Julius Caesar's divinity is highly debated,[63] it is clear that, by the time of Augustus, Julius Caesar was commonly known as *Divus Iulius*. The titles given the Caesars are similar to those of the Divine Men of Greek mythology, and Alexander the Great. One source says of Julius Caesar: "τόν ἀπὸ Ἄρεως καὶ Ἀφροδειτης θεὸν ἐπιφανῆ καὶ κοινὸν τοῦ ἀνθροπίνου βίου σοτῆρα."[64] Julius Caesar is associated here with two gods of the Greek pantheon. Further, he is called a "savior" (σοτῆρα) and "god manifest" (θεὸν ἐπιφανῆ), as were the Ptolemaic rulers. Again, we read, "ὁ δῆμος ὁ Καρθαιέων τόν θεον καί αὐτοκράτορα καί σωτῆρα τῆς οἰκαμένης Γάϊον Ἰούλιον Καίσαρα."[65] There can be little doubt that in both the East and the West, Julius Caesar was venerated as god.[66]

Augustus was hailed, and it appears, deliberately framed himself as a traditionalist. Rather that implements drastic, unfamiliar traditions, he sought to resurrect the old ways.[67] What developed under Augustus, in terms of the reference and worship of the emperor, persisted in the empire for three hundred years. Gaius Octavius Thurnus was eighteen when Julius Caesar, his grand-uncle, was assassinated in 44 BCE. Fourteen years later,

---

61. Kreitzer, "Apotheosis of the Roman Emperor," 212.

62. Ibid.

63. Gradel, *Emperor Worship and Roman Religion*, 54–70; Taylor, *Divinity of the Roman Emperor*, 58–99.

64. SIG 760: "The manifest god from Mars and Aphrodites, and the universal savior of human life."

65. IG 12.5, 556–57: "The Carthaean people honor the god and emperor and savior of the inhabited world Gaius Julius Caesar."

66. Kreitzer, "Apotheosis of the Roman Emperor," 212.

67. Momligliano, "How Roman Emperors Became Gods," 187.

after some political maneuvering, Octavian became the emperor of Rome. His skillful defeat of Marc Antony earned him the throne and his name was changed to Caesar Augustus— "Caesar" after his adopted father Julius Caesar, and "Augustus" meaning "revered one."

Although the belief that Augustus was deified in Rome only after his death is generally accepted, Egypt and parts of the East did see him as a divine king during his life.[68] This trend was predictable; Augustus was "more of a god in his absence, than in his presence."[69] In the areas that he rarely visited, worship seemed to blossom at rate that was not equaled in his home territory. More than likely, it was Tiberius, Augustus successor who initiated his *apotheosis* in a similar fashion to the approach of Augustus to Julius Caesar's deification. Van Eck explains what occurred shortly after this:

> After the assassination of Julius Caesar in 44 BCE, Augustus also seized on the so-called Julian star that appears during the games—organized by a young Octavian in honor of Julius Caesar in spite of senatorial opposition—as the *apotheosis* of Julius.[70]

After defeating Marc Anthony and Cleopatra, Octavian stayed in Alexandria for one year. It was during this time, while holding absolute power, that the Egyptian and Hellenistic model of divine honor was bestowed upon him. In regard to this development, Taylor writes:

> The land (Egypt) had for thousands of years been under the rule of divine kings, and every conqueror had established his supremacy by accepting the titles and the cult that had belonged to the ancient Pharaohs. Octavian was above all else a practical statesman.[71]

In the Asian provinces, Augustus was honored with continued cult activity. Some cities even went so far as to request the rights to build temples dedicated to his name. Historians at the time record that, in Rome, however, Augustus rejected cult worship.[72] Augustus drew a clear line between the worship permitted in the East and the worship permitted in Rome. The only honors allowed in Rome were those directed towards his stepfather, Julius Caesar. However, with the increase of Augustus' infamy and popularity

---

68. Mowery points out that Augustus was only hailed as *divus* after his death in: Mowery, "Son of God in Roman Imperial Titles," 102. See also Charlesworth, "Some Observations on Ruler-Cult," 22–28; Taylor, *Divinity of the Roman Emperor*, 142–62.

69. Momligliano, "How Roman Emperors Became Gods."

70. Van Eck, "Mission, Identity and Ethics in Mark," 2.

71. Taylor, *Divinity of the Roman Emperor*, 142.

72. Suetonius *Aug.* 52

came an increase in various cult activities in his honor in Rome. The ritual of pouring libations to Augustus's genius came into practice in 12 BCE; this was highly significant. Taylor reasons that this practice created a link to the hero worship of the Greeks and forged a path for future cultic practices that would later develop into emperor worship.[73] It is likely that Augustus' hesitant acceptance of Roman cult worship was rooted in a desire for political stability; he based his authority to rule on the nature and view of Julius Caesar, rather than on his own divinity. However, as the growth and stability of the empire thrived under Augustus, an increasing level of comfort in regards to cult worship developed. After all, once the senate recognizes Julius Caesar as a divine person, the same would naturally be said about his heir—Augustus.[74]

A number of records demonstrate that Augustus maintained a close link to Julius Caesar:

> Καίσαρος αὐτκράτωρ θεός ἐκ θεοῦ[75]
> Καίσαρα θεοῦ υἱὸν θεὸν[76]
> Θεὸν θεοῦ[77]

And the Latin:

> *Imperator Caesar divi filius Augustus*[78]

As mentioned, as the *Pax Augusta* began to take hold, the zeal and frequency of emperor worship grew. An inscription found in the Greek city of Priene, dated at about 9 BCE, called the Priene Inscription is an important source of information about the language being used to talk about Augustus.[79] What we gather from this inscription and others is that the original meaning to the term "good news" had political concepts in mind rather than soteriological.[80]

---

73. Taylor, *Divinity of the Roman Emperor*, 152–53.
74. Van Eck, "Mission, Identity and Ethics in Mark," 2.
75. SB 8895: "Emperor Caesar, god from god."
76. IGR IV, 309: "Caesar son of god." See also IGR IV, 311, 1173, and 1302.
77. IGR IV, 315: "god from god."
78. SB 401; BGU 628: "Emperor Caesar Augustus, son of god." This same concept has been found on coinage: "*DIVI F DIVOS AUGUST*"—"Son of the Divine Caesar, the Divine Augustus." See: Kreitzer, "Apotheosis of the Roman Emperor," 216.
79. This inscription is evaluated by Evans, "Mark's Incipit and the Priene Calendar Inscription"; Van Eck, "Mission, Identity and Ethics in Mark," 3.
80. Van Eck, "Mission, Identity and Ethics in Mark," 2.

Evans also brings attention to an inscription found in Pergamum, which has been reconstructed from five pieces of broken marble.[81] In writing about the mysteries that developed around *Divus Augustus*, Pleket notes that although emperor worship only infrequently had anything even approaching set-form rituals or established rites, there were lamp rituals that functioned as cult instrument.[82] The rituals demonstrate that the fusion of older, established religious practices were being joined with new expression of cult worship. Pleket continues, and agrees with Nock that a "deepening sentimentality" surrounding Augustus was present within 150 years of his death.[83]

It is clear that a religious belief system, which incorporated both the public and private spheres of life, held significance in the time of Augustus. The apotheosis of Augustus also bolstered the position of his successors. Because his two adopted sons—Gaius and Lucius—died, Augustus adopted another son. His step-son Tiberius succeeded him and reigned from 14–37 CE. The Roman world's view of Augustus cannot be defined by titles alone, it went much further than this. Aside from the outright titles "Son of God," "Lord," and so forth, all good things could be said to come from him in some form or other.[84]

Tiberius also made claims that were similar to the ones by Julius Caesar and his stepfather Augustus:

Τιβέριος Καίσαρ Σεβαστός θεοῦ υἱὸς αὐτοκράτωρ[85]
Τιβέριος Καῖσαρ νέοσ Σεβαστός αὐτοκράτωρ θεοῦ Διός ἐλευθερίου[86]

Due to the Senate's extreme dislike for him, Tiberias continually brought up his filial relationship to Augustus and used it as the basis of his legitimacy to rule. He, more than any other emperor, relied heavily on his paternal roots. The phrase "Son of Augustus" was often used.[87]

Tiberius's adopted nephew, Gaius Julius Caesar Germanicus, continued the Julio-Claudian dynasty. Gaius, more commonly known as Caligula,

---

81. [. . .] ΟΡ [. . .] ΑΙΣΑΡΑ [. . .] ΕΟΥΥΙΟΝΘΕΟΝΣΕΒΑΣΤΟ [. . .] ΓΗ [. . .] ΑΙΘ [. . .] ΛΑΣΣΗΕ [. . .] Π [. . .] Τ [. . .]. It is translated "The Emperor Caesar, son of a god, the god Augustus, the overseer of every land and sea."

82. Pleket, "Aspect of the Emperor Cult," 343.

83. Ibid., 346.

84. Van Eck, "Mission, Identity and Ethics in Mark," 2.

85. SB 8317: "Emperor Tiberius Caesar Augustus, son of god."

86. SB 8895: "Emperor Tiberius Caesar, New Augustus son of Zeus the liberator."

87. For a collection of inscriptions and documents, see Kim, "Anarthrous υἱὸς θεοῦ," 233.

did not force the deification of his adopted uncle on the senate. Caligula, instead, advanced his own deification and "went far beyond the example set by Augustus."[88] He is said to have dressed as various gods.[89] He was referred to as a "νέωι θεῶι"[90] and as "νέον Ἄρη"[91] and even frequently referred to himself as a god.[92]

Tiberius Claudius Caesar Augustus Germanicus, more commonly known as "Claudius," was also deified.[93] Claudius, although he refused cult worship in some instances, still allowed a priest to be dedicated to his honor in Asia Minor.[94]

> Claudius' grand-nephew, Nero, took the throne in 54 CE and reigned until 68 CE Nero was called "the liberating Zeus Nero, for all eternity."[95]

Additionally, it was recorded of Nero:

> Νέρων Κλαύδιος Καῖσαρ . . . ὁ σωτήρ καὶ εὐεργέτης τῆς οἰκαμένης[96]
> Ἀγαθός Δαίμων τῆς οἰκουμένης ἀρχὴ ὤν τε πάντων ἀγαθῶν[97]
> Τόν υἱὸν τοῦ μεγίστοθ θεῶν[98]

The centrality of divine sonship appeared to be fading during the latter part of the Julio-Claudian dynasty. Augustus claimed divine sonship many times but it was not until Nero that this formulation began to reappear. Mowery notes that the phrase "Θεοῦ Κλαυδίου υἱος" and the two-word formula "θεοῦ υἱος" occur frequently in Nero's reign.[99]

---

88. Taylor, *Divinity of the Roman Emperor*, 240.

89. Speaking of Gaius, Philo writes, "But the madness and frenzy to which he gave way were so preposterous, and so utterly insane, that he went even beyond the demi-gods, and mounted up to and invaded the veneration and worship paid to those who are looked upon as greater than they, as the supreme deities of the world, Mercury, and Apollo, and Mars." See also Philo (*Eternity* XL).

90. IGR IV, 1094: "new god."

91. CIA 3.444: "new Ares."

92. Dio Cassius (*Hist. rom* LIX. 2, 4).

93. See SB 4331; PSI 1235; P.Oxy. 713.

94. Price, *Rituals and Power*, 72.

95. ILS 8794.

96. OGIS 668: "Nero Claudius Caesar . . . the savior and benefactor of the inhabited world."

97. P.Oxy. 1021: "The good god of the inhabited world, the beginning of all good things."

98. "The son of the greatest of the gods." See Kim, "The Anarthrous υἱὸς θεοῦ," 235.

99. Mowery, "Son of God in Roman Imperial Titles," 103.

Nero was the last of the emperors in the Julio-Claudian dynasty. Following the infamous "year of the four emperors" was the Flavian dynasty which was comprised of Vespasian, Titus, and Dominitian. Each of these three emperors (69–96 CE) was either deified or claimed divinity for himself.[100]

Before 70 CE, a number of emperors from the Julio-Claudian dynasty, including Augustus, Tiberius, and Nero, claimed to be "θεοῦ υἱός." These emperors were the subjects of cult worship and various honors as they ruled the entire known world. They did not invent the notion of divine-kingship, but rather continued in a similar, though be it different vein as it was understood by the Persian, Greek and Egyptian cultures that predated the *Pax Romana*. Thus far in this chapter, we have demonstrated that divine sonship was a concept that was familiar to those in the Hebrew and Greco-Roman World. But what about the Christian communities in the early church that began to spring up after the crucifixion of Jesus? It is obvious that these early Christians were influenced by their respective cultures, though they did come to a number of novel and startling conclusions about the identity of Jesus that were at odds to the broader cultural expectations placed on one called the "son of god." The next part of this study will examine the early Christian documents and what they had to say about Jesus as the Son of God. Special attention will be given to the writing of Paul, perhaps the most prominent early church theologian and pastor.

SON OF GOD IN PAULINE LITERATURE

Some of first observations of early Christian theology can be made in the writings of Paul. It is interesting to note that Paul uses the title "Son of God" rather sparingly as compared to other titles given to Jesus. Various commentators have found significance in the number of occurrences of the title "Lord" and "Son of God" in Paul's writing (υἱός 15 times; κυριὸς 184 times).[101] Werner Kramer contends that Paul's use of "Son of God" always occurs after the mention of God and therefore has no real theological significance but merely fits within the context of his writings.[102] Kramer goes on to say that

---

100. For Vespasian, see P.Oxy. 1439; 257, for Titus see P.Oxy. 369, 1028; and for Domitian P.Oxy. 2186. For an overview of Titus and Domitian's claim to being "θεοῦ υἱός," see Mowery, "Son of God in Roman Imperial Titles," 104–6.

101. Numbers taken from Kramer, *Christ, Lord, Son of God*, 183; Hengel, *Son of God*, 7. The fifteen uses are: 1 Cor 1:9; 15:28; 2 Cor 1:19; Rom 1:3, 4, 9; 5:10; 8:3, 29, 32; Gal 1:16; 2:20; 4:4f; 1 Thess 1:10. See Dunn, *Theology of Paul the Apostle*, 224, who argues for seventeen uses including Colossians.

102. Kramer, *Christ, Lord, Son of God*, 183.

there are no "particular themes which call for the title 'Son of God,' nor does its presence in any way influence the course of the argument."[103] He does acknowledge, however, that there may exist a "tending towards the idea of pre-existence" in some of the uses.[104]

Hengel holds an opposite view. He remarks that, for Kramer, "the title 'Son of God' and the ideas with it are of relatively minor importance."[105] Hengel believed that the importance of the title to Paul's theology cannot be determined by statistics alone. Rather, he suggests that the context in which the title is used should be factored in.[106] Observation of the use of the title in Romans (Rom 1:3, 4, 9; 8:3, 29, 32) reinforces his argument that Paul's central emphasis is one of soteriology.[107] He proposes that the title's importance should be understood in view of the fact that Paul uses the title to introduce his letter (Rom 1:3, 4, 9) and at the climax of his epistle (8:3, 29, 32). The technique of referring to Christ's sonship in the introduction and at the climax of the epistle is again seen in the first letter to the Corinthians (1 Cor 1:9, 15:28). Hengel's argument seems more likely for understanding the usage of the "Son of God" title than Kramer's because Hengel gives careful consideration to the specific instances where the title is used. Bruce emphasizes that, in Acts 9:20, Luke encapsulates Paul's earliest Christian testimony about Jesus with the words, "He is the Son of God."[108] Likewise, Bruce points to Gal 1:15 and argues that it appears obvious that the "appreciation of Jesus as the Son of God" is central to Paul's conversion experience.[109] Collins and Collins, reflecting on the letters to the Thessalonians and Galatians, write, ". . .it is likely that here, too, 'Son of God' is equivalent to 'messiah.'"[110] Schoeps, along with Hengel and Bruce, see this title as important to Paul's theology, and does not understate its relevance as Kramer does. Schoeps concludes his examination of Paul's Christology with this statement,

> The real content of the Pauline Christology, which far exceeds the ideas of the Jerusalem church but is akin to Johannine Christ-mysticism, consists in the fact that the Messiah as the Son of God in a literal sense, pre-existed in heaven, came into the world by self-deprivation of the divine form of His being,

---

103. Ibid.
104. Ibid.
105. Hengel, *Son of God*, 7.
106. Ibid., 8.
107. Ibid.
108. Bruce, *Paul*, 118.
109. Ibid.
110. Collins and Collins, *King and Messiah as Son of God*, 106.

PLACING "SON OF GOD" IN HISTORY, RESEARCH, AND CONTEXT

in order to fulfil [sic] His redemptive mission, and then again ascend to heaven.[111]

Having demonstrated that the importance of the title to Paul's theology cannot be determined by statistics alone, and that it did serve as an important feature of his Christology, his exact usage will now be considered.

Son of God and Paul's Usage

Of the instances where Paul uses the title "Son of God," four appear to reference the Old Testament relationship between Abraham and Isaac. James Dunn proposes that this usage appears to rest on the idea that Jesus was the "beloved Son of God" who was sacrificed just as Abraham was willing to sacrifice his only son. He says, "Certainly, in Rom 8:32, Paul seems deliberately to echo Gen 22:16."[112]

Paul's first letter to the Thessalonians, which is the earliest letter we have, refers to Jesus as the "Christ" ten times. Although it is used frequently, Paul does not explain the title. The title "Christ" appears to be used almost as a personal name in the book of 1 Thessalonians. However, to guard against viewing it as a de facto proper name, Collins and Collins remark that ". . .it can probably be understood as an epithet or title signifying authority. It also served to make the point that there is only one anointed person in the last days, only one messiah."[113] Since, as we have seen before, the king of Israel is, in his authority and leadership, God's son (see Old Testament and Dead Sea Scrolls) the idea of divine sonship is likely informing the usage of the title "Christ" in Paul's writings.

Some of Paul's most developed teaching on the person and work of Christ can be found in the book of Romans. This may be the case because this letter was written before Paul had visited the church in Rome. He may, therefore, have felt it necessary to introduce himself and outline his understanding of the Gospel.[114] Romans 5:10 and 8:3 reveal an association between the "Son of God" and his crucifixion, and a link is seen in Galatians as well (Gal 2:20; 4:4–5). Dunn remarks, "Paul may possibly have intended an allusion to the vineyard tenants (Mark 12:1–9), where the death of the 'beloved son' is given some emphasis."[115] Either way, Dunn and Hengel

---

111. Schoeps, *Paul*, 51.
112. Dunn, *Theology of Paul the Apostle*, 224.
113. Collins and Collins, *King and Messiah as Son of God*, 102.
114. Fitzmyer, *Romans*, 85.
115. Dunn, *Theology of Paul the Apostle*, 224.

view the usage of "Son of God" as being principally soteriological. Paul "proclaims" the Son (2 Cor 1:19); God "revealed" his Son (Gal 1:16); God reconciled "by the death of his Son" (Rom 5:10); God "sent" his Son (Rom 8:3). Evidently, then, the soteriological significance of the title Son of God cannot be ignored. Dunn contends that a look at Rom 8:32 makes this apparent: "he did not spare his own son, but gave him up for us all."[116] Hengel also views the death of the son as pivotal to the apostle's theology.[117]

Jesus is not only the "beloved" son in Paul's theology—he is the "exalted" son as well. Dunn refers to this as the "Son of God in power."[118] Romans 1:3–4 says,

> Concerning His Son, who was born of a descendant of David according to the flesh, who was declared the Son of God with power by the resurrection from the dead, according to the Spirit of holiness, Jesus Christ our Lord.

We cannot overlook the centrality of the resurrection in these verses. We observe similar thoughts in 1 Thess 1:9–10, where the church was urged to place their hope in the resurrected Son of God. Again, in 1 Cor 15:28, the Son is exalted, having "all things in subjection to him." Paul's argument in 1 Cor 15 is that Jesus' resurrection and subsequent exaltation is the foundation on which all things become subject to Christ.[119]

The emphasis placed on the preexistence of the Son can be seen as the third aspect of Paul's "Son of God" theology. Two Pauline passages, Phil 2:6–8 and 2 Cor 8:9, are worthy of noting in regards to this aspect. The Philippians passage reads:

> Who, being in the form of God,
> did not reckon equality with God as something to be exploited,
>   but emptied himself,
> Taking the form of a servant,
> Coming in human likeness.
> And being found in appearance as a man,
>   he humbled himself, becoming obedient to death—
>   even death on a cross.

---

116. See also Gen 22:16, where the MT uses "only," and the LXX "beloved." See also Hengel, *Son of God*, 11.

117. Hengel, *Son of God*, 12. See also: Schreiner, *New Testament Theology*, 321–23.

118. Dunn, *Theology of Paul the Apostle*, 242.

119. Ibid.

Although some have refuted the idea that this passage provides evidence of a theology of preexistence concerning the son[120] Gathercole's exegesis of the text is persuasive, and his argument in favor of a preexistence theology, carefully laid out. His treatment of the text follows the logical implications and flow of the Philippians hymn. First, he points out that the hymn refers to Christ in two ways right at the outset, first as "being in the form of God," and then, as "taking the form of a servant."[121] This, he contends, suggests "a prior state, or preexistence . . . and then a subsequent 'form of a servant.'"[122] Second, Gathercole suggests, based on the depiction in Philippians of Christ voluntarily taking on of the form of a servant, that Christ "is not merely the passive envoy of the Father."[123] In this hymn, the preexistence of the "Son of God" is evident. The language and imagery of the Philippians hymn is echoed in 2 Cor 8:9 when it states, "he emptied himself." Rather than being emptied by the Father, Paul maintains that Jesus emptied himself. The depiction of a voluntary act in this verse speaks to the preexistence of the Son of God.

In Hengel's influential book, *The Son of God*, preexistence plays an important role in the development of his "Son of God" theology.[124] Hengel forms his argument by looking at the relationship between Christ's preexistence, his mediation, his creating of the material world, and his being sent into the world. He writes that, because of Jewish tradition concerning wisdom and logos, "there was an inner necessity about the introduction of the idea of pre-existence into Christology."[125] His presentation of the formation of this theology and the context within which preexistence was attributed to Christ, is sound. He disputes the history-of-religion's claims that Greco-Roman culture and religion were the foundational forces behind the development of Christian theology. Hengel argues instead that "the Jewish Christians were always the driving force which determined the content of the theology." Thus, the foundation for the formation of a preexistence understanding of Christ's identity can be found in the Jewish ideas of wisdom and the logos. This is important, since the preexistence of the Son of God is a crucial aspect of Paul's "Son of God" theology.

In summation, Paul's identification in his letters of Jesus as "*the Messiah*" is beyond dispute. The progressive relationship between the Messiah

---

120. Ibid.
121. Gathercole, *Preexistent Son*, 24.
122. Ibid., 25.
123. Ibid.
124. Hengel, *Son of God*, 66–76.
125. Ibid., 67–71.

as king and divine sonship is demonstrated in both the Old Testament and Qumran documents. Thus, according to Paul, Jesus was both the Messiah and the Son of God.

SON OF GOD AND SYNOPTICS

While almost all scholars would agree that Jesus is understood by the Synoptic Gospel writers to be the Son of God, what exactly this signifies is the crux of the matter. On the issue of Jesus' preexistence alone there is considerable debate. Collins and Collins, in their book *King and Messiah as Son of God* (2008), argue against Gathercole that the "I have come" sayings of Jesus indicate his preexistence. The disagreement centers on whether or not these "I have come" sayings are idiomatic or whether they do, in fact, point to some level of purpose in coming, thus suggesting that to come with a purpose necessitates a previous existence from which to come.

Two interesting additions to Mark's Gospel can be seen in Peter's confession in the parallel accounts: Matt 16:13–23; Luke 9:18–22. In Mark, Peter's confession stands as: "You are the Christ." But in Matthew, Peter confesses, "You are the Christ, the son of the living God." Luke's Peter confesses, "You are the Christ of God." For Matthew, in light of his use of Hos 11:1 in Matt 2:15, Jesus as the true Israel, the Messiah, and the son of David seems to be in view. Since, as we have seen in our study of the Old Testament's notion of divine sonship, the Messiah was conceived of as being God's son is a distinct way, it seems likely that this is the best way to understand Matthew's usage of the term. This proposition is strengthened by the opening section of Matthew, where the Messiahship of Jesus is brought to the forefront of the book and sets the tone for the remainder of the work. Schreiner explains Matt 16:16: "The titles 'Christ' and 'Son of God' were synonyms, denoting that Jesus was the Messiah of Israel."[126]

Assuming Markan priority, one would expect there to be similarities between Mark's usage and the manner in which Matthew and Luke make use of the title "Son of God" and that they would be consistent with the broader manner of use in the New Testament. However, one of the most significant and clearest passages concerning Synoptic Christology can be seen in a Q passage, Matt 11:25–27 = Luke 10:21–22. We will therefore give special attention to this particular passage. In Matthew's account, the Q passage reads:

---

126. Schreiner, *New Testament Theology*, 236.

> At that time Jesus declared, "I thank you, Father, Lord of heaven and earth, that you have hidden these things from the wise and understanding and revealed them to little children; yes, Father, for such was your gracious will. All things have been handed over to me by my Father, and no one knows the Son except the Father, and no one knows the Father except the Son and anyone to whom the Son chooses to reveal him."

Some of the questions that arise from a pre-Easter Synoptic tradition from Q are explained by Dunn in this way: "This Q passage may thus indicate one of the shoots which grew into the full Johannine bloom. But it also may indicate that the development was already well underway in Q."[127] In view of this Q passage, a cursory reading of the text naturally leads one to a "high-christological" understanding. However, some contend the opposite.

Bousset, for example, argued that this passage was born out of a late Hellenistic influence on Christianity.[128] George Eldon Ladd responded to this contention by referring to J. Jeremias' work on the Semitic nature of this particular passage. Ladd's choice quote from the work of Jeremias is worth repeating here as he responds to Bousset and others from the history-of-religions approach: "If we reject it [the passage], it must be on the grounds of our general attitude to the person of Jesus, not on the ground that its form or language is 'hellenistic's [sic]' in any intelligible sense."[129] Additionally, Craig Keener observes that because this passage is from Q, the exalted view of Jesus' identity has given scholars reason for doubt.[130] He notes other scholars argue this Q passage is merely communicating a normal father-son relationship and that there is no cause to assume anything unique or essentially divine. Keener, however, refers to the work done by Schweizer in *Jesus* (1971) to argue against the idea that the passage points only to a normal father-son relationship.

Matthew 11:27 provides a significant parallel. Jesus explains that in the same way that the father knows the son, so the son knows the father. A totally unique essence of relationship exists between father and son. On this, Ladd writes, "It is very clear that this knowledge possessed by the Father is not an acquired knowledge based on experience, but a direct, intuitive and immediate knowledge."[131]

---

127. Dunn, *Jesus Remembered*, 719.
128. Bousset, *Kyrios Christos*, 84.
129. Jeremias, *Prayers of Jesus*, 45.
130. Keener, *Gospel of Matthew*, 347.
131. Ladd, *Theology of the New Testament*, 143.

Both Matthew and Luke record the virginal conception of Jesus (Matt 1:18-25; Luke 1:26-35). The inclusion of the virginal conception, among other things, in Matthew and Luke serves to reinforce the teaching that Jesus was no ordinary human conceived naturally; he was a unique person who was both divine and human.

In order to present a complete study of Matthew's presentation of the "Son of God," we must recognize the importance he places on Jesus' obedience, and its relation to his being the "Son of God." In this vein, D. B. Bauer summarizes Matthew's concern with obedience: "Jesus is the Son of God primarily in the sense that he perfectly obeys the will of his Father, especially the will of God that the Messiah must suffer and die."[132] The subject of obedience is found in the baptism account (Matt 3:13-17), the temptation (Matt 4:1-11), Peter's rebuke of Jesus (Matt 16:22-23), and in the Garden of Gethsemane (Matt 26:39, 42)—all of which present Jesus as acting in obedience to the Father.

The Gospel of Mark is much the same. Stein is right when he notes that "Mark's portrayal of Jesus Christ, the Son of God, is multifaceted."[133] In Mark, Jesus is presented as a miracle worker (Mark 1:29-31, 40-45; 2:1-12; 7:31-37; 8:22-26). He heals the sick; gives sight to the bling casts out evil spirits. He claims for himself a unique authority that is so great; it causes the individuals around him to express astonishment (Mark 1:22). This same authority is mentioned in regards to Jesus' selection of the Disciple in Mark 3:13,14. Jesus' authority in Mark extends to matters of interpretation of the Torah. Jesus has the authority to redefine the understanding of cleanness and uncleanness (Mark 1:40, 45), observance and the nature of Sabbath rest (Mark 2:22-26; 3:1-6), and to commonly held prejudices against ethnic outliers (Mark 7:24-30).

Mark presents Jesus as coming in the eschatological expectation of the Hebrew Scripture. This can be seen in the opening few lines of Mark (see also Old Testament quotation in Mark 1:2, 3), and the constant motifs and language that harken back to the sacred writing and history of Israel (more on this is found in chapter 4). Collins understands the portrayal of Jesus in Mark's Gospel as being one with features a significant prophetic component.[134] Jesus is, according to Collins, likely cast in the vein of the Old Testament prophets (specifically Elijah) and bares some relationship to the understanding of the prophetic Messianic figure found in the documents

---

132. Bauer, "Son of God," 773.
133. Stein, *Mark*, 21.
134. Collins, *Mark*, 46.

from Qumran.[135] Schreiner makes notes that the presentation of Jesus a prophet is fairly straight forwards since Jesus preaches and predict future events (Mark 8:31; 9:9; 14:30).[136]

The loftiness of the Christology of Mark may not be that of John's Gospel, but it nevertheless presents Jesus as something more than a simple prophet. On this reality, Moritz contends,

> From his first-century perspective the most pertinent claim is that somehow Christ embodies the returning God of Israel. Along with his fellow writers, he stops far short of ontological speculations about either the natures of Christ or the inner-trinitarian position of Christ.[137]

As this study argues, the central christological title that Mark makes use of is "Son of God." The other titles that are used in Mark also significant, but it appears that for Mark, the central and most significant christological title by which the reader is expected to understand the identity of Jesus is "Son of God."

Luke, also, shares many of the christological nuances that are found in Matthew and Mark. One aspect that is especially pronounced in Luke is the theme of promise and fulfillment. This can be seen in the constant allusions or citations of the Old Testament that both the narrator and characters make use of.

Luke's infancy narrative also contains some unique, though not contradictory, notes about his Christology. In this section of his work (Luke 1:5—2:52) Jesus is portrayed in a regal manner. His birth is announced in the heavenly realm (Luke 1:26–38) by a herald, and the words spoken by Zechariah seem to reinforce a regal interpretation of Luke's presentation of Jesus (Luke 1:8–25).

Like Matthew and Mark, Luke highlights the prophetic nature of Jesus' person on a number of occasions. Take for example, his sermon at Nazareth (Luke 4:16–30, or the manner in which Jesus is held adjacent to Elijah and Elisha (Luke 4:25–27). Additionally, Luke makes use of the titles and epithets, "son of David" (Luke 1:27, 32, 69; 2:4, 11; 18:38–39), "Son of God" (Luke 1:35; 2:49; 3:31, 38; 4:3, 9, 41; 9:35), and the "teacher" (Luke 7:40; 8:49; 9:38; 10:25; 11:45; 12:13; 18:18; 19:39; 20:21, 28, 39; 21:7; 22:11).

Another tenant of Christology that Luke shares with the other canonical Gospels is the powerful actions and deeds of Jesus. There are a number

---

135. Ibid.
136. Schreiner, *New Testament Theology*, 177–79.
137. Moritz, "Mark," 47.

of instances where Jesus heals (Luke 4:31–41; 5:12–16; 7:1–10; 8:26–39; 40–56), casts out demons (Luke 8:26–29; 9:37–43), and even forgives sins (Luke 7:48).

Matthew, Luke, and Q all present a unique relationship between Jesus and the Father. This presentation is also in line with Mark, John, and the letters of Paul. It seems clear at all points that these authors were relying predominantly on the Old Testament and Second Temple Judaism's understanding that, in some distinct and significant way, the Messiah was God's Son.

SON OF GOD IN JOHN

John has long been a fundamental book for the Christian faith because of its rich theological nature. It has had a profound influence on the understanding of the person and work of Jesus. A number of explanations are offered by scholars for the high Christology found in John.[138] Whatever the reason, whether "developmental" or "evolutionary,"[139] the significance of the relationship between the book of John and an understanding of New Testament Christology can hardly be overstated. It is no surprise that, in the book of John, emphasis is given to the important doctrine of the divine sonship of Christ. Statistical data recorded by Köstenberger and Swain reveals that Jesus is referred to as the "son" forty-one times in the book of John, and as the "one-of-a-kind" (μονογενῆ) son four times (John 1:14, 18; 3:16, 18).[140] He is called the "Son of God" a total of eight times (John 1:14; 3:18; 5:25; 10:36; 11:4, 27; 19:7; 20:31).

John's use of the description "one-of-a-kind" (μονογενῆς) son is unique to his Gospel. Köstenberger and Swain argue that John's use of this term can be seen as a parallel to the title "beloved" found in the Synoptics.[141] The LXX's use of "μονογενῆς" in place of "ἀγαπητός" for the Hebrew "יחיד" demonstrates the plausibility of this contention.[142] Fundamentally then, the description communicates the same tone of intimacy that exists between the Father and the Son.

---

138. McGrath, *John's Apologetic Christology*, 4. He also presents a well-researched bibliography for each school of thought.

139. The analogy of evolution and development is the work of C. F. D. Moule, *Origin of Christology*, 1–11.

140. Köstenberger and Swain, *Father, Son and Spirit*, 76.

141. Ibid., 77.

142. Cf. Gen 22:2, 12, 16; Amos 8:10; Jer 6:26; 8:42; 9:38.

PLACING "SON OF GOD" IN HISTORY, RESEARCH, AND CONTEXT 77

The first time that Jesus is called the "Son of God" in John is by Nathaniel in 1:49. The next instances are in 3:18 and 5:25, then in 10:36 and 11:4 again. In 11:27, Jesus is again referred to as the "Son of God." Finally, the concluding verse of John's Gospel, 20:31, refers to Jesus in this way.[143] In John, to be the Messiah is equivalent to being God's Son.[144] This can be inferred from a number of passages, but is seen clearly in two places. First, in John 11:27: "Yes, Lord," she replied, "I believe that you are the Messiah, the Son of God, who is to come into the world." The second instance is in the closing section of the book, 20:31, where the author of John explains his motivation for writing a Gospel to his audience: "These signs are written in order that you may believe that Jesus is the Messiah, the son of God. . .."

The idea that Jesus is the "Son of God" is a central aspect of John's Christology. John demonstrates that Jesus maintains a unique and intimate relationship with the Father. Further, John seems to infer that Jesus has a oneness or shared essence with the Father, thus highlighting Jesus' divinity. That John has something akin to divinity in view in relating to Christ's sonship seems clear from the few passages noted above. Without a doubt, John presents the fullest and highest Christology of the Gospels. In John 10:30 the son and Father are said to be equal. Schreiner remarks on the importance of this passage: "The equality in view cannot be limited to unity of purpose and aim, for the Jews took up stones to put Jesus to death for blasphemy."[145] Additionally, Jesus says in John that whoever hates the son hates the Father also (John 15:23–24). The unity between Father and son is stressed repeatedly in John and is a theme that the author returns to again and again and presents in a number of different contexts.

CONCLUSION

A few thoughts are worth noting as this part of the study comes to a close. It is clear that the concept of divine sonship was fairly common in the Hellenistic world. Although there are thematic overlaps between what it seems to mean in the Greaco-Roman World and the New Testament for what it means to be called the "son of god," there are differences as well. In Hellenistic thought and literature of day, there was room for many sons of god. Zeus, for example, was known to have fathered many offspring. This stands

---

143. Left out is the reference in John 19:7, where the title is used in a hostile manner by the opposition at Jesus' trial. See also Köstenberger and Swain, *Father, Son and Spirit*, 76.

144. Collins and Collins, *King and Messiah as Son of God*, 179.

145. Schreiner, *New Testament Theology*, 244.

in contrast to the New Testament understanding of the uniqueness of Jesus' divine sonship. Furthermore, the notion of "Divine Men" was not as fixed in antiquity as was often argued by those advocating the History-of-Religions approach. The notion of divine sonship was quite dynamic and thus nothing in the Hellenistic world offers a direct parallel to the manner in which Jesus' divine sonship was presented in the Gospels.

More closely aligned with the New Testaments presentation of Jesus as the Son of God is manner in which the themes of Messiahship, authority and the kingship as God's son relate in the Old Testament. The Hebrew tradition, along with what we find at Qumran closely link the concept of Messiah and God's son. What is not at play, however, in any part of the Old Testament, is an ontological dimension to the conversation. We see that developing in the later New Testament, but suffice to say that for Jesus to be Israel's Messiah meant he was the king, and as such had right to be called God's son in light of 2 Sam 7 and Ps 2, among other passages.

In the Gospel of Mark, Jesus is presented as the "Son of God" before he does anything significant. Typically speaking, in the Greaco-Roman World divine sonship was closely linked to great feats of strength of valor. Gathercole has argued that the Synoptics also present Jesus as preexistent, lending a unique element to his sonship.[146] Gathercole's interpretation has been challenged, as was discussed, however, the arguments given against his view only gain force when each Gospel is examined in overt isolation. If one approaches Mark looking for explicit claims to preexistence and ontological dimension to Jesus' divine sonship, one will be looking amiss. However, if one listens closely to the text, there are echoes of preexistence, or, in the very least, some unique aspects to Christ's sonship that go beyond the Divine Mam concept in Hellenism.

For Paul, the divine sonship of Jesus was significant to his theology despite the fact that, numerically speaking, it is referred to far less often than the concept of Jesus as "Lord." Moreover, in his writings, Paul came back to the preexistence of Jesus a number of times. The Synoptics present Jesus as the "Son of God" in a fashion that is close to Mark's. The Q passage in Matt 11:25–27 and Luke 10:21–22 is of particular importance for Synoptic Christology. Even in Q, Jesus was portrayed as possessing a unique intimacy with the father. In John, the sonship of Jesus is a major theme. John demonstrates that Jesus possessed a shared essence with the Father and therefore offers some of the most developed Christology in the New Testament.

The purpose of this chapter is to place the concept of Son of God within its broad, local, and immediate context. We have seen that the concept existed

---

146. Gathercole, *Preexistent Son*.

in some form in Hellenistic world, in the Old Testament, and in the New Testament writers. The most proper foundation from which to understand and approach the concept would undoubtedly is the Old Testament, as our Study has argued. Upon that premise, the study will continue as the chapter 4 investigates the Gospel of Mark's usage of "Son of God" in detail.

4

Son of God in Mark

INTRODUCTION

THIS CHAPTER WILL LAY out the data that is available to us in the Gospel of Mark regarding the divine sonship of Christ. Each and every instance of this title will be investigated. Both the immediate context of these occurrences and their broader literary properties will be examined. To prevent against the often leveled charge towards narrative criticism—that it ignores the historical-critical components of the text—questions of this nature will be asked and insights given. Each instance will be examined historically-exegetically *and* literarily. While this chapter lays that data before the reader, the next chapter will seek to form a synthesis of the data that does justice to both the historical critical and literary dimensions of the text. To begin, the flow and overall structure of the book of Mark will be highlighted; there is no use missing the forest for the trees. The text as a whole must be emphasized.

OVERVIEW OF MARK'S GOSPEL

Mark opens with the line, "The beginning of the gospel of Jesus Christ, the Son of God." The narrator immediately seeks to follow up this pronouncement with a few guideposts. The "gospel" or "good news" that Mark is referring to here is to be anchored, according to him, in the person of Jesus and in the Hebrew Scriptures. He follows this introduction with a conglomerate quote from Isaiah and Malachi. John the Baptist comes preaching a "baptism of repentance for the forgiveness of sins." In the initial few verses (1:1–15) both Jesus and John the Baptist's ministries are introduced and their respective messages recounted. John the Baptist is baptizing in the Jordan River and Mark 1:9 recounts the extraordinary baptism of Jesus: "At that time Jesus came from Nazareth in Galilee and was baptized by John in the Jordan." His baptism is not an ordinary event because, as Jesus is coming up out of the water, he is declared to be God's Son by a voice from heaven.

After his time of temptation in the wilderness (1:12–13), Jesus begins "proclaiming the good news of God" (1:14). He explains in Mark 1:15 that the "time has come" and that the "kingdom of God has come near!" In the next verses, Jesus is depicted as gathering his first disciples (1:16–20). After this (v. 21–28), he begins his signs, miracles, and healings, beginning with driving out an impure spirit whom he commands and who subsequently yields to his authority. His notoriety is said to be growing through this time. In this encounter, we see that Jesus is in the synagogue on the Sabbath. This, coupled with the echoes of Old Testament apocalyptic expectation present in the Isaiah and Malachi quotes, and the coming of the "kingdom of God," demonstrates that Jesus is standing in continuity with redemptive-history as found in Second Temple Jewish life and thought. It serves to anchor him more in the line of the prophets and leaders of the Hebrew Bible than in Hellenistic Divine Mam traditions.

As the story continues, Jesus is seen healing, teaching, and forgiving different people. He heals a man with leprosy (1:40–45), and a man suffering paralysis (2:1–12) whose sin he also forgives. He eats and initiates relationships with the "sinners" (2:15–17). Jesus is thrust into conflict with the religious leaders. This continues to be a dominant theme throughout Mark. First, the "teachers" draw issue with Jesus' offering of forgiveness to the paralyzed man. The conflict continues to escalate as the teachers—who are revealed to be Pharisees—see him eating with "sinners." The tension increases to the point that the Pharisees are "looking for a reason to accuse Jesus" (3:2). After witnessing yet another healing on the Sabbath, they join forces with the Herodians and begin to plot to kill Jesus.

At this point in the narrative, a few things stand out. First, Jesus, the Messiah, is said to be the "Son of God" (1:1, 11). He is a powerful worker of miracles, a healer, an authoritative teacher, and he stands in the tradition of the Hebrew Scriptures. He has gathered a group of disciples to be around him, and he stands in frequent conflict with the Pharisees, who we learn are planning to kill him. Already, by 3:6, we have the majority of the plot in play, save for the passion narrative. Mark 3:7—14:43 displays basically more of the same types of elements that we find in 1:1—3:6. That is not to say, in the least, that these chapters are unimportant. They are, and they develop the plot, feel, and contour of the realities already in play. Mark is a fast moving work, and the narrator wastes little time in laying out the essential information about Jesus the Messiah, the Son of God.

The plot continues and Jesus persists in his healing and teaching ministry. His power seemingly knows no end since in 4:35-41 he tames the forces of nature and calms a raging storm, and in 5:21-43 he raises a little girl from the dead. Nearly every commentator and interpreter of Mark recognizes that Mark 8:27 functions as a hinge, or transition point in Mark. Here, Peter, the *primus inter pares* of the disciples, proclaims that Jesus is, in fact, "the Christ." Immediately following this pronouncement, Jesus predicts his death. He does this two other times (9:30-37; 10:32-34). This heightens the tension and expectation in the second half of the book. Jesus and his disciples begin the trek to Jerusalem, the place which he has already predicted he will die. When he arrives at Jerusalem, he is welcomed by the crowds who proclaim: "Hosanna," and confer blessing on him and cry out that he is coming "in the name of the Lord" (11:1-11).

After the cleansing of the temple in 11:12-17, we are told that the chief priest and the teachers of law are plotting, with renewed vigor, to have Jesus killed. At the last supper, Jesus institutes the new covenant (14:12-26) and then predicts Peter's betrayal (14:27-31). After this, the garden of Gethsemane becomes the scene of the betrayal by Judas (14:43-51), and Jesus is arrested. He is taken before the Sanhedrin and eventually Pilate, and the verdict is pronounced: crucifixion (14:53—15:15). He is led away and crucified. In his final moment, one final cosmic event takes place. The curtain of the temple is torn in two, and the centurion who is standing near the cross proclaims, "Surely this man was the Son of God" (15:38-39). Jesus, now dead, is buried in a tomb. A short time later, when a group of women come to the tomb to anoint Jesus' body, they are met not with a sealed tomb, but with an open door (16:1-4). When they enter the tomb, Jesus' body is gone and they see a man in white sitting there, who says, "You are looking for Jesus the Nazarene, who was crucified. He has risen! He is not here" (Mark 16:6). The women leave in fear and trembling, and the story ends (Mark 16:8).

In Mark, Jesus is called Messiah, Son of Godm, Son of Man, Teacher, Rabbi, Prophet, Lord, Son of David, and King of the Jews. Space and time do not permit an exhaustive treatment of all of these titles; though, in due course we will refer to the majority of them in the exegetical sections.

For Mark both the identity of Jesus as the Messiah, and Jesus as the Son of God, can only be understood in light of the cross. After Peter's confession in 8:29, Jesus explains that he must suffer and be rejected by the elders. Additionally, after the experience of Peter, James, and John at the transfiguration, Jesus commands them not to recount the event until *after* the resurrection (9:1). After this preliminary overview of the contents and flow of Mark's narrative, we will now turn our attention to each occurrence of the title Son of God found in Mark. Each use of the honorific will receive special attention and be examined from an exegetical and narrative-critical vantage point.

MARK'S INCIPIT AND FOUNDATION

The opening of the book of Mark is theologically rich and serves to set the stage for what follows. The words read:

- The beginning of the gospel of Jesus Christ, Son of God (ESV, NASB, KJV, NET)

- The beginning of the good news about Jesus the Messiah, the Son of God (NIV)

- Greek text: Ἀρχὴ τοῦ εὐαγγελίου Ἰησοῦ χριστοῦ [υἱοῦ θεοῦ] (UBS)

Mark 1:1 serves to introduce and summarise his Gospel as a whole.[1] Malina and Rohrbaugh make an interesting point from a social-scientific approach. Unlike Matthew and Luke, Mark does not point to Jesus' genealogy as a source for his status or honor—rather "Mark immediately identifies Jesus as Son of God, giving him a status unavailable through the line of Joseph."[2]

In the fourth edition of the United Bible Societies' Greek New Testament (1994), the final two words "Son of God" appear in brackets.[3] This is also the case with Nestle-Aland's *Novum Testamentum Graece* (2012).[4] They have given it a grade of "C" in the textual apparatus, believing it is unlikely that it is original. The SBLGNT (2010) omits the words from their edition of the Greek text of Mark.[5] Commentators are divided on this. Generally speaking, they are divided between two views. One group sees the textual apparatus as definitive and cannot, in good conscience, accept the inclusion of these two words. The other group argues on contextual grounds that the words are likely original. These scholars believe that, although the words are

1. Collins, *Mark*, 130.
2. Malina and Rohrbaugh, *Social-Science Commentary*, 145.
3. Aland and Aland, *UBS Greek New Testament*.
4. *Novum Testamentum Graece* (NA28).
5. Holmes, *Society of Biblical Literature*.

missing from some manuscript traditions, the flow and structure of the book of Mark itself seems to lend credence to the view that the words be included. Scholars in the first group, who lean toward rejecting their authenticity based on external evidence, include Collins, Ehrman, Marcus, and Schweizer.[6] Those who argue that the words are authentic include Guelich, Gundry, Mann, Kim, Stein, and Van Eck.[7] The debate surrounding the inclusion of these two words continues to be a popular topic in scholarly discussion. A comprehensive bibliography on the debate is offered by Wasserman.[8] Wasserman also presents the variant readings that are found in the manuscript tradition for Mark 1:1. Wasserman counters Croy's assessment that there are as many as nine different variant readings of Mark 1:1 which indicates, in Croy's view, that Mark originally circulated without any stable opening.[9] Croy's argumentation assumes that the Patristic Fathers had a somewhat fixed manner in which they incorporated or quoted the New Testament. But this is really not the case, since finding a uniform pattern of Patristic Scripture usage is all but impossible. Once these are removed from Croy's list of nine variant readings, there are two primary readings that remain:

1. Ἀρχὴ τοῦ εὐαγγελίου Ἰησοῦ χριστοῦ
2. Ἀρχὴ τοῦ εὐαγγελίου Ἰησοῦ χριστοῦ (τοῦ) υἱοῦ (τοῦ) θεοῦ

The longer reading does feature two stylistic variations. Wasserman explains these as having very little ability of casting doubt on the longer reading. The reason for this is that the minuscule differences underlying the variants are likely secondary and are absent from the earliest witnesses. After assessing the Patristic evidence for tradition, Wasserman ends his external evidence investigation with this summary:

> In sum, the longer reading is attested by the following versions: Old Latin and Vulgate, Gothic, Peshitta, Philozenien, and Harklean Syrian; at least two Sahidic Coptic textual groups and the Bohairic Coptic; the second Georgian recession; Ethoipic; and Slavonic. Moreover, it is attested by sixteen of seventeen Arabic MSS.

---

6. Collins, *Mark*, 130; Ehrman, "Text of Mark in the Hands of the Orthodox," 149–52; Marcus, *Mark 1–8*, 141; and Schweizer, *Good News according to Mark*, 30.

7. Guelich, *Mark*, 6; Gundry, *Mark*, 24; Mann, *Mark*, 194; Kim, "Anarthrous υἱὸς θεοῦ"; Stein, *Mark*, 52; and Van Eck, "Mission, Identity and Ethics in Mark," 7. We should note Kim argues from 15:39 back to 1:1. His approach is more concerned with the Greek grammar than the textual issue.

8. Wasserman, "'Son of God' Was In the Beginning."

9. Croy, "Where the Gospel Text Begins," 107–8.

The shorter reading is attested by these versions/MSS: one valuable Sahidic Coptic MSS (P. Palaau Rib. Inv. Nr. 182); Christian Palestinian Aramaic; Armenian the first Georgian recession; and one valuable Arabic MS (Sin. Ar. N.F. Parch 8). *Thus, the versional evidence on the whole is clearly in favor of the long reading, but at the same time confirms the impression that both readings are widespread.*[10]

The shorter version is attested to by Codex Sinaiticus (א). Lane argues that since א may have been based off texts preserved and transported by Origin, the two greatest witnesses against the longer reading "are, perhaps, reduced to one."[11]

Although the external evidence may, at best, lean towards the inclusion of the "Son of God," the internal evidence seems more absolute. Both Gundry and Wasserman refer to Rudolf Schnackenburg's assessment that the anarthrous nature of Mark 1:1 and 15:39 favor the longer reading.[12] Another layer of internal evidence in favor of the longer reading is that, for Mark, "Son of God" is the most commonly used title for Jesus, much more so than "Christ."[13] Van Iersel comments that whether or not "Son of God" was original is immaterial since, as soon as one turns the page, the voice from heaven proclaims Jesus as the "son" anyway.[14] His point is well taken and, in a similar vein, Gundry notes that the proclamation from heaven at the baptism "provides a much less closely matching inclusion with 'Son of God' in 15:39."[15] Hooker concludes, "the phrase is keeping with Mark's own belief, and forms an appropriate heading to his book."[16] Additionally, Mann comments, "Whether the text of 1:1 is original—in whatever sense—in its present form . . . it undergirds the whole gospel."[17] Boring, along with Mann, accepts the phrase as likely original since the common scribal error of *homoioteleuton* could be a factor in this case.[18]

---

10. Wasserman, "'Son of God' Was In the Beginning," 39 (emphasis added).

11. Lane, *Mark*, 41.

12. Gundry, *Mark*, 39; Wasserman, "'Son of God' Was in the Beginning," 23; Schnackenburg, "Das Evangelium' Im Verständnis Des Altesten Evangelisten," 321–23.

13. Stein, *Mark*, 41; Wasserman, "'Son of God' Was in the Beginning," 42.

14. Iersel, *Mark*, 91.

15. Gundry, *Mark*, 39.

16. Hooker, *Gospel according to St. Mark*, 34. This same point is made by Schweizer, *Good News according to Mark*, 30, who argued that, although it was "added later," it is "in conformity to Mark's linguistic style (15:39)."

17. Mann, *Mark*, 105.

18. Boring, *Mark*, 30; Mann, *Mark*, 105.

The textual issue that underlies Mark 1:1 is a difficult one. Scholars have yet to reach a consensus. This study, in agreement with Schnackenburg, will proceed by tentatively accepting the inclusion of "Son of God." At this point, having examined the textual difficulties that surround Mark 1:1, and arguing for its inclusion, a second question comes to mind.

The second significant issue that arises from the first verse in Mark is whether or not the Roman Imperial cult is in view and is being challenged. As was noted in chapter 3, the words "beginning," "gospel," and "son of God" were linked together and used in reference to Augustus. Does Mark 1:1 constitute a challenge of sorts to the Roman emperor? Because the word "gospel" was commonly used in Imperial propaganda, Myers believes that Mark 1:1 functions as a "declaration of war upon the political culture of the empire."[19] Craig Evans, in his study of the Priene calendar inscription, explains the Roman usage of "gospel":

> The emperor's reign or victory was announced as "gospel" or "good news" (εὐαγγέλιον or εὐαγγελίζεσθαι). The good news was celebrated as a religious event. For example, cities rejoiced and offered sacrifices to the gods upon receiving the good news (εὐαγγελίζεσθαι) of the royal heir's coming of age.[20]

In this study, before going on to survey the entire narrative of Mark, it is prudent to examine Evans's comments regarding the similarities between Mark 1:1 and the Priene Calendar inscription. According to Evans, both the Priene inscription and Mark's incipit refer to the "beginning" (ἀρχή in Mark; ἄρχομαι in Priene) and "the good news" (εὐαγγέλιον in Mark; εὐαγγέλια in Priene). He further points out that, in both, a divine agent brings the "good news." As mentioned in chapter 3, Augustus was often called the son of god. Van Eck has noted additional similarities stemming from the usage of the word "good news." Van Eck writes, the Priene inscription demonstrates

> support for Augustus' achievements was not only limited to Rome. In the inscription and its preamble Augustus is hailed as most divine Caesar and savior of the world whose birth (epiphany) was the beginning of a new creation of the world that brought peace to mankind.[21]

These facts further highlight the similarities between the two records. Additionally, Mark records Jesus as demonstrating a number of similar themes

---

19. Myers, *Binding the Strong Man*, 124.
20. Evans, "Mark's Incipit and the Priene Calendar Inscription," 7.
21. Van Eck, "Mission, Identity and Ethics in Mark," 3.

and activities (e.g., healing, omens, divine names, and sitting with the gods) to what was also attributed to the emperors.

A first century Roman audience would certainly sense the contrast between Mark's presentation of Jesus and the manner in which they viewed the emperor. Mark's incipit would be a direct contradiction to the Imperial cult. With it, Mark provides the context in which to read his book: The true commencement of the good news (εὐαγγέλιον) is not found in the person of Augustus the son of god, but in Jesus, the Jewish Messiah, who is the true Son of God.

In his incipit, Mark is undoubtedly addressing the audience in a manner that would grasp their attention and provide similarities between what he writes and what they were experiencing.[22] He places Jesus in direct contrast with all that the Roman audience knew with his use of the popular religious and cultic language of the Imperial cult. Mark's intention of re-educating his Roman audience concerning the identity of the true Son of God is obvious in his Gospel. For the Roman audience, the introduction functions as a direct challenge to the idea of the Roman emperor being the source of "glad tidings" and the son of god. Mark's theologically driven narrative will continue to underscore these ideas and present Jesus as the true Son of God.

Not only does Mark's incipit remind readers of their present situation, but it also gives them clues about the forthcoming content and emphasis of the Gospel. The Son of God motif, in reference to Jesus, will continue to be established throughout the narrative, and the theology of Mark 1:1 is not fully understood by Jesus' contemporaries until Mark 15:39 when an unlikely individual (a Roman, also the first human to do so) finally repeats the words of Mark's incipit.

Yet, despite the similarities in Mark's incipit and the Roman cult, it should be noted once more that the most pertinent locale from which to understand Mark's intention with the usage of the title "Son of God" can be found in Old Testament thought and theology. This is where the notion of an indefinite audience is important. Surely there were readers who interpreted "Son of God" as standing in distinction to the emperor, but the point Mark is making is that Jesus is the "Son of God" in a way that no emperor could ever claim to be and that the best way to understand what it really means for Jesus to be the "Son of God" is found, not by looking at Greaco-Roman mythology or Divine Men, but in reflecting on the history of Israel and the Messianic dimensions of Christ's identity.

22. The presence of the Roman gospel can be found in Mark. Van Eck notes that in Jesus' interactions and assessment of the Herodians, Pilate, and Herod Antipas, there are hints at the violence through which Rome achieved her gospel. Ibid., 5–7.

The reader is informed that the coming of Jesus is the "beginning" (Ἀρχὴ) of the gospel. This may indicate the "beginning of a new reality."[23] Alternatively, it is possible that the good news begins, not with the birth of the emperor, but with Jesus.[24] Arguing that the idea of "source" is also in play, Boring agrees but notes that something even larger is in view. "The point is not that the story of Jesus begins with his baptism by John, but that the gospel proclaimed by the church of Mark's day had its beginning and origin in the events narrated in Mark as a whole."[25]

The word "gospel," or "good news" (εὐαγγελίου), was used before Mark by Paul in 1 Cor 15:3–5 to specifically talk about "the good news of God's saving acts in the death and resurrection of Jesus."[26] By the time of Mark's writing, this familiar word (εὐαγγελίου) had been borrowed from the Roman World and applied to the Christian message. The LXX uses "εὐαγγέλιον," though not in its singular form (2 Sam 4:10). It also uses the plural of "εὐαγγέλια," a form not known in the New Testament (2 Sam 18:20, 22). Additional uses (1 Kgs 1:42; Jer 20:15; Ps 40:9; 68:11; 96:2; Isa 41:27; 52:7) refer to, broadly speaking, Yahweh's uncontested victory over the world. Increasingly in these usages, a heightened emphasis on the messenger along with the message that they proclaim is seen. It is not simply the "what" of the good news, but the "what" and "who." A similar line of thinking may be present in Mark 1:1. The grammar here is ambiguous. It is unclear whether the genitive "of" is objective or subjective.[27] Hengel understood it to be primarily objective, yet still understood it as having a "comprehensive character; it contains the whole saving event which begins with the forerunner, John the Baptist, and culminates in the death of Jesus for many and his resurrection."[28] The ambiguity may be intentional, however, the use of "gospel" in the New Testament almost always refers to the good news about Christ.[29] Regardless of how 1:1 functions in Mark, its intent is rather clear. It is a message of proclamation.[30] It is not just the "what" of the proclamation,

---

23. Mann, *Mark*, 194.

24. Van Eck, "Mission, Identity and Ethics in Mark," 2; Elliott and Reasoner, *Documents and Images for the Study of Paul*, 366.

25. Boring, *Mark*, 21.

26. Ibid., 31. See also Rom 1:1, 9, 15–16; 2:16; 10:16; 11:28; 15:16, 19–20; 16:25; 1 Cor 1:17; 4:15; 9:12, 14, 16, 18, 23; 15:1 for additional uses and forms of εὐαγγέλιον.

27. Guelich, *Mark*, 9.

28. Hengel, *Studies in the Gospel of Mark*, 53. Some questions that relate to what the term "gospel" meant and its relationship to the "gospel" preached by the early church (specifically Paul and Peter) are addressed by Hengel on pp. 54–56.

29. Gundry, *Mark*, 32; Stein, *Mark*, 40.

30. Malbon, *Hearing Mark*, 11.

but also the "who." Myers notes the word "gospel" was commonly known to be a word that referred to the "technical terms for news of victory."[31] This seems to be the case in this instance.

The question most commentators of Mark begin with is whether 1:1 functions as a title or as part of an introduction or prologue to what follows.[32] It appears best to consider it part of an introduction.[33] As Guelich notes, as a stand-alone title, the sentence would need to be "grammatically independent" and "καθώς never introduces a sentence in Mark or the rest of the NT documents."[34] The first three verses of Mark serve as an introduction to the first micro-narrative of John the Baptist, and, as an introduction to the work itself. These verses serve a number of functions in the broader context. First, they serve to draw attention to the central character that is revealed in the work: Jesus Christ, God's Son. Second, in linking what follows to the tradition of the prophets of Israel's history, the author indicates that the "gospel" of Jesus Christ is the breaking in of the new order on the old.[35]

It may be best to understand 1:1 as an introduction to the micro-narrative of 1:1–15 and as an introduction for the book.[36] There are two sections to this first micro-narrative, namely 1:1–8 and 1:9–15. The first section introduces the protagonist Jesus, and links the good news about him to the prophetic tradition of Israel. Mark 1:2–3 should be linked with 1:1 rather than with 1:4.[37] "As" (καθώς), especially when linked with "it is written" in Mark and elsewhere, depends on what precedes rather than what follows.[38] The quotation from the Old Testament that Mark cites is a conglomerate of three different passages: Exod 23:20; Mal 3:1; and Isa 40:3. Here, Mark cites only Isaiah perhaps because the Isaiah quote is longest, or perhaps because of the high esteem Isaiah enjoyed during the time period. Mark's quotation is,

> As it is written in Isaiah the prophet,
> "Behold, I send my messenger before your face,

31. Myers, *Binding the Strong Man*, 122.

32. An extensive structural study and argument is offered by Boring, *Mark*.

33. *Contra* Boring, *Mark*, 50–53; Marcus, *Mark 1–8*, 143.

34. Guelich, *Mark*, 7.

35. Witherington, *Gospel of Mark*, 68.

36. This view is taken by Mann. He writes, "It is only when the eschatological conflict between the Tempter and Jesus has been joined and decided that any ministry of proclamation is possible." Mann, *Mark*, 193. He follows Keck, "Introduction to Mark's Gospel." *Contra* Taylor, *Gospel according to St. Mark*; Lane, *Mark*, 59–61.

37. Gundry, *Mark*, 30.

38. See Gundry, *Mark*, 30, for citations and examples. See also Guelich, *Mark*, 6; Marcus *Mark*, 17–18; and Stein, *Mark*, 42.

who will prepare your way,
the voice of one crying in the wilderness:
'Prepare the way of the Lord,
make his paths straight.'"

This passage is taken from:

Exod 23:20	"Behold I send my messenger before you."
Mal 3:1	"Who will prepare your way."
Isa 40:3	"The voice of one calling out in the wilderness: 'Prepare the way of the Lord; make straight his paths.'"

This is one of Mark's most evident redactoral actions. Nowhere else in his work does he refer to the fulfillment of Scripture. In the original, the "your" of Exod 23:20 refers to the nation of Israel. In Mark, however, it refers to Jesus, and the "messenger" to John the Baptist. The Exodus quotation is followed quite seamlessly by a similar quotation from Malachi. In Malachi, the text reads: "Behold, I send my messenger, and he will prepare the way before me" (Mal 3:1). The "me" of Malachi (speaking of the LORD; Mal 2:17) is replaced by "your" referring to Jesus. Following Malachi is the quotation from Isaiah primarily from the LXX in which the translation of Isaiah connects "in the wilderness" with "the voice of one crying."[39] By presenting the double rendering of "prepare the way" (Mark 1:1, 2), Mark presents them as parallels. Thus, preparing "your" way (that is Jesus') is preparing the way of "the Lord." What Mark has done here with this quotation is connect the gospel of Jesus Christ to the long-standing prophetic anticipation that is found throughout the Hebrew Bible. The quotation indicates both Jesus and John's ministries are not something new, but stand in continuation with the Hebrew Bible. This conglomerate quote serves a narrative purpose as well. Richards, in his 1974 publication of D. J. James Lectures at University College of Swansea, helpfully summarizes the role of the first few lines of Mark,

> The simplicity of the opening words of the narrative is deceptive, for they do more than set the events to be recorded within the sphere of God's purposes, they also re-create the mental and spiritual environment of the age in which they took place, helping us to understand why it was that when John appeared large crowds were drawn to the Jordan, why is was that men responded to his call to repent, why it was that they confessed their sins and accepted baptism at his hands. All this happened because these men and women, although they might not have

---

39. Van Iersel, *Mark*, 95.

been thinking in terms of fulfillment of a particular prophecy or prophecies, were convinced nevertheless that they were witnessing a renewal of the activity of God in their midst.[40]

The scholarship surrounding Mark and his relation to the Old Testament is summarized succinctly by Watts.[41] Watts, after surveying the different views scholars take on the issue, offers a few thoughts with which this study is inclined to agree. Jesus' authority to at once pronounce judgment on religious leaders for not obeying the Old Testament Law, and at the same time recasting or reinterpreting the Old Testament is a central theme in Mark.[42] In agreement with Kee and Hooker, Watts proposes, rather than providing direct editorial insertions (excepting 1:2–3), Mark records Old Testament quotations coming from the lips of Jesus himself. In this, he asserts the Torah is used by Jesus to reinterpret the Law, Isaiah and Zechariah to reinterpret God's community of people, and Isaiah and Daniel to recast redemption. These themes—the interplay and fluidity that exist between the Old Testament and Mark's (through the character of Jesus) reinterpreting of the Old Testament—are elements this study will continue to build upon.

Collective experiences, or a shared history, have direct influence on the way we communicate and the way we understand what is being said. If two men stand opposite one another and someone shouts out, "Let's get ready to rumble," those familiar with American professional wrestling will understand the situation, have certain specific expectations, and understand that, most likely, a fight or match is immanent. Those with virtually no exposure to American wrestling will find this statement confusing and, most likely, unhelpful for providing context or a framework to understand the situation at hand. It is the same with the shared history and expectations of Israel. One would not be so naïve as to ignore the complexities and diversity that existed in Israel at the time of Christ but, nevertheless, Isaiah and the New Exodus expectation is a point that cannot be dismissed. Watts summarizes this view well:

> Retuning to Mark, I suggest that his "grand piano" is a schematized interpretive "map" of Israel's "history" and that his OT part-citations or allusions may function as "grid references" to

---

40. Richards, *Jesus, Son of God and Son of Man*, 42.

41. Watts, *Isaiah's New Exodus in Mark*, 9–28. In addition, see Anderson, "Old Testament in Mark's Gospel," 307; Beale, *Handbook on the New Testament*, 111–30; Watts, "Mark."

42. Watts, *Isaiah's New Exodus in Mark*, 27.

that map which gives expression and order to Israel's interpretation of her history, namely that of the OT.[43]

Malina and Rohrbaugh highlight the significance of Mark's quotation: "In oral societies the ability of the writer and speakers to quote tradition conferred honor upon them, especially if they could use it creatively as Mark has done here."[44] Yet, Mark as the authority, or implicitly as the omniscient narrator, uses this authority to point to the greater authority of the Son.

The proclamation offered in Mark 1:1 casts a shadow over the events in the first section of the micro-narrative (and the whole narrative, for that matter). The reader is not sure what to expect, only that it will be significant. The scriptural quotation, followed by the words of John the Baptist, continues to build a sense of anticipation towards the introduction of the protagonist. It is interesting that Mark mentions Jesus in Mark 1:1, yet John the Baptist is the first character that speaks and appears on the scene. This choice by Mark does not serve to deflate the expectation of the introduction of Jesus, but to heighten it because John's words increase the anticipation surrounding the authority and power of Jesus.

The opening that is offered by Mark is not part of the narrative or story that follows. Rather, it is the essential information that the reader needs in order to frame his or her interaction with the story that is to come. Before jumping into the narrative, Mark wants his readers to be aware of who Jesus is.[45] He "tips his cards" so to speak.

Kingsbury has noted that there are essentially three characters introduced in the first micro-narrative of Mark; God, John the Baptist, and Jesus.[46] God designates John as the messenger that goes ahead of Jesus and prepares his way (1:2). Additionally, according to the quotation that Mark presents, God has also designated Jesus as "Lord" (cf. 1:3 to 1:1).[47] Accordingly, both John and Jesus do what they do in the narrative under the commissioning and authority of God himself.

---

43. Ibid., 33.

44. Malina and Rohrbaugh, *Social-Science Commentary*, 175.

45. Kingsbury writes, "Rhetorically, this verse is critical already in informing the reader of Mark's own conception of Jesus (i.e., his own 'evaluative point of view' concerning Jesus' identity). Addressing the reader both directly and programmatically, Mark tell him that he holds Jesus to be the 'Messiah, the Son of God.' The reader has no grounds for assuming, or even suspecting, that these titles for Jesus are 'false' or 'defective.' While Mark can be expected to elaborate them in the course of his story, they are nonetheless 'correct.'" Kingsbury, *Christology of Mark's Gospel*, 56.

46. Ibid., 57.

47. Ibid.

This introduction is noteworthy for a number of reasons. First, the titles that are ascribed to Jesus are not without exegetical and narrative significance. Right from the beginning, the narrator ensures that the reader understands who Jesus is, even before he does anything. This makes the reader expect something grand or significant to follow; after all, the story is centering on God's Messiah, his Son! Second, by anchoring the story of Jesus within the Old Testament eschatological expectation, the author protects against diverse and varied understandings of what it means to be the "Son of God." It is clear from the words chosen in Mark 1:1 and the conglomerate quotation in 1:2 and 1:3 that the context of understanding what "Son of God" means is not in the Hellenistic ruler cults, but rather in the Old Testament tradition of divine sonship. To this point, Schweizer explains,

> If we wish to discern what it is that Mark is trying to say, we must observe the way he uses his material. He places these two Old Testament citations at the beginning so that although they refer only to the 1:4–8, they still function as a preface to the whole book an introduce everything that follows as fulfillment of God's dealings with Israel.[48]

Third, by adding the "voice" of God to his own narration, the author increases the weight behind his assertion about Jesus and indicates that not only in "his" eyes is Jesus the Son, but also in the eyes of God. Already, in the first eight verses, the narrator, God, the Old Testament Scriptures, and John the Baptist stand in support and continuation of the titles ascribed to Christ in the first line of the Gospel. This "authority" afforded by the narrator through his omniscience is ratified through the inclusion of the previously mentioned voices.

This approach is found throughout the Gospel of Mark. The narrator leads his readers by means of "asides."[49] Rhoads explain the significance of the omniscient narrator of Mark well:

> Because Mark's narrator is not a character in the story, there is no identity, social location, or place in time specified for the narrator. The narrator simply begins the story in the past tense and proceeds to tell it without drawing attention to the act of narration itself. This effacing of the narrator's identity and presence enables the narrator to assume a position of authority in relation to the story being constructed.[50]

---

48. Schweizer, *Good News according to Mark*, 29.

49. For the significance and placement of these "asides," see Rhoads, Dewey, and Michie, *Mark as Story*, 40.

50. Ibid.

94 ALLEGIANCE, OPPOSITION, AND MISUNDERSTANDING

The final few verses of the introduction (1:4–8) continue the direction started in 1:1–3. In 1:4 John is introduced as the messenger of preparation for Jesus.[51] With typical prophetic boldness and authority, John claims, "after me comes he who is mightier than I, the strap of whose sandals I am not worthy to stoop down and untie. I have baptized you with water, but he will baptize you with the Holy Spirit" (1:7, 8). John's language is strong and further serves to heighten the expectation and interest for the introduction of the protagonist mentioned in Mark 1:1. Already, only a few lines in, a significant amount of information has been given by Mark: Jesus is the Messiah, and in some sense or other, he is God's son. He brings the "good news" that was foretold by the prophets of Israel. The messenger that goes before him is John the Baptist. He is found in the desert, leading a rather large movement and baptizing many. Yet, this leader proclaims that Jesus is mightier than he, and will come and baptize the people with the Holy Spirit.

John's description is not without purpose. The reader is given the information about his dress and diet because they are expected to have read the biblical stories about the prophets of Israel. In the words of Malbon, "he dresses like Elijah (2 Kgs 1:8; compare Zech 13:4), he eats like Elijah, and we know that Elijah is coming before the end times (Mal 4:5)."[52] This, again, anchors the introduction in the Scriptures and expects that the readers will understand the narrative in that context.

MARK 1:11: THE BAPTISM OF JESUS

The next micro-narrative (Mark 1:9–13) has two parts, of which the second (1:12–13) is often undervalued by commentators. With the proclamation by John that a "mightier" eschatological figure is soon coming, the readers of Mark's Gospel are quickly introduced to Jesus. Here again, the characters in the story are not led on the same journey of anticipation or discovery as the readers of the Gospel are. Jesus is baptized by John in the Jordan, imbued with the Spirit, and a voice from heaven declares that Jesus is "my beloved son, in whom I am well pleased" (1:10). Yet little additional information is offered, and no formal commissioning is given to Jesus. Instead, the Spirit drives him into the wilderness, and while there, he is tempted by Satan and ministered to by angels. Unlike Matthew and Luke, or even John, the author of Mark offers nothing about Jesus' lineage, family heritage, or pre-existence. For Mark, the priority from the beginning is on who Jesus is,

---

51. Edwards, *Mark*, 29.
52. Malbon, *Hearing Mark*, 14–15.

his ministry, and his death. To properly interpret this micro-narrative, these two sections must be treated together.

In Mark's account of the baptism the vision of the heavens being opened and the voice that speaks from heaven is a private affair. Only Jesus, in the story, is privy to this revelation. Again, the reader is given the "inside scoop" about who Jesus is. The reader is aligned with Jesus, God himself, and the narrator as those who are to be considered "in the know." This alignment continues throughout Mark's narrative.

The transitional phrase found in 1:9, "in those days," indicates a departure from a focus on the ministry of John the Baptist, to the ministry of Jesus. The context of 1:2 makes it clear that Jesus was the "Lord" referred to, and thus, his appearance on the scene is permeated by expectation and anticipation. As Collins notes, "The statement that Jesus was baptized by John in the Jordan provides narrative continuity."[53] It is not explicitly stated in the text, but it is implied that the baptism of Jesus in the Jordan is the fulfillment of John's prediction in 1:7 that a "mightier" one is coming. Rather than explicitly stating the fulfillment, it is left to the reader to "discover it for themselves."[54] The order in Greek is also significant here. The words "in the Jordan" precede "John" and further demonstrate that the focus has shifted from John the Baptist—the one who stands in the prophetic tradition of the Hebrew prophets—to Jesus, the divine Messiah. Add to this Marcus' point that, in this micro-narrative, Jesus becomes the subject of all the main verbs, and it becomes clear that the character of John is quickly and deliberately being eclipsed by Jesus.[55]

Additionally, the Greek of 1:9, (Καὶ ἐγένετο ἐν ἐκείναις ταῖς ἡμέραις ἦλθεν Ἰησοῦς) would likely have been familiar to the readers of Mark's Gospel. Parrallels to this abound in the Hebrew Scripture (cf. Exod 2:11; Judg 18:31) and, as Marcus notes, the phrase has an eschatological essence as well because "in those days" indicates an eschatological period that was referred to by the prophets (Jer 31:33; Joel 3:1).[56]

Mark 1:10–11 describe the details of Jesus' baptism by John: "Immediately coming up out of the water, He saw the heavens opening, and the Spirit like a dove descending upon him and a voice came out of the heavens: 'You are my beloved Son, in you I am well-pleased.'" At this point in the story, the narrator, the Hebrew Bible, and John the Baptist have all spoken in unity that Jesus is the Son of God; now the author recruits God himself

---

53. Collins, *Mark*, 148.
54. Gundry, *Mark*, 47.
55. Marcus, *Mark 1–8*, 163.
56. Ibid.

to reinforce this claim. The voice from heaven reiterates what the narrator begun the Gospel with. Mark 1:10 is the first usage by Mark of his well-used "εὐθύς."[57] It propels the story forward in dramatic fashion. Mark does not allow the reader to have even a moment's pause or tension. He refuses to allow his audience to wonder or question whether the lofty claims about Jesus are to be accepted as authoritative or not because "immediately" God adds his endorsement.

Coming up out of the water, the heavens are "torn open"—a dramatic verb (σχιζομένους) used only here and in 15:38. Both Matthew and Luke choose a less dramatic word in "open" (ἀνοίγω), and Collins notes that this is the word most commonly used in "theophanic, epiphanic, or revelatory" situations.[58] In Matthew's rendering, the second person pronoun "you" is changed to the demonstrative "this is." The agreement of Matthew and Luke against Mark may be due to their being aware of a pre-Markan oral formulation or it may be simple happenstance.[59] What can be understood from Mark's rendering here is that he is deliberately attempting to frame the baptism in an eschatological framework.

Regarding the phrase "the Spirit descending on him like a dove" (1:10), coming to grips with the exact meaning of the text is difficult. The "Spirit," as Bultmann has noted, is most often indefinite in its usage, but this usage is not absolute, as has been contradicted by finds at Qumran.[60] An additional argument against Bultmann's assertion is that the definite "Holy Spirit" or "the spirit" are referred to in the verses that precede (1:8) and follow (1:12) the baptism-narrative. This, coupled with the fact that the Spirit came "from heaven," make it hard to avoid the conclusion that Mark is likely meaning "the Holy Spirit," as opposed to meaning "one's inner spirit" or something akin to "unclean spirit." Second, the complication is compounded because the simile of the dove is difficult to understand. The simile is present in all four Gospels.[61] Additionally, the apocalyptic nature of the word "like" in Mark 1:10 is an aspect that must feature into our interpretation. It has been noted that ὡς occurs more often in Revelation than any other book.[62] So why did Mark include the reference to the dove? Perhaps it was simply part of the tradition that he received.[63] Another view is that the dove is

---

57. Used in total forty-one times by Mark. Cf. Stein, *Mark*, 57.
58. Collins, *Mark*, 148; Mann, *Mark*, 200.
59. Stein, *Mark*, 57.
60. Bultmann, *Theology of the New Testament*, 251.
61. The debate and uncertainty surrounding the dove image is summarized in an impressive fashion by Collins, *Mark*, 148; Mann, *Mark*, 200.
62. Marcus, *Mark 1–8*, 159.
63. Stein, *Mark*, 57.

being contrasted with the Roman eagle. This is keeping with the trajectory that the narrator started in 1:1 of simultaneously teaching about Jesus and demonstrating the disjunction between he and Rome. This view argues that since the Roman World esteemed the eagle, Mark is here depicting Jesus as a "counter-emperor."[64] In the end, no clear parallel exists that helps in the interpretation of the dove simile. Guelich summarizes the point well, "The absence of clear precedent for identifying the dove symbolically with the Spirit, despite the extensive literary use of the dove in ancient literature . . . makes any symbolic explanation of the dove's role in the pericope . . . tenuous at best."[65] It seems best to agree with Guelich in this.

The Spirit, and even the image of the dove may not, in the present day, carry the same significance as it would to the original readers. Boring puts it well: "The coming of the Spirit is not a soft, warm-fuzzy image . . . 'Spirit' connotes power, eschatological power, as in Isa 11:1–5."[66] Mark's shortening here of "Holy Spirit" (1:8) to "Spirit" does not change the meaning of the usage.[67] The same "Spirit" mentioned by John has come upon Jesus.

The word "heaven" in Mark typically constitutes that which is inherently upward or other worldly. It is the "other place" that stands above and beyond the earth. The baptism scene is, in essence, the in-breaking of the apocalyptic on the present. Heaven, or the "other place," is pressing in on the world inhabited by the readers. This happens because the heavens are "torn" or "ripped" open (σχιζομένους) and the Spirit, promised by the forerunner John the Baptist, "comes down."

In Mark it is Jesus alone who hears the voice from heaven. This is the first hint at the secrecy motif in his Gospel and, also, the first indication of what is meant by "Son of God." The reader has already been informed that Jesus is the Son of God, and this disclosure heightens the expectations of the reader. The reader thinks, "if Jesus is the 'Son of God,' then surely something significant is going to happen very shortly." The reader has been "tipped off," so to speak, and eagerly awaits some additional disclosure or public demonstration of Jesus' divine sonship. Yet, what occurs is unexpected; Jesus alone hears the voice (along with the readers). Kingsbury argues that the motif of secrecy is more closely related to the divine sonship of Jesus than him being the Messiah.[68] He is correct in this and more than just a motif of

---

64. Van Eck, "Mission, Identity and Ethics in Mark," 7, quoting Peppard, "Eagle and the Dove," 450.
65. Evans, *Mark*, 33.
66. Boring, *Mark*, 45.
67. Mann, *Mark*, 200.
68. Kingsbury, *Christology of Mark's Gospel*, 14.

secrecy, Mark has created a privileged-perspective motif of secrecy in which the readers are brought in on the narrator's point of view and in which the characters in the story remain ignorant.[69]

Many commentators note the progression in the text is from seeing to hearing[70] First, a sign is seen, followed by a voice that is heard. The voice from heaven serves to dispel any doubt from the reader's mind about what the narrator said in Mark 1:1. The voice returns in Mark 9:2–8 where the divine sonship of Jesus is reinforced once again. The voice from heaven calls out,

- ESV: "you are my beloved Son; with you I am well pleased."
- GNTSBL: Σὺ εἶ ὁ υἱός μου ὁ ἀγαπητός, ἐν σοὶ εὐδόκησα

The "voice" (φωνή) from heaven forms a couplet with Mark's quotation of Isa 40:3 in 1:3. First, in 1:3, a "voice" calls out in the wilderness (ἐρήμῳ) preparing the "way of the Lord." Next, a "voice" (φωνή) is heard in the wilderness (ἐρήμῳ; 1:4). This time, however, it is not the forerunner, but God himself who speaks.

A few points are worth noting here. First, the "you" (σύ) is likely emphatic due to its placement at the beginning of the line. The first part of the pronouncement from heaven is a very close quotation from Ps 2:7 LXX, the only major difference being the placement of the "you."[71] The second clause may be taken from Isa 42:1. The word "beloved" in Mark 1:11 may be taken from there though its exact origin is hard to surmise.[72] The second clause, "with you I am well pleased," may have been taken from a copy of the LXX that Matthew and Mark had available to them.[73] There is also another intertextual connection between Mark 1 and Isa 42:2 in the reference to the "spirit."

Next, the question that is often presupposed by this pronouncement from heaven is whether the understanding of sonship in the text is one of adoption, or if it is identifying Jesus as the Son.[74] The link between Mark 1:11 and Mark 1:1 and the twin usage of "Son of God" seem to argue against

69. That the motif of secrecy is primarily focused on the sonship of Jesus will be examined in greater detail in chapter 6. For now, however, we note the reader is already being invited to take part in the narrator's omniscient viewpoint.

70. Edwards, *Mark*, 37; Gundry, *Mark*, 49; Stein, *Mark*, 58.

71. Gundry, *Mark*, 49.

72. Collins, *Mark*, 150.

73. Ibid.

74. Schweizer rightly notes that even if an adoption of sorts is taking place, it is not the primary issue under consideration for Mark. The question of who Jesus was before his baptism is not one the text is trying to answer. Schweizer, *Mark*, 41.

an adoptionistic understanding of sonship here. Just as Mark 9:7 does not constitute a second adoption, the usage in 1:11 is likewise unlikely to be an adoption. The context and contents of the passage also argue against a view of adoption. Jesus has yet to do anything significant or special. He has not warranted an adoption in any sense of the word. In the words of Stein, "He is not the Son of God because he does certain things, he does certain things because he is the Son of God. Who he *is* determines what he does, not vice versa."[75] It is also possible that in these verses readers note a Jesus-as-representative Israel motif being developed.[76]

The voice from heaven declares that Jesus is the "beloved" (ἀγαπητός) son. This word can mean "only" as is likely the case in Mark 12:6 since the "beloved" son is the heir to estate.[77] This same type of meaning can be found in the LXX where the Hebrew (יָחִיד) is translated as ἀγαπητός (Gen 22:2, 12, 16). It is uncertain whether the meaning of ἀγαπητός in Mark 1:11 indicates something akin to John's "only begotten" (John 3:16) or "chosen" stemming from a linguistic link to Isa 42.[78] Regardless, it is clear that the voice from heaven is declaring Jesus his Son in a unique and highly significant way. The phrase, "with you I am well pleased" likely finds its source in Isa 42:1b. Here, it appears that Mark is following the MT against the LXX since the MT's "delight" is closer than the "helps" (ἀντιλαμβάνω) of the LXX's rendering of Isa 42:1.

The use of Isa 42 and the declaration of sonship by God in Mark 1:11 have a number of important christological points worth reflecting on. By uniting Ps 2:7, a royal Psalm, and Isa 42, about the suffering servant, Mark presents Jesus as both the Messiah and the servant of God.[79] Here, we have three lines of revelation. Jesus is Messiah (Mark 1:1), suffering Servant, and Son of God. All of this is something the reader is privy to. It is not something the characters in the story are aware of.

God tears the heavens open, and the Spirit is sent down to empower and lead Jesus in his ministry. There is an undeniable eschatological essence to these actions. Something cosmic and new is happening at the arrival of Jesus. But the new act is not something that does not have any precedence. The words spoken by the narrator (1:2–3) and God himself (1:11) are words from Israel's Scripture. This new act is anchored in the eschatological hope of Israel's prophets. Too often studies that focus on the divine sonship of

75. Stein, *Mark*, 58.
76. Mann, *Mark*, 201.
77. Stein, *Mark*, 59.
78. Collins, *Mark*, 150.
79. Ibid.

Jesus, approach the question from an almost entirely Hellenistic or Greaco-Roman vantage point. The number of allusions, references, and motifs that originate in Israel's past make it far more beneficial to invest in study on this contextual horizon.

A brief review of Mark's literary approach thus far is in order. Van Iersel notes that the "tension" in the text that Mark has already setup is that the reader knows significantly more than the characters of the story.[80] Rhoads, Dewey, and Michie, comment on this tension:

> Hearing Mark's story for the first time is like watching a Hitchcock film in which the viewer is aware of a threatening situation at the opening of the film, then nervously watches the unsuspecting characters in the story become aware of the situation for themselves.[81]

The reader knows before Jesus says or does anything that he is God's Son. With eagerness and expectation, the reader awaits the time when this revelation is made known to the characters in the story. How will they respond? Surely, if God's Son is among them, they will rejoice and embrace him. What powerful, cosmic actions will the Son of God perform? The reader naturally asks these questions and many more. With these questions in mind, the reader continues, and awaits clarification as to what being the Son of God entails for Jesus.

THE TEMPTATION

The next instance in which the title "Son of God" occurs in Mark is in 3:11. However, to jump from the baptism to the third chapter is to commit the "word-concept" fallacy. Just because the words "Son of God" do not appear in the intermittent verses, does not mean that concepts, themes, or motifs surrounding sonship are not present. There is much in the passage in between that will illumine the present study. We can take, for example, the temptation narrative. Since the opening verses in Mark leave open the Jesus-as-representative Israel, and since Israel was commonly known and referred to as God's Son, a corporate story line (of Israel) may be being applied to the life of Jesus.

Mark introduces his short temptation narrative with "immediately" (εὐθύς), thus creating a close link with the baptism account that preceded

---

80. Van Iersel, *Mark*, 101.
81. Rhoads, Dewey, and Michie, *Mark as Story*, 43.

it.[82] There are a number of significant differences between Mark's account and the way the temptation narrative is rendered in Matthew and Luke.[83] The same Spirit that Jesus would baptize with, and the same Spirit that came down as a dove from heaven now takes an active role in the story. The Spirit "drives" (ἐκβάλλω) Jesus into the wilderness (ἔρημος) for forty days where he is with the "wild animals."[84] Mark's use of the term wilderness is interesting. In indicates the barren places that God is now invading and bringing life to.[85] First, a voice is heard in the "wilderness" (1:3), then a voice preaches in the "wilderness" (1:4), then God's voice is heard in the "wilderness" (1:11; Jordan area where John was baptizing), then Jesus is "driven" out into the "wilderness" to be tested. The desert appears five times in the first 13 verses of Mark. The "wilderness" cannot be any real defined geographical place for Mark since Jesus goes from wilderness to wilderness. The narrator has already indicated that John was baptizing in the wilderness, and right after Jesus was baptized he leaves that region, called the "wilderness" to go to the "wilderness."

The LXX renders "ἔρημος" 241 of 345 occurrences of "מִדְבָּר." There is a two-fold understanding of the "desert" in the Old Testament. It is the place where God often reveals himself, and the place where demons and evil spirits threaten humans; it is at once a place of revelation and a place of desolation. Examples abound of God revealing himself to humans in the wilderness (1 Kgs 19:4-6; Exod 3:1). Likewise, the desert is also the place of danger (Deut 8:15; Num 21:4-9). This same understanding about the nature of the desert is found in the writers of the Synoptics. Through Mark's account of the baptism and temptation of Jesus, we see both of the elements in play. God reveals from heaven that Jesus is his Son in the desert (1:11). Next, Jesus is tempted by demonic forces in the desert (1:13).

What is curious about the temptation narrative is the way in which it is not essentially Satan against God (with Jesus in the fray), but rather is effectively Satan against Jesus. The cosmic struggle between good and evil pits God's Son against the arch evil-one, Satan. As God's Messiah and Son, Jesus is his representative and does battle with God's enemies, just as he fulfills God's mission.

---

82. Stein, *Mark*, 62.

83. See Gundry, *Mark*, 55.

84. Some of the Second Temple literature Mark may be drawing on in this instance, specifically in the mention of "devil," "wild animal," and "angels," is offered by Schweizer, *Mark*, 42.

85. For a brief explanation of Mark's use of "desert," see Mann, *Mark*, 195, 203.

The symbolism in this passage is highly debated. Is there an Adam-Christ comparison taking place in Mark,[86] where Jesus is overcoming Satan through resisting temptation?[87] Or is there a Christ as the new Israel being demonstrated?[88] Regardless of the way one reads the temptation narrative, either with a Christ-Adam or a Christ-Israel theological backdrop, what is beyond dispute is the deep and unmistakable Old Testament roots and connections. It does seem best, however, to see Mark as presenting Jesus as the culmination of Israel's history and as the True Israel.[89] A few points demonstrating this are worth noting.

The sequence of the events in Mark are significant. Jesus comes up through the waters, is addressed by God from heaven, and proceeds to be led into the wilderness for forty days to be tested. Israel, is a similar vein, was delivered through the waters (Red Sea), addressed by God in the giving of the Law, and then proceeded to go into the wilderness for forty years for a time of testing. Israel is God's Son (Exod 4:22) and so is Jesus, thus their journeys share a number of characteristics. The New Exodus-theology in Mark has been highlighted and observed by Watts.[90] It is in the context of the baptism narrative that the links become clear between the manner in which Mark renders the story and New Exodus-motif. The thematic overlap between Isa 63 and the baptism narrative are highlighted by Watts.[91] These further demonstrate the New Exodus-motif in Mark since the passage in Isaiah has clear overtures of this expectation.

However, in favor of an Adam-Christ, or paradise motif, there are a few points. Both Christ and Adam were tested when they were at peace with the wild animals (Gen 1:28; 2:19–20; Mark 1:13b). The temptation of Adam succeeded and brought a curse that led to enmity between Adam and the created order (Gen 3:14–20). Additionally, the mention of the angel in Mark 1:13b is often thought to indicate some form of food delivery since "serving" is most often used in this way.[92] A similar usage of angels and serving is found in Elijah's story (1 Kgs 19:1–8), But, as Guelich remarks, "A closer analogy comes from the Jewish reference to the angel's sustenance of Adam and Eve in the Garden."[93]

---

86. Illustrative of this is Mann, *Mark*, 203.
87. Guelich, *Mark*, 39.
88. France, *Mark*, 85.
89. Schreiner, *New Testament Theology*, 236–38.
90. Watts, *Isaiah's New Exodus in Mark*.
91. Ibid., 107.
92. Guelich, *Mark*, 39.
93. Ibid., 29.

Despite the points in favor of an Adam-Christ contrast or typology, it seems best to place the temptation narrative in the context of the first chapter of Mark. Here we see that the use of Exodus, Isaiah, and Malachi, along with Messianic overtures throughout the passage, lead one to conclude that Mark most likely had an interest in portraying Jesus as the True Israel, rather than as some type of second Adam (see Rom 5:12–21). Waetjen remarks, "he becomes the embodiment of Israel, who will be escorted into the promise land of the new creation by God's messenger."[94]

The connection of the temptation narrative with the baptism is used by Mark to connect Israel's history with that of Jesus. It solidifies the contextual horizon as being primarily in the locale of Israel as opposed to the Divine Men or ruler cult. Although Jesus is not explicitly referred to here as the "Son of God," his actions are cast as a shadow of Israel's, who is referred to as "God's Son" in the Old Testament (Exod 4:22). Mark is presenting Jesus as Israel. The temptation is also the first introduction of evil forces in Mark. Satan is "testing" Jesus in the wilderness, and these evil forces will make appearances later in the Gospel as well. This will be the next area the study will examine.

MARK 3:11: THE SON OF GOD AND THE DEMONIACS

The next time the divine sonship of Jesus is explicitly referred to is in Mark 3:11. Here, and in 1:24 and 5:7, we see the evil forces being addressed by Jesus. Jesus begins his ministry with preaching (1:14–15). He then calls disciples and they follow him (1:16–20). In Capernaum, he enters the synagogue on the Sabbath and begins to teach "as one who had authority and not as the scribes" (1:22). Mark's repeated usage of the word "immediately" functions as a literary punch—during Jesus' authoritative teaching that is being recognized and apparently celebrated in some sense by the crowd, the man with an "unclean spirit" (πνεύματι ἀκαθάρτῳ) calls out. The phrase "unclean spirit" may be related to the account of the story of fallen angels from Gen 6:1–4.[95] But more than pointing the reader back to the Old Testament, the words "unclean spirit" point the reader to the "Holy Spirit" mentioned in Mark 1:8 and 11. In the temptation Jesus and the arch-enemy of God are pitted head to head. Here, something similar is happening. The Holy Spirit in Jesus confronts the unclean spirit in the man. The question that naturally arises in the conflict is simple: who will win the day? Who is more powerful, the Holy Spirit in Jesus, or the unclean spirit that confronts

---

94. Waetjen, *Reordering of Power*, 74.
95. Collins, *Mark*, 167.

him? The words of the demoniac remove all doubt about who possesses the greater power: "What have you to do with us, Jesus of Nazareth? Have you come to destroy us? I know who you are—Holy One of God" (1:24). The plural "us" as opposed to "me" in 1:24 is likely a reference to evil spirits as a whole, rather than to some schizophrenic union of the man and the spirit. The words, "have you come" also likely refer to something larger than the immediate situation of Jesus' entrance to the Capernaum synagogue, but rather, likely refer to Jesus' "coming on the scene" (cf. 1:38, 29; 2:17; 10:45). The "stronger one" that John the Baptist pointed to has evidently appeared on the scene. The evil and unclean spirits that wreak havoc and bring about physical and spiritual bondage are about to be "destroyed" by the work of the Son of God. The idea that the unclean spirit was seeking to gain power over Jesus through knowledge of his name is doubtful.[96] Rather than displaying an attempt to gain control, it appears in some sense that it is functioning as a christological confession of sorts.[97] Perhaps Mark uses it for both purposes. The unclean spirit may have been used by Mark to highlight Jesus' authority (since his attempt to gain authority over Jesus fails) and to offer yet another christological confession. Naturally, the question is, then, what type of confession? One of divine sonship, or one of a Messianic secret kind? Regarding this question, William Wrede argued that the confession was not originally part of the story but was most likely from the hand of Mark the redactor, seeking to further develop the Messianic secret motif in his work.[98] However, against Wrede, it should be noted that the words "Holy one of God" appear nowhere else in Mark's Gospel and so seem an unlikely redactoral addition by Mark.[99]

Jesus rebukes the unclean spirit and commands it to leave the man (1:25). The command "Be silent" is, according to Wrede, reinforcing the Messianic secret motif. However, Mark presents Jesus as of such authority that he need not rely on word games, set incantations, or any other type of pagan magical work to exorcise the demon. So, more likely than not, Mark is highlighting Jesus' authority as the "Holy one of God" more than working on developing his Messianic motif. Authority is the focus, not secrecy. In the synagogue, there is room for only one teacher with authority, and Mark presents Jesus as that one. The people are amazed, yet their response to this miracle is simply a repeat of their previous statements. They are amazed at

---

96. *Contra* Collins, *Mark*, 169; Gundry, *Mark*.
97. Stein, *Mark*, 88.
98. Wrede, *Messianic Secret*, 24–25.

99. Interestingly, Bultmann views these words as "protective words" that were commonly used in demonic situations in an attempt to gain control over another. Bultmann, *History of the Synoptic Tradition*, 209.

his teaching and authority (1:27; cf. 1:22). After this encounter, Mark expresses that Jesus' fame spread throughout the region.

Bartlett, in his dissertation on exorcism in Mark, presents the five typical stages or elements of exorcism in Mark.[100] They are:

1. The presentation of the demoniac
2. The demoniac's cry—an attempt to ward off Jesus
3. Jesus' exhortation, in opposition to the demoniac
4. The spirit departs with appropriate signs, proving effectiveness of exorcism
5. The awestruck response of the crowd.

Bartlett examines each instance in Mark where an exorcism occurs and gives special attention to the ways in which redactoral omissions or additions shed light on Mark's theological or didactic aims. In light of the words "I know who you are—the Holy One of God" (1:24), Bartlett sees a Semitic formula that offers "reminiscence of the Elijah story in 1 Kgs 17:18."[101]

The question of identity, knowing and recognizing who Jesus is, functions significantly here in this passage. Mark writes that whenever the unclean spirits "saw" Jesus, they responded this way. Mann is correct in noting that to "see" in this sense does not simply mean to glance at, or casually take notice of something, but rather imply "something more."[102] When the unclean spirits see, really see, who Jesus is—that he is God's Son, they responded by falling down and correctly identifying him.

Mark 3:11: Editorial Comment on Exorcism

The editorial comment of 3:11, "and whenever unclean spirits saw him, they fell down before him and cried out, 'You are the Son of God,'" encapsulates all the encounters that Jesus has with evil spirits. The progression in this text is worth examining. First of all, Mark writes that these significant events occurred whenever the unclean spirits "saw" Jesus. It was not a matter of a long showdown between Jesus and the unclean sprits, or a case of back and forth give-and-take. The spirits needed only to "see" Jesus and the process of exorcism began. In short order, the reader comes to 3:27 and reads about the "stronger man" who is able to plunder the "strong man's house." The

---

100. Bartlett, *Exorcism Stories in the Gospel of Mark*, 45.
101. Ibid., 42.
102. Mann, *Mark*, 246.

unclean spirits, as superhuman beings, have an awareness of Jesus' identity that remains hidden to the characters in the story. These unclean spirits have authority over humans, and supernatural knowledge, yet whenever they "see" Jesus they fall before him.

The word here, translated as "fall down," is προσέπιπτον and is used again in 5:33 and 7:25. Both instances continue the idea of submission and "falling" before. The word "cry" (ἔκραζον) in Mark is often used in connection with the cry of those afflicted by unclean spirits (1:23; 3:11; 5:5, 7). In this scene, we have the same type of occurrence as we saw in 1:23, but intensified. Regardless if one saw some form of name/authority mastery in 1:23–24 or not, nothing of the sort is given in this account. The authority of Jesus is beyond question. Stein makes the note, "Mark indicates that the demons are reliable spokespersons for understanding who Jesus is, and because of their supernatural insight, they know better than Jesus' contemporaries his identity."[103] Boring comments about 3:11 being more than just a ministry summary:

> Jesus is acclaimed as the Son of God by demons, who prostrate themselves before him, but he orders them to be silent precisely because they—in contrast to the admiring crowd—know his true identity. In this scene, Jesus does not cast out the unclean spirits, and there are no pictures of people rejoicing in their deliverance from demons. The reader sees another indication that the account is not merely informational, as the narrative camera focuses on only one aspect of the scene: the demons prostrate themselves before Jesus and cry out that he is the Son of God.[104]

In Mark, exorcisms play a fairly prominent role, appearing throughout the narrative (1:21–28, 34; 3:11; 5:1–20; 6:13 [through commissioning disciples]; 9:14–29, 38 [through the unnamed exorcist]). Exorcisms are more highly concentrated, though, at the beginning of the narrative. From the first of these encounters to the last, we see that Jesus has authority over the spirits. He is the Messiah, the Son of God and, as such, his authority is startling to the crowds and demons alike. Jesus as God's representative, commissioned by the Spirit (1:11), stands as the stronger one (3:27) who has authority and power over all the supernatural agents of the strong one, Satan (3:23–28). Yet despite the important revelatory and theological dimensions of these accounts, it is only the reader that is given this "privileged information."[105] The human characters in the story, however, remain in the

---

103. Stein, *Mark*, 88.
104. Boring, *Mark*, 98.
105. Ibid.

dark about the true identity of Jesus. Additionally, Marcus connects the narrative and christological elements in play: "In Mark's conception then, 'Son of God' is not simply a title for Jesus as the human Messiah . . . but a designation suggesting that he participates in God's sovereignty over evil supernatural forces."[106]

MARK 5:7: JESUS, SON OF THE MOST HIGH

The next encounter with unclean spirits is found in 5:7. In Mark, this is the more fully developed and complete encounter with unclean spirits. Whereas it was introduced in 1:13–28 and alluded to in 3:11, this encounter is drawn out. While Bultmann and Taylor see Mark's hand as a redactor functioning in 5:8 only, others see a much heavier hand at work.[107]

When Jesus arrives at the region known as the Gerasenes, a man "immediately" meets him with an unclean spirit.[108] At this point, the narrator gives an aside and offers a bit on the history of the individual. The reader is told that things are not going well for this man, and have not in a long while. The reader is told that the man lived among the tombs and was unable to be bound with shackles or chains. Apparently this was continuous both "night and day" (5:5). When the man with the unclean spirit sees Jesus, he runs to him and cries out, "What have you to do with me, Jesus, Son of the Most High God" (Τί ἐμοὶ καὶ σοί, Ἰησοῦ υἱὲ τοῦ θεοῦ τοῦ ὑψίστου; 5:7). Jesus interacts with the demons and permits them to enter a group of nearby pigs. The pigs instantly self-destruct, running off a cliff of sorts and drowning in the sea (5:13).

For the present study, the most significant point of this episode is the words of the demoniac. Collins understands this title as being particularly interesting for a Roman reader.[109] She argues that it is possible that a Semitic background to the word τοῦ ὑψίστου is in play because that is how the Hebrew Elyon (עליון) is translated in the LXX (Gen 14:18, 19, 20, 22; Ps 56:3). Because ὑψίστου is so often used of Zeus in Asia Minor into Egypt, she states plainly, "Thus, for members of Mark's audience familiar with this cult, the demon's address of Jesus is equivalent to 'son of Zeus.'"[110] Collins's

---

106. Marcus, *Mark 1–8*, 261.

107. Bultmann, *History of the Synoptic Tradition*, 210; and Taylor, *Gospel according to St. Mark*, 272; cp. Guelich, *Mark*, 273.

108. For an explanation of the variants related to "Gerasenes," see Guelich, *Mark*, 275; Marcus, *Mark 1–8*, 342.

109. Collins, "Mark and His Readers."

110. Ibid., 90.

familiarity and interaction with Greco-Roman sources and religion is laudable. However, in this case, it appears she claims too much. The Hebrew "God Most High" (עליון) is found thirty-one times in the Old Testament and fifteen times in the Dead Sea Scrolls.[111] Edwards suggests that "God Most High," "*establishes the uniqueness of Jesus' position* in relation to God Almighty and *universality of his power*."[112] If a reader were to hear this episode detached from the context of the narrative—what came before and what came after—then yes, it could be read that "Son of the Most High" equaled "son of Zeus." However, the contents of Mark lead the reader, without pretense of subtlety, to a different conclusion. There are a number of Old Testament and LXX references to "Most High." Mark, as a narrator, has tried to anchor Jesus' divine sonship to his Messianic identity. In this, Mark is placing Jesus squarely in the stream of Old Testament eschatological expectation. Martin Hengel rightly notes the disjunction between Hellenistic or Greaco-Roman conceptions of "Son of God" and the manner in which Jesus is presented in the Gospels.[113] To be sure, it is not impossible that a reader interpret the epithet in such a way, but it seems unlikely, given Mark's efforts to securely anchor Jesus in Old Testament thought and theology rather than Hellenism. Perhaps the usage of title has more to do with the characters in the story being non-Jewish thus Mark presents the demoniac as using the vocabulary found in the LXX.[114]

Narrative Assessment of Mark 1:1—8:27

The first four chapters of Mark are rich in theology, narrative, and development. Since we do not want to miss the forest for the trees, it is worth pausing and reflecting on the material covered thus far.

There is a tension in Mark regarding Jesus' identity as the Son of God. The very first line of the Gospel introduces Jesus as the Son of God, and as Messiah. Naturally, the implied reader is excited and interested that the protagonist of this *bioi* is God's Son and that his entrance into history means "good news" (Mark 1:1). The reader, however, is not left wondering what "Son of God" means, or the context from which they are to interpret this quasi-cryptic title. The narrator wastes no time firmly anchoring the notion of divine sonship in Israel's history and Scriptures. The Old Testament quotation given in Mark 1:2–3 point forward to the coming of God himself

111. Bertram, "Hypsistos," 602–20.
112. Edwards, *Mark*, 156. Italics original.
113. Hengel, *Studies in the Gospel of Mark*, 22.
114. Guelich, *Mark*, 279; Stein, *Mark*, 250–55.

in human history. John, the forerunner, appears in the tradition of Elijah and declares that the one coming will "baptize with the Holy Spirit" (1:8).

The narrator is not "objective" in the sense that he does not have any agenda or purpose in writing. Neutrality is not his aim. The narrator unites, as it where, his voice with the prophetic tradition of Israel and the voice from heaven. The narrator begins with a proclamation and quickly progresses his story to avoid losing steam. His narrative begins to reveal what it means for Jesus to be the Son of God.

Before Jesus even appears on the scene, the stage is set. No doubt the reader anticipates the appearance of Jesus on the scene to be something akin to a triumphal entry. The reader at no point experiences the confusion or uncertainty that the characters in the account are facing. From the onset, the reader is aware of Jesus' "secret identity" and sees the case building as he or she works his or her way through the first few chapters of the Gospel. The reader knows Jesus' identity, and so to do the demoniacs. The characters in the story, however, are presented as having a difficult time understanding who Jesus is. Evidently, the Jewish leaders are unclear as to who Jesus is. We see this in the way they constantly question his actions and his authority (2:8, 16; 3:24). Likewise, the crowds are confused (2:19).

The reader is privy to the important note by the narrator in 1:1, the private voice from heaven (1:11), and the words of the demoniacs (who were commanded to silence in 3:12). The tension inherent in this reality is significant. No one "gets" who Jesus is, yet the reader is made aware from the onset and thus feels a growing sense of expectation that someone somewhere will eventually recognize Jesus for who he is. The reader eagerly awaits this event.

There are three characters revealed in 1:1–11 that lend credence to and reveal Jesus's identity to the reader. They are the narrator (1:1), John the Baptist (1:8), and the voice from heaven, presumably God himself (1:11). The authority of these characters in the text reinforce the punchy opening line. It is not the unidentified crowds who understand Jesus' identity, but the "voice calling out in the wilderness" (1:3; cf. 1:8) and the "voice" from heaven (1:11). The narrator, John the Baptist, and God himself have placed their stamp of approval on Jesus. Here, the narrator has given the reader information about Jesus through "telling" and "showing." We are told exactly who Jesus is by the omniscient narrator, and we are shown who he is by being privy to the events that occurred in the heavens at the baptism. There can be no doubt from this first scene that the author is interested in presenting Jesus in a specific manner—the Son of God. Readers are led, and expected in some sense, to align their point of view with that of the narrator. The reader empathizes with John the Baptist because he stands in fulfillment of the Old Testament eschatological hope of a forerunner. The reader does the same for the voice that "tears" the heavens open to pronounce a blessing on Jesus.

The first few sections (1:1–11, 12–45) served to introduce the protagonist and extol his power and authority, additionally, it serves to inform the reader that this is not another gospel, as if there were many, but is in fact, "*the* gospel—*the* good news—the figure of Jesus, and not Augustus, is the announcement of God's triumph; in Jesus, the Son of God, a new age has dawned—the kingdom of God."[115] The next section of Mark (2:1—3:12) serves a different function. As is common in all forms of narrative or story, a degree of confrontation and conflict arises. That is exactly what we see develop next. Up until Mark 2:7, it seems that Jesus' authority is such that it is beyond question. After all, he is the Son of God (1:1, 11), he stands in Old Testament eschatological anticipation and prophetic tradition (1:2, 3; "fulfilled" language in 1:15), he opposes and overcomes Satan and demons (1:12, 13, 21–28), heals all manner of sickness (1:34, 41; 2:1–12) and teaches with authority (1:28). However, the mission of Jesus is not long left unopposed. As the story grows, it seems more and more evident to the reader that to side with Jesus is to side with the "right" or the "good" point of view.[116] The reader, no doubt, anticipates the authorities to fall in line with God's (and Jesus') agenda. Such is not the case, however. In 2:7 Jesus is accused of blasphemy.

Van Eck explains the interplay between the presentations of the various characters in Mark's Gospel as such:

> The protagonist of the narrative is the main character, Jesus. As help in his mission, the protagonist calls helpers, the disciples. The target of the protagonist (and his helpers) is the crowds. The antagonists in the narrative, who are opposed to the mission of the protagonist are, on Galilean soil, local scribes and Pharisees, and the Herodians, as well as scribes and Pharisees who come from Jerusalem and Galilee.[117]

His assessment relates to the narrative of Mark as a whole, but it is seen to be especially helpful as a grid by which to understand the first few scenes in Mark. What the narrator is doing in 2:7 is showing that not all are in-tune with God's agenda. There will be some who understand and respond properly, but there will be some who do not. The tension, however, is that the charge of blasphemy—and thus the failure to recognize Jesus' identity—is

---

115. Van Eck, "Mission, Identity and Ethics in Mark," 7.
116. Rhoads, Dewey, and Michie, *Mark as Story*, 44–46.
117. Van Eck, *Galilee and Jerusalem*, 278.

found not on the lips of a Gentile, but on the lips (or, rather, in the minds) of the scribes. Van Eck's statement, quoted above, is helpful because it distinguishes between the crowds and the protagonist. In the calling of the disciples (1:16–20), his interactions in Capernaum at the synagogue (1:21–28), and various healings, the crowds, or general public, are seen to interact favorably with Jesus.

This is not the first time the group designated as "scribes" has appeared in Mark. They are mentioned, only in passing, earlier in 1:22. Here, Jesus is held up in contrast to the scribes. Jesus is said to "teach with authority, and not as the scribes." The superiority of Jesus over the Jewish religious leaders is established in 1:22, and this is, in a sense, to be expected. Jesus is, after all, the "Son of God," so of course his teaching brings a different and higher authority than the religious leaders of the day. The tension arises in Mark 2:7 when the scribes rebuke Jesus. Here is the first glimpse of division or conflict in the story of Mark. It will factor in significantly throughout the rest of the narrative.[118]

An interesting contrast in presented in 3:1–12 between the response of the Jewish leaders and the response of the unclean spirits to Jesus' authority and power. When Jesus reveals himself to the Pharisees, they (with the Herodians) go out and plot to destroy him (3:6). When he does the same to the unclean spirits, they fall down before him (3:11). Those who should have known the truth about Jesus—the Pharisees and Jewish leaders—did not. There is almost always (following Aristotle's take on Greek tragedy) a turning point in which the identity of the protagonist is revealed. Here, we have an interesting collision of expectation, insider knowledge, and ignorance of the characters in the story. The unclean spirits, as supernatural agents, share, in some sense, a similar vantage point as the omniscient narrator in the story. Mark's use of irony here is important. It is not that the Pharisees are just unaware of Jesus' identity and are therefore confused, they are against him. The point is clear, privileged position and religious pedigree are not what make someone "with" or in line with God's agenda.

At this point in the account, only two groups in the story are aware of the true identity of Jesus: the forces of good (1:11) and the forces of evil (3:11). Other than these supernatural voices, the characters in the story struggle and misunderstand who Jesus is.

---

118. The role of conflict and development of plot in Mark is examined by Van Eck and Van Aarde, "Narratological Analysis," 782–88.

Transition Point in Mark's Gospel

In the first half of Mark, Jesus is presented as a uniquely commissioned and powerful individual.[119] The constant admonition after Jesus exhibits his power is "don't tell anyone." After Jesus heals the man with an unclean spirit (5:1–20), he demonstrates his power and abilities in a number of healing episodes (5:21–43; 6:53–56; 7:31–37), two feeding events (6:30–44; 8:1–10), and some unparalleled teaching sessions (7:1–23; 8:14–21). Mark reveals that Jesus is the Son of God through "telling" and "showing" in the first half of the narrative. Throughout this section, the tension and conflict with the Pharisees and religious leaders continues to develop. By this point, the reader is confident that a simple and peaceful solution to the conflict is unlikely. The natural questions are: What will happen to the Son of God as he is rejected by the leaders and rulers? What does it mean for him to be the Son when he is rejected by God's people?

The natural hinge in the Gospel is Mark 8:27.[120] Scholars have noted that the second half of the Gospel revolves around a three step pattern: (1) predictions of the suffering, death, and resurrection of the Son of Man (8:31; 9:31; 10:32–43); (2) misunderstanding on the part of the disciples (8:34–37; 9:32; 10:35–41); (3) instruction on discipleship (8:34–37; 9:33–37; 10:42–45).[121] While the first half of Mark has Jesus being misunderstood and facing opposition, the second half features the misunderstanding growing more frustrating to the reader, as well as the vehemence of the opposition becoming alarming. It seems clear that Jesus' identity is unknown to all but the supernatural characters in the story. The level of misunderstanding only grows as Jesus becomes even more explicit in his teachings about himself. The human characters in the story continue in their blindness. About this second section, Kingsbury writes, "the disciples become even more 'uncomprehending,' until they at last fall away from Jesus."[122] Danove, in investigating the rhetorical presentation of the disciples in Mark's Gospel, notes a number of words or phrases that are negatively associated with the disciples including: discuss, rebuke, not know, understand, and fear.[123] The occurrence of these five verbs is most frequently located in the first eight chapters of Mark.

---

119. Malbon, *Hearing Mark*, 55.

120. Collins, *Mark*, 297; Hooker, *Gospel according to St. Mark*, 200.

121. Peterson, "Point of View in Mark"; Rhoads, Dewey, and Michie, *Mark as Story*, 74–97; Kingsbury, *Conflict in Mark*, 27–29; Collins, *Mark*, 397.

122. Kingsbury, *Conflict in Mark*, 11.

123. Danove, *Rhetoric of Characterization*, 93–97.

Time and time again in the first half of Mark, individuals who encounter Jesus fail to understand. Mark's Jesus expresses his frustration and concerns in a number of instances.

- Mark 3:5: Jesus is "grieved at their hardness of heart"
- Mark 4:13: "Do you not understand the parables?"
- Mark 4:34: "He did not speak to them without a parable"
- Mark 4:40: "Why are you afraid? Have you still no faith?"
- Mark 6:6: "And he marveled because of their unbelief"
- Mark 7:18: "Are you also still without understanding?"

Likewise, the editorial asides and narrative points demonstrate that understanding Jesus' identity was apparently beyond the grasp of the human characters in the story. For example, the Pharisees, the crowds (2:19-22), the Herodians (3:6), Jesus' family (3:20-21, 31-35), and the scribes (3:22) all misunderstand or misconstrue Jesus' identity.

There is no wonder, then, that many commentators see a symbolic essence to the healing of the blind man in 8:22-26.[124] Perhaps Mark is using the blind man as a metaphor for the blindness of the disciples. It took the man a little time to regain his sight fully. The argument goes that this same concept is true for the disciples; they too had "stages" of understanding. We see in Mark, time and time again, the disciples (and others) misunderstanding what is happening and who Jesus is. Another indication that the healing in 8:22-26 should be interpreted symbolically, is just how opposite in form it is from the healing in 10:45-52. In the end, it may be that the healing account functions symbolically in Mark's narrative. However, being confident of this is difficult.

Generally speaking, Mark's redactoral additions to this healing account are thought to be isolated to the introductory verse in 8:22a.[125] Jesus' only dialogue in this healing account comes in the form of a question and a command: "What do you see?" (8:23) and, "Do not even enter the village" (8:26). From a form critical perspective, this healing account and the one found in 7:31 share a number of similar characteristics. Stein charts a number of these similarities of form in his commentary on Mark.[126] These similarities have caused speculation that a variant or doublet is present. The differences between these two accounts, however, have led the majority

---

124. Waetjen, *Reordering of Power*, 99; Van Eck, *Galilee and Jerusalem*, 392.
125. Guelich, *Mark*, 429.
126. Stein, *Mark*, 388.

of scholars to conclude that they are different traditions[127] Collins writes that since 8:22 is a quotation of sorts of Jer 5:21 ("having, eyes, do you not see?"), it most likely is being used by Mark in a symbolic manner referring to the disciples' blindness.[128] Gundry, after examining the arguments both in favor and against the symbolic reading, settles on the view that nothing of this nature is in play in the text.[129] The data is, unfortunately, not entirely clear. It is worth noting that in the first century it was common for healing stories that featured a blind man to have a symbolic meaning.[130] There are a number of arguments in favor of a symbolic reading, but there are also many difficulties in reading it this way. It seems best to leave the ambiguity as it stands and note that such a phenomenon may be in play in the scene.

Regardless of the manner in which we understand the healing account of the blind man at Bethsaida, the significance of 8:27–30 for the present study is such that it demands close attention. In this section, Jesus asks his disciples on the way to Caesarea Philippi two searching questions. The first is: "Who do people say that I am?" The second is a direct question to the disciples, "Who do you say that I am?" (8:29). Bultmann views the passage as an Easter confession pulled back and inserted into the life of Christ by Mark.[131]

As was mentioned above, the disciples are presented as being confused about Jesus' true identity. Here, Jesus directly asks his disciples, "Who do people say I am?" The answers that Mark places on the lips of the disciples are varied. First of all, the disciples indicate that some thought Jesus was John the Baptist (first mentioned in 1:4). John had been arrested (1:14) and executed by Herod (6:16). Apparently, Herod himself agreed with this view because Mark has Herod fearing that the rumors he was hearing about Jesus were actually being caused by John being raised from the dead. The next answer that the disciples offer is "Elijah." The crowd also (6:15) seems to understand the true identity of Jesus as bring "Elijah" or "a prophet."

The manner in which the various opinions about Jesus are presented is important from a narrative critical perspective. Compare the words of the narrator in 6:14 and 15 and the words from the disciples in 8:28:

> Mark 6:14–15: King Herod heard of it, for Jesus' name had become known. Some said, "John the Baptist has been raised from the dead. That is why these miraculous powers are at work

---

127. Collins, *Mark*, 390.
128. Ibid.,
129. Gundry, *Mark*, 421.
130. Malbon, *Hearing Mark*, 57.
131. Bultmann, *History of the Synoptic Tradition*, 257.

	in him." But others said, "He is Elijah." And others said, "He is a prophet, like one of the prophets of old."
Mark 8:28:	And they told him, "John the Baptist; and others say, Elijah; and others, one of the prophets."

The same three opinions are given in each account. It appears that Mark is deliberately setting up the dialogue of 8:28. He gives attention to the misunderstanding of the crowd by disclosing it through means of his ability to play omniscient narrator, then turns and presents the disciples, especially Peter, as having a greater degree of understanding than the crowds.

Peter responds to Jesus' direct question about who they thought he was by saying, "You are the Christ." This is highly significant for a number of reasons and functions as a turn in the narrative structure of the Gospel of Mark. As soon as Peter utters these words, the reader instantly hearkens back to the initial line of the Gospel, "The beginning of the gospel of Jesus Christ, God's Son" (1:1). What the reader was given from the get go has taken the human characters in the story nearly half the book to understand. The narrator identified Jesus with the title "Christ" and Peter has just been elevated as one of the only human characters that understands, at least in part, who Jesus is. In the first half of Mark, the title "Christ" occurs only here and in 1:1, but it occurs a number of times in the second half of the narrative (9:41; 12:35; 13:21–22; 14:61; 15:32). Obviously, the epithet "God's Son," from Mark's incipit, is not included in the confession of Peter in 8:22. Regardless of this omission by Peter, it is clear that, as spokesman for the group, Peter's confession reveals that the disciples are, at least in part, beginning to understand Jesus' identity. However, whatever ground was made in the readers' evaluation of the disciples is quickly shaken when, within a few lines, Peter is referred to as "Satan" by Jesus (8:33)! Such a negative assessment of Peter's character by Jesus serves as a powerful literary device. The reader has been led to adopt Jesus' point of view of reality. His assessment of Peter, then, is also to be accepted by the reader.

The first of three prediction announcements by Jesus occurs directly on the heels of Peter's confession. It is used by Mark to show that, although Peter (and the disciples by extension) has some understanding of who Jesus is, he still has a far way to go in arriving at the same level of understanding that the reader is already privy to (1:1). Apparently, the notion of Jesus suffering, being rejected and killed, and being raised again is a significant part of Jesus' identity that he wishes his disciples to understand (8:31) but clearly, Peter still lacks understanding.

The narrative of the transfiguration also plays a significant role in Mark's narrative of Jesus. After Peter's confession (8:27–30), Jesus offers his first passion prediction, explaining to his disciples that he will "suffer many things and be rejected by the elders and chief priests and the scribes and be killed, and after three days rise again" (8:31). Peter, as spokesman for the group, rebukes Jesus. Malbon puts is correctly: "Peter's confession has become Peter's confusion."[132] After calling Peter "Satan," and telling him to get behind him, Jesus begins teaching the larger group (crowds) about what it means to be his disciple and "follow him" (8:34). Jesus explains that the path of discipleship is somewhat paradoxical—if one desires to save one's life, one must lose it. It is unclear if the five statements on discipleship originally existed together or were placed in this sequence by Mark.[133] The historicity of the passion prediction has been debated. While many deny its possibility,[134] increasingly, some scholars are recognizing that, due to the opposition he was facing, Jesus could have foresaw events transpiring in such a way that ended in his death.[135] Regardless of one's understanding and view of the historicity of the prediction, the role it plays in the narrative lends the reader to perceive the direction that Jesus is headed, and his death and crucifixion are not supposed to surprise the reader.

MARK 9:2–10: THE TRANSFIGURATION OF THE SON OF GOD

The next christological highpoint of the narrative is the voice from heaven that reveals, again to the reader, and this time to characters, that Jesus is his "beloved son" (9:7). The account is rich in narrative and literary motifs and symbolism. It requires a close reading. Though some have argued that it is a post-Easter insertion into Mark's narrative, Schweizer helpfully notes that nowhere in the post-Easter accounts are similar elements found ("divine voice," "heavenly companions," "visible glory of Jesus") and nowhere in Mark's transfiguration account is there a mention of death or resurrection.[136]

The account begins, "And after six days." Naturally, the question is, "six days after what?" Although it has been argued that the temporal indicator here is one which the reader is expected to be anticipating a significant event on the seventh day, it seems more likely that the narrator is offering an

---

132. Malbon, *Hearing Mark*, 59.

133. Best, *Mark*, 31.

134. Bultmann, *History of the Synoptic Tradition*, 152; Wrede, *Messianic Secret*, 87; Collins, *Mark*, 403.

135. Evans, *Mark*, 101; Hooker, *Gospel according to St. Mark*, 204.

136. Schweizer, *Good News according to Mark*, 180.

allusion to the account of Moses on Mount Sinai (Exod 24:16).[137] Additional elements are present that seem to strengthen the view that an allusion is present. For example, there are the mentions of the "mountain," "Elijah and Moses," a "cloud," and a "voice" from the cloud. These are all elements found in the aforementioned passage in Exodus. Additionally, the mention of both "Moses" and "Elijah" seems to indicate, in some fashion at least, a symbolic nature to the event.[138] The most plausible explanation of the appearance of Moses and Elijah (or, as Mark puts it, "Elijah with Moses") is "their role in salvation history in the past and the expectation that they would each play a role in eschatological denouement."[139] The voice from heaven reiterates a foundational Markan christological truth—Jesus is God's Son and the disciples are to "listen" to him (ἀκούετε). The most common explanation of the reference to these two Old Testament characters is that they represent the "Law" and "the Prophets."[140] Additional explanations include Moses representing the old covenant, and Elijah representing the "fulfillment of all things,"[141] or a general apocalyptic, Midrash based union of these two stalwarts.[142] Regardless of the exact function or reason for their inclusion in the account, as characters, they are obviously subservient to Jesus. This can be seen in the voice's words to "listen" to Jesus, and the final scene in which only Jesus remains; the disciples are to listen to Jesus, not offer a misguided act of building "tents" to the other two (9:5).

The transfiguration, along with the baptism and crucifixion, function as the three pillars upon which the narrative of Mark is built.[143] They each reinforce and reiterate that Jesus is the Son of God. In the baptism, the voice from heaven, clearly God's voice, lays his seal of approval on Jesus and his mission. Here, in the transfiguration, a similar act occurs. The reader is again given privy information about the identity of Jesus. The careful reader, at this point, is not surprised at the voice from heaven; they are on the "in." The characters in the story, however, are "terrified" (9:6). The mention of two central Old Testament leaders further anchors the interpretive context

---

137. Boring, *Mark*, 260. Alternatively, Waetjen's view is that "after six days" serves as a "time reference that intimates completion of fulfillment." Waetjen, *Reordering of Power*, 148.

138. Mann, *Mark*, 355.

139. Boring, *Mark*, 261. For a form critical and structural discussion of the appearance of Moses and Elijah, see Gundry, *Mark*, 471. An overview of the various interpretations that scholars have offered is summarized by Mann, *Mark*, 356.

140. Stein, *Mark*, 417.

141. Lane, *Mark*, 319.

142. Evans, *Mark*, 36.

143. Myers, *Binding the Strong Man*, 390.

of Jesus' divine sonship in the Old Testament itself, rather than in Greco-Roman or Imperial cult worship contexts.

MARK 12:1-11: THE PARABLE OF THE TENANTS

The parable commonly known as the Tenants is likely one of the "most debated—and misunderstood—parables of Jesus."[144] Interpretation of the parable aside, the historicity of the parable is also highly debated.[145] Some posit that the earliest version is found in *Gospel of Thomas* 65.[146] Additionally, the original form of the parable and what redactoral insertions Mark made is also a matter of discussion[147] as are the linguistic links to the LXX and the Qumran documents[148]

The parable is a response from Jesus to the question regarding his authority (11:28). In response to the question, Jesus tells the story of the leased vineyard. The story goes like this: A man plants a vineyard, leases it to tenants, and departs from the region. Eventually, he sends a servant back to get some of the goods from the vineyard, and the tenants turn on the servant and beat him. It escalates, because the next time the owner sends a servant, the tenants kill him! Eventually, the owner sends his own son, (ἀγαπητόν) thinking, "they will respect my son." Such is not the case, because the evil tenants kill the son. Jesus then asks, "What will the owner do? He will come and destroy them!" The Jewish leaders do not miss the directness of the parable—"they perceived that he had told the parable about them" (12:12).

It appears that the language and concept surrounding the vineyard is taken from Isa 5:1–7.[149] The most germane section for our present study is the words, "ἕνα εἶχεν, υἱὸν ἀγαπητόν"; "he still had one other, a beloved son" (12:7). The meaning of the word "beloved" (ἀγαπητός) has found little consensus among scholars. Some see it as a Markan addition in which the

---

144. Snodgrass, "Recent Research," 177.

145. Bultmann, *History of the Synoptic Tradition*, 205.

146. Van Eck, "Tenants in the Vineyard." In this article, Van Eck approaches the parable from a realistic and social scientific perspective. He interacts with the work of Kloppenborg, *Tenants in the Vineyard*. Kloppenborg believes that from what is known of agrarian practices in Mediterranean culture, *Gospel of Thomas* 65 is most likely the closest to the original. This view is assessed by Lane, *Mark*, 416. Additional notes on the manner in which *Gospel of Thomas* interprets and makes use of the transfiguration is given by Mann, *Mark*, 458–63.

147. Gundry, *Mark*, 682–83.

148. Evans, *Mark*, 224.

149. Lane, *Mark*, 417; Evans, *Mark*, 220–24.

language from the baptism and transfiguration are placed in the parable.[150] Or, it could be a reference to Gen 22:2 where Isaac is called the "beloved son" (LXX: τὸν υἱόν σου τὸν ἀγαπητόν, ὃν ἠγάπησας; MT: אֶת־בִּנְךָ אֶת־יְחִידְךָ אֲשֶׁר־אָהַבְתָּ). Or, it is possible that that the term is borrowed from the Isaiah passage that the vineyard motif is built upon (Isa 5:1: "beloved"; LXX: ἀγαπητοῦ; MT: לִידִידִי). This, Gundry believes, is not an option, due to God himself being the one offering the son.[151] Myers notes the irony of Jesus' parable, "Jesus tells a story in which the Jerusalem leadership, who were *in fact* the absentee landowning class, appear as *tenants* of an absentee landlord—that is Yahweh."[152]

At the conclusion of the parable, Jesus references Ps 118:22–23. His quotation, *verbatim*, is from the LXX.[153] The Jewish leadership easily grasp the point that Jesus was, in fact, telling a parable against them (12:12). Although the parable serves, at best, as an indirect reference to Jesus' divine sonship, the reference is worth noting. Mark (along with Luke) speak of the "beloved son" which reminds the reader of the term's usage in the baptism (1:11) and the transfiguration (9:7). Was the "beloved son" a self-reference to Jesus? Or, as Mann proposes, was the "son" speaking of John the Baptist—the one who was rejected by the "tenants"?[154] It seems though, that whatever the original form of the parable, Mark is using it not to point to John but to Jesus. The whole matter at hand is the authority of Jesus, not the authority of John. The question that is first directed at Jesus is about his authority (11:28). Jesus is the one who introduces John into the account (11:30). After confounding the leaders, Jesus then brings the topic back to his own authority in his response: "Neither will I tell you by what authority I do these things" (11:33).

It was well known at the time that Israel was God's "vineyard."[155] The parable highlights that the owner sent messengers who were mistreated, and he eventually sent his "beloved" son to confront the evil tenants. There is no mistaking that Mark, in light of presenting Jesus as the "beloved son," is making another pointed statement about Jesus' identity and doing so in such a way that he is drawing attention to the opposition he faces from the Jewish leaders. Those who are aware of Jesus' identity (indefinite or implied audience) see this as yet another opportunity for the characters in the story

150. Jeremias, *Prayers of Jesus*, 73–74; Stein, *Mark*, 535.
151. Gundry, *Mark*, 686.
152. Myers, *Binding the Strong Man*, 308.
153. Rahlfs and Hanhart, *Septuaginta*.
154. Mann, *Mark*, 463.
155. Malbon, *Hearing Mark*, 81.

to align with God's point of view. Yet, the reader, likely, in some sense is not surprised that things continue to go poorly for Jesus in the narrative. After all, the very group that Jesus has put together to "be with him" includes a betrayer (3:19) and the enemies of Jesus are apparently going to kill him (8:31–33). In Mark's Gospel there is only one who is presented as the "beloved son," and it is Jesus. It seems likely then, that the reader, who has been given the privy information that Jesus is God's "beloved son," is going to understand the parable in line with what has already been revealed in the narrative.

MARK 12:35: "WHOSE SON IS THE CHRIST?"

After hearing the parable of the Tenants, the Pharisees commission a few of their own to trap Jesus with a question about paying taxes. After Jesus deflects the question and leaves them marveling, the Sadducees try their hand with a question regarding the resurrection. The passage continues with questions from the scribes about what commandment is the greatest. After this, another question is asked, but this time, it is Jesus asking the question: "How can the scribes say that the Christ is the son of David?" (12:35).

This pericope features the first temporal marker for quite some time (11:27).[156] Jesus is teaching in the "temple" and, here again, comes to some degree of confrontation with the religious leaders and rulers. From the "chief priest," "scribes," and elders (11:27), to "them" (12:1), to the "Pharisees" and "Herodians" (12:13), to the "Sadducees" (12:18), to "one of the scribes" (12:28), it is clear that Jesus is facing a religious establishment that is hostile through and through. Mark presents Jesus in 1:1 as the "Christ;" what he had done throughout his narrative, and especially here in 11:27— 13:1, is highlight the degree of animosity and further heighten the sense of foreboding for the future. Remember, the omniscient narrator has already given inside information that the leaders are plotting against Jesus (3:6). This same narrator has indicated that Judas would betray Jesus (3:19) and has Jesus predict his forthcoming death (8:31). All of this serves to make Jesus' question even more probing from a narrative standpoint. In 10:47–48 Jesus is called the "son of David" by Bartimaeus. In 11:9, 10, when Jesus is entering the Jerusalem, some from the crowd cry out, "Blessed is the coming kingdom of our father David."

In citing Ps 110, Jesus is requesting that his audience (and Mark as narrator is requesting that his audience) approach again the conceptual link between the Messiah and the "son of David." What he is asking is, "In

---

156. Collins, *Mark*, 578.

what manner can the Messiah be called David's son?" It is evident, from as early as 2 Sam 7:12, that there was an expectation of a kingly leader, or son(s) of David who would rule and lead the nation.[157] In later literature (*Pss. Sol.* 17:21), the two identities, Messiah and son of David, are linked: "O Lord, raise up their king, the son of David that he may reign over Israel thy servant." Evans notes that the promise in Jeremiah of a coming branch being raised up (Jer 23:5; 33:15) clearly identifies this as having progeny in view and that the usage of "branch" by both Isaiah (Isa 11:1) and Zechariah (Zech 3:8; 6:12) is being used as a Messianic epithet.[158] By the time of Mark's Gospel, these two titles seem to be unified as a general Messianic expectation.[159] In this passage, Jesus is not deemed the "Son of God" as he is in other passages in Mark, but nevertheless it is still important for understanding Mark's Christology.

In the broader context, Mark shows the diverse approaches of Jesus' antagonists. A number of difficult questions are leveled at Jesus in the hopes of seeing him say something self-incriminating. Jesus is up to this challenge, however. He responds with his own complex and compelling question about the lineage of the Messiah. In the end, Jesus seems to be hinting that the title "son of David," although fitting for the Messiah, is insufficient or incomplete. For Mark, the most fitting familial context from which to understand the true identity of Jesus is not just his royal lineage through the line of David, but his being the Son of God.

MARK 13:32: "NOT EVEN THE SON"

The importance of chapter 13 in Mark's Gospel can be demonstrated by the immense amount of scholarly discussion and debate that it has produced.[160] Bultmann argued that the passage was a Jewish apocalypse, which features "Christian editing."[161] The composition and sources that underlie

157. This is, in many ways, exactly what Peter managed to understand in Mark 8:27–29 before being depicted as missing the rest of the question about Jesus' divine sonship.

158. Evans, *Mark*, 273.

159. Lane, *Mark*, 435.

160. For an overview of the academic literature and views on Mark 13, see Beasley-Murray, *Jesus and the Last Days*, 32–79; Mann charts the linguistic and conceptual backing of Mark 13 to the Old Testament and to the other Synoptics. In the end he points to Daniel and 2 *Esdras* sharing the most allusions with Mark. Mann goes so far as to say that other than a few references to Jesus added in by redactoral means, the apocalypse of Mark 13 does not appear to be a "distinctively Christian origin." Mann, *Mark*, 500–504.

161. Bultmann, *History of the Synoptic Tradition*, 125. Here, Bultmann proposes

the passage are uncertain and a number of views are offered, however, a consensus has yet to be reached.[162] The primary question is whether Mark is functioning as a compiler or a composer. Regardless of the sources at Mark's disposal, there is little doubt, in light of the manner in which Mark uses Old Testament allusions and quotations to achieve certain narrative aims rather than haphazardly throwing sources together, that he is intentionally furthering his narrative in deliberate ways.

The chapter features a number of stark and significant predictions about the destruction of Jerusalem and its temple. Evans, in his commentary on Mark, offers a number of predictions about the temple's destruction that are found in intertestamental literature.[163] The number of predictions that are found on the lips of Jesus in this chapter are used to further enforce the view that Jesus is a prophet.[164] The coming of the Son of Man in clouds (13:25) is clearly taken from Dan 7:13. That this "Son of Man" will "send his angels" signifies a tremendous level of authority (13:27) bestowed on this individual.

Especially significant for our present study is 13:32: "But concerning that day or that hour, no one knows, not even the angels in heaven, nor the Son, but only the Father." The indication that the Son does not know the day or hour was, according to Evans, "an embarrassment to early Christians."[165] He argues, on the criterion of embarrassment, that the early Christian community would never invent such a saying.[166] Thus, Evans argues that the saying most likely went back to the historical Jesus.[167] Luke omits this sentence in his Gospel. Again, the present Study is concerned, primarily, with the literary dimensions of the text rather than the historical. Here it appears that Mark is allowing the historical Jesus to speak, and is using his words to further his christological understanding. In Mark, Jesus is the

---

an analogy to the manner in which, in his estimation, the "Didache takes over Jewish Prophecy."

162. Collins, *Mark*, 594–95, succinctly presents the differing views regarding the composition of Mark 13. The aside in 13:14, "Let the reader understand" has only served to complicate the issue at hand. Also see Collins' reference to the fullest treatment of this parenthetical comment as being by Fowler, *Let the Reader Understand*. The likelihood that the gospel was intended to be read aloud adds an additional issue on a compositional level since it would be odd for the writer to refer to the reader, when it is really the listener that is in view. cf. Malbon, *Hearing Mark*.

163. Evans, *Mark*, 296.

164. Gundry, *Mark*, 734.

165. Evans, *Mark*, 336.

166. Ibid. For Bultmann's approach to this text, see his *History of Synoptic Tradition*, 123.

167. Evans, *Mark*, 366. See also Mann, *Mark*, 539, for a similar line of argumentation.

Son of God; this has been demonstrated time and time again. This is an important christological title because of the manner in which "son" (υἱὸς) and "Father" (πατρὸς) are juxtaposed. Earlier, in 8:38, Jesus calls himself "Son of Man" and refers to "his Father" (τοῦ πατρὸς αὐτοῦ). In 11:25, after giving his disciples ethical instruction, he encourages them to pray to their "Father" (ὁ πατὴρ ὑμῶν). The only other clear reference to "the Father" by Jesus is the Gethsemane prayer in 14:36. Although Mark does not make use of the title "Father" for God in relationship to Jesus' divine sonship, the concept is abundantly clear. The implied apologetic is this: Jesus is the Son of God, and that makes (in some sense or another) God his father. Here, the fatherhood of God is not meant to be taken necessarily in an ontological sense, but rather is used to enforce the teaching that Jesus is the Son of God in a unique and unparalleled way. On this verse, Kingsbury summarizes the point well:

> "The Son" in 13:32 is Jesus' designation for himself. It appears only here, and this alone makes it unlikely in the extreme that Mark would have the reader regard it as introducing a "new [sic] Christology."[168]

To summarize, this particular passage further demonstrates the centrality of the divine sonship of Christ for Mark's Christology. As a writer, Mark has more finesse as an authors than just resorting to using the explicit epithet "Son of God" over and over. He uses indirect methods such as this to communicate and strengthen the case that Jesus is the Son of God in a unique way.

MARK 14:36: "ABBA FATHER"

After the discourse in chapter 13, the plot against Jesus will reach new levels. In the first section of this chapter, Mark says that the chief priests and scribes were seeking to kill Jesus (14:1, 2). Jesus is then anointed at Bethany by an unnamed woman (14:3–9). Judas, "one of the twelve," once and for all sides himself with the antagonists and agrees to betray Jesus (14:10, 11).[169] After instituting the new covenant (14:22–25), and predicting that Peter will deny him (14:26–31), Jesus goes to Gethsemane to pray (14:32–42) and, finally, is betrayed (14:43–50). Mark's Christology is presented in a significant fashion in Jesus' prayer in Gethsemane. It is worth considering in detail.

---

168. Kingsbury, *Christology of Mark's Gospel*, 138.

169. For an examination of the significant irony and characterization occurring in these passages, see MacDonald, "Characterization of a False Disciple," 110–35.

Bultmann understood 14:32–42 to be of a later Christian tradition imposed on Mark and was clearly legendary.[170] Regardless of what tradition, if any, underlie this pericope, Mark is advancing his Christology by the specific words that come from Jesus' lips. In the midst of his anguished prayer, Jesus calls out to "Abba Father" (αββα ὁ πατήρ) (14:36). The usage of "Abba" here is the Greek transliteration of the Aramaic vocative (אב).[171] This is the only use of "Abba" in the Gospels, though Paul does make use of the title in Rom 8:15 and Gal 4:6 with the same doublet as is in Mark (αββα ὁ πατήρ). The most monumental study on this construct was published by Joachim Jeremias first in German (1966) and then translated into English (1967) and titled, "Prayers of Jesus." Jeremias argued that the title "Abba" demonstrated a unique level of intimacy with God that was not used widely at the time. He also contended that it was a diminutive usage due it being the word a child uses for a father.[172] Barr disagreed and presented his counter arguments with an article simply titled "Abba isn't Daddy," published in 1988 in the *Journal of Theological Studies*.[173] Mann sees it as most likely indicating that the original audience of Mark's Gospel was bilingual.[174] Although the consensus has yet to be reached on what exactly is in view in these words, the usage by Mark's Jesus is distinctive if not entirely unique.

It seems evident that Mark would anticipate his audience understanding this passage in light of what has passed. Even if a reader (or listener) only managed to have access to half of Mark's Gospel, there seems little doubt that they would understand this passage as reinforcing the divine sonship that is present in the rest of the narrative. In light of the back and forth between Jesus and his Father through indirect references (the unnamed voice from heaven in 1:11 and 9:7 designating Jesus as "son") and Jesus speaking about or to his "Father" (13:32; 14:36) it seems clear that Jesus is the Son of God. Really, any other interpretation requires a twisting of the natural reading of the text.

To review, although there is ambiguity about what "Abba" means and what Mark intended with its use, there can be little doubt that this is yet another instance where Jesus' divine sonship is developed and brought back

---

170. Bultmann, *History of the Synoptic Tradition*, 268. Cf. Kelber, "Mark 14:32–42."

171. For some of the historical and exegetical considerations see Schweizer, *Good News according to Mark*, 312–13.

172. Jeremias, *Prayers of Jesus*, 11–65.

173. Barr, "Abba Isn't Daddy." For an additional challenge to Jeremias's work, see Brown, *Introduction to the New Testament Christology*, 84–87; Stein, *Mark*; Stein, *Method and Message of Jesus' Teachings*, 83–86. On the probability of these titles being authentic, see: Evans, *Mark*, 412; Gnilka, *Jesus of Nazareth*, 262; Gundry, *Mark*, 863–64.

174. Mann, *Mark*, 590.

to the reader's mind. It should also be noted that, here again, only the reader is privy to this intimate scene between Jesus and his Father. The narrator of the Gospel is not clear on how, exactly, this scene was left for posterity, but the point is left standing: the reader is being led to understand that there can be no doubt that Jesus is the Son of God in a unique sense, and although this is missed by the characters of the story, the reader is continually reminded.

MARK 14:61: "ARE YOU THE SON OF THE BLESSED?"

After being betrayed (14:43–50), Jesus is brought before the chief priests, elders, and scribes (14:53) and accused.[175] Some confusion ensues when the witnesses against Jesus are unable to present a unified testimony (14:59). To cut through the confusion, the high priest asks Jesus about the destruction of the temple. When Jesus responds with silence, the high priest asks another, more direct question.[176] It is the question the implied reader has been waiting for since the first line of the Gospel. The high priest asks Jesus outright: "Are you the Christ, the Son of the Blessed?" (σὺ εἶ ὁ χριστὸς ὁ υἱὸς τοῦ εὐλογητοῦ) (14:61). It appears that Jesus is cast by Mark as the suffering servant in Isaiah.[177]

From a form critical perspective, a number of interpretations have been offered about 14:53–65.[178] Gnilka sees the Markan additions to the story as being primarily confined to 14:54–55.[179] Some, such as Donahue argue that the additions are much more extensive.[180] The historical accuracy of the account is also debated. Bultmann, along with Dibelius argue that the historical question is essentially moot since an eye witness account is unlikely if not impossible.[181] Collins goes so far as to say, "From the point of

---

175. For a helpful overview of the interactions between Jesus and his accusers, see Campbell, "Engagement, Disengagement and Obstruction."

176. The significance of Jesus responding with silence is highlighted by Collins. Collins identifies the silence as a presentation by Mark that Jesus is suffering in accordance with Scriptures. "Just as the prototypical king, David, suffered, so must the messiah." In support of this view, she offers the tenure of Psalm LXX 37:14–15; 26:12; and LXX 31:11. Collins, *Mark*, 704. See also Boring, *Mark*, 412.

177. Myers, *Binding the Strong Man*, 278.

178. Evans, *Mark*, 439–41.

179. Gnilka, *Jesus of Nazareth*, 267–77.

180. Donahue, "Jesus as Parable in the Gospel of Mark," 65–94. For an additional assessment of Mark's redaction, see Pryke, *Redactional Style in the Marcan Gospel*, 147, 173.

181. Bultmann, *History of the Synoptic Tradition*, 269; Dibelius, *From Tradition to Gospel*, 213.

view of historical reconstruction, Mark's account of a trial before the Judean council is not based on any historically reliable tradition."[182]

The question from the high priest is not two; but one. He is not asking, "are you the Messiah," and "are you the son of the Blessed." Instead, "son of the blessed" (ὺ εἶ ὁ χριστὸς ὁ υἱὸς τοῦ εὐλογητοῦ) modifies "Messiah."[183] The question in view is, in essence, "Are you the Messiah of David's line?" The importance of David's lineage was covered above in chapter 3. However, it is worth repeating that only David's sons could be rightly deemed sons of God because of 2 Sam 7:12 and 14. The Qumran documents reinforce this line of thinking.[184] The usage of the title, "Blessed" instead of the more direct "God," has been understood as a somewhat common Second Temple custom in which the name of God was avoided.[185]

The reader has been "in the know" about Jesus' true identity from the beginning. When the high priest asks this question, it is a bitter-sweet moment. In one sense, it appears as the first instance in which Jesus may be publically identified by the religious establishment as the Son of God, something the reader has known all along and eagerly awaited to see revealed. On the other hand, the reader is also aware of the long-standing antagonism against Jesus that has been present all thought the narrative. The reader eagerly waits for, first of all, Jesus' answer, and secondly, the high priest's response.

Jesus answers in the affirmative: "I am, and you will see the Son of Man seated at the right and of Power, and coming with the clouds of heaven" (Ἐγώ εἰμι, καὶ ὄψεσθε τὸν υἱὸν τοῦ ἀνθρώπου ἐκ δεξιῶν καθήμενον τῆς δυνάμεως καὶ ἐρχόμενον μετὰ τῶν νεφελῶν τοῦ οὐρανοῦ; 14:62). With these powerful words, Jesus asserts what has been known to the reader since the beginning of Mark's narrative; Jesus is the Christ, the Son of God. Boring rightly notes the impact of Jesus' words as a narrative highpoint: "These are the climatic words of Jesus in the whole Gospel. Jesus' *egō eimi* makes the trial into an *epiphany* scene."[186] Gundry is helpful in his assessment of the manner in which Mark's reader (he supposes a Roman provenance) would understand the question. Gundry lays out the argument that, in light of the constant emphasis on Jesus' miracles, power, and authority, a Roman audience would interpret the question with a much higher theological context than could be historically present in the high priest's words.[187] He suggests

---

182. Collins, *Mark*, 699.
183. Evans, *Mark*, 448.
184. See, for example, the number of references offered by Evans, *Mark*, 449.
185. Collins, *Mark*, 704.
186. Boring, *Mark*, 413.
187. Gundry, *Mark*, 909.

that although the historical context had a "divine appointment" of sonship in view, the implied reader may understand it as "divine nature" sonship.[188]

The words that Mark has Jesus speak indicate something of his own christological aims. His initial affirmation, "I am" (Ἐγώ εἰμι) is not a reference to the divine name.[189] but rather a simple, straightforward "yes." Jesus' response is a combination of the images found in Ps 110 and Dan 7:13–14. The use of "thrones," "come with the clouds," and "in judgment" is taken from Dan 7, while the reference to being "seated at the right hand," until his "enemies" are made a "footstool" are taken from Ps 110. Jesus's use of the title, "Son of Man" in reference to himself has appeared before in the Gospel (2:10, 28; 8:31, 38; 9:9, 12, 31; 10:33, 45; 13:26; 14:21, 41).[190]

Mark uses this instance in two significant ways. First of all, Mark uses this title to illustrate the level of misunderstanding that exists among those who are antagonizing and opposing Jesus. The very people who should have known best the Messiah's identity are unable to see clearly. The implied reader, however, is clear on this truth from the beginning of the narrative (1:1). The privileged "insiders" (high priests and rulers) remain firmly on the other side, far from the truth. Even though they, along with the disciples, have had direct revelatory encounters regarding Jesus' identity, they miss one of the central tenants about Jesus' identity.

Secondly, Mark uses this encounter as another point to reveal the authority and power of the Son of God. The "Son of Man" will come with the clouds of heaven and will be seated at the right hand of Power. This demonstrates a surprising level of power and authority. Here, it appears that yet again, Mark is leading his audience to interpret the divine sonship of Jesus from an Old Testament context. The use of two Old Testament references gives the reader the framework from which to understand the title. Further, the setting lends to this view as well. Jesus is being tried by the very individuals charged to carry out and protect the Scriptures. The high priest's questions indicate that the common expectation of Second Temple Judaism regarding the union of the office of Messiah and "Son of God" is in play, and, coupled with the answer given by Jesus, there seems little doubt about what is in view.

188. Ibid.
189. Evans, *Mark*, 450.
190. The scholarly debate and dialogue about what exactly the title "Son of Man" means shows no sign of waning. Illustrative of recent scholarship on the issue, see: Bauckham, "Son of Man," 23–33; Hooker, "Expression 'Son of Man,'" 651–52; Kim, "'Son of Man' as the Son of God"; Leim, "In the Glory of His Father," 213–32; Moloney, "Constructing Jesus and the Son of Man," 719–38. For a classic treatment, see Perrin, "Son of Man in the Synoptic Tradition."

Throughout Mark's narrative, the revelation has been made known in a number of ways. The characters in the story are almost surprisingly slow to comprehend and accept the truth that the implied reader understands from the onset. God himself speaks from heaven and pronounces his acceptance of Jesus as his son (1:1; 9:7), demons understand Jesus' true identity (1:24; 3:11; 5:7), Jesus has hinted and suggested in fairly direct ways that he is the Messiah, Son of God (12:1, 2, 35; 13:32; 14:36), yet through all of this the characters in the story are still unclear. The only instance in which we have a character in the story (apart from the centurion which will be examined shortly) offer any kind of assessment of Jesus' sonship, the assessment is total rejection (14:61, 62).

MARK 15:39: SOMEONE UNDERSTANDS—"TRULY THIS MAN WAS THE SON OF GOD!"

The final reference to the divine sonship of Jesus in the Gospel of Mark, along with the first, proves to be the most significant. It is in this final usage that we see even more about the author's intention and the deliberate nature with which he shapes his narrative. Up until this point in the narrative, no human character has understood or accepted what has been evident to the reader from the start: Jesus is the Son of God.

According to Mark, the crucifixion of Jesus is a cosmic event. After being beaten (15:15) and mocked (15:19), Jesus is taken to Golgotha and crucified (15:22–24). The charge is listed as "The King of the Jews" (15:26). Mark reiterates that a great degree of mocking and humiliation are occurring by mentioning that even "those who passed by" mocked (ἐβλασφήμουν) him (15:29). Not only is it the religious leaders who reject Jesus and scorn him, it is also the population at large.[191] The deriding continues and, after a misunderstanding about the intentions of his words, Jesus dies. The narrator then offers an aside that no characters in the story immediately seem to be aware of: "And the curtain of the temple was torn in two, from top to bottom" (15:38). In response to seeing the manner in which Jesus died, an unnamed Roman centurion exclaims, "truly this man was the Son of God" (15:39). The scene then shifts to focusing on the women who were following Jesus, and then, to the burial process (15:40–45). The entire scene seems to moves quickly. Mark accomplishes this through repeated use of the conjunction "and" (καὶ), and the historical present tense.[192]

---

191. Myers, *Binding the Strong Man*, 286–88.
192. Gundry, *Mark*, 943.

The crucifixion scene is, obviously, highly significant in Mark's Gospel. There are a number of aspects of the account that are important for this study. The first of these is the constant and unrelenting Old Testament allusions and citations.[193] In the early Christian movement, the crucifixion was often viewed in terms of Jesus functioning as the archetypal righteous sufferer.[194] Evans makes reference to Marcus's presentation of a number of allusions in the Passion narrative:[195]

Mark	Topic	Psalm
15:24	division of garment	22:18
15:29	mockery, wagging head	22:7
15:30–31	Save yourself!	22:8
15:32	reviling	22:6
15:34	cry of dereliction	22:1
15:36	gave him vinegar to drink	69:1
15:40	looking on at a distance	38:11

Evans also notes a few other proposals that are offered concerning the possible chiastic structure of the Passion narrative,[196] but they are not compelling enough to require much further attention. What is clear, however, is that the context that Mark is requesting, even leading, his reader to understand the person of Jesus in is the Old Testament tradition of Messiah and righteous sufferer.

The scene is rich in irony and the theatrical elements of the account are hard to miss.[197] The actions of the soldiers are, to the sympathetic reader, deplorable.[198] First, the soldiers mock Jesus by giving him a purple cloak, placing a crown of thorns on his head, and offering fake homage (15:19). The "purple cloak," which Matthew renders "scarlet" (κοκκίνην) in 27:28, heightens the irony and dramatic nature of the account since purple was considered a royal color.[199] Additionally, there is irony in what Mark says is

---

193. See, for example, the impressive, detailed study by Moo, *Old Testament in the Gospel Passion Narratives*; Ahearne-Kroll, *Psalms of Lament in Mark's Passion*.

194. Edwards, *Mark*, 467–68.

195. Evans, *Mark*, 298; Marcus, *Way of the Lord*, 175.

196. Evans, *Mark*, 499.

197. Myers, *Binding the Strong Man*, 379.

198. Belo, *Materialist Reading of the Gospel of Mark*, 330–31.

199. Gundry, *Mark*, 942. Additionally, see the tradition coming out of the East concerning conquerors, leaders, and rulers wearing purple in procession, as noted by Collins, *Mark*, 726.

written on the placard, but it is a sort of double irony. Pilate asks Jesus if he is the King of the Jews. Jesus answers in the affirmative (15:2). The soldiers mockingly refer to Jesus as "King of the Jews." Yet, in the end, the characters mockingly ascribe to Jesus the very title that Mark leads his reader to see as true. Jesus is called "King of the Jews" in jest, but the reader has been led to accept that this is a fit title for Jesus.[200] Kingsbury comments on the use of the title "King of the Jews,"

> Mark imbues this title with the quality of irony throughout chapter 15, but nowhere does this come to the fore with greater clarity than in the passages 15:18 and 15:32: what Gentile and Jew say "in mockery" (15:20, 31) is—in Marcan perspective—true, namely, Jesus is in fact the "king of the Jews," or "the Messiah, King of Israel."[201]

Jesus' death does not catch the reader by surprise. In three instances, Jesus predicts his death (8:31; 9:31; 10:33–34). When Jesus expires, Mark notes that the "curtain of the temple was torn in two, from top to bottom" (καὶ τὸ καταπέτασμα τοῦ ναοῦ ἐσχίσθη εἰς δύο ἀπ' ἄνωθεν ἕως κάτω; 15:38). Scholars are not in consensus as to which "curtain" this verse refers since the temple had at least two. There is what is referred to as the "inner veil" and the "outer veil." One of the lines of reasoning that some have given for the veil in Mark's mind to of necessity be the outer veil is that the centurion's response seems to be indicating that he was witness to the event.[202] Despite this physical and spatial reality, it seems clear that Mark is presenting the centurion's response as being primarily to Jesus' death, and not to the supernatural events at the temple. The words used by Mark seem to clearly lean this way: ἰδὼν δὲ ὁ κεντυρίων ὁ παρεστηκὼς . . . ὅτι οὕτως ἐξέπνευσεν (15:39). It reads that the centurion was "facing him," not "facing the temple." The word for curtain used here is present in the LXX to refer to the veil between the Holy Place and the Most Holy Place (Exod 27:16).[203]

Earlier in this account, the reader is introduced to "soldiers" (στρατιῶται; 15:16) and next, to the centurion (κεντυρίων; 15:39). Unlike the position of a regular "soldier," the centurion's role, prestige and social standing in the historical context are hard to surmise. The word "centurion"

---

200. Additional notes on the use of irony in Mark, especially in Mark 15, is offered by Shiner, "Ambiguous Pronouncement of the Centurion."

201. Kingsbury, *Christology of Mark's Gospel*, 128.

202. Illustrative of this view are Gundry, *Mark*, 950–51; Ulansey, "Heavenly Veil Torn," 124.

203. See also the usage of the word in Philo, *Moses*, 2:128. The theological dimensions of this insertion into the narrative is examined by Chronis, "Torn Veil."

in Greek is a loan word from the Latin *centurio* that means literally an overseer or commander of a hundred. A centurion was a known and respected position similar to a "captain."[204] Johnson summarizes,

> Centurions had reputations not only of experience and perspicacity but also one of bravery and loyalty. The centurions were masters of discipline and they were the ones expected to fill the breach. Since they served in the army from the time they were young men until they were well into their fifties or sixties, they were among those who maintained the perpetuity of Roman military tradition.[205]

It has been demonstrated that in the Roman world a centurion was often promoted up through the ranks and thus not necessarily Roman by birth.[206] Collins notes, however, that even if someone in this position were not Roman by birth, they would likely be thoroughly Romanized.[207] Mark seems to inferring that one who commands a hundred—the centurion—was the one actually in charge of other soldiers that are seen mocking Jesus earlier. The centurion does not "pass by" (15:29) Jesus, but stands "facing him" (15:39).

The natural questions that arise from this text are: How does Mark use the character of the centurion as a device in his narrative; and secondly, how does Mark anticipate his audience will understand the words of the centurion. These two important questions will be addressed shortly. The question, however, about whether or not a centurion would realistically say such a thing as is recorded by Mark is irrelevant to the discussion at hand. Johnson, in a 1987 article in *JSNT*, argued that since Roman soldiers took religious oaths to the Emperors as "sons of god," it would be "unlikely that Mark's readers would find it believable that a professional soldier would risk his career in order to worship a crucified man."[208] His additional arguments include the reality that Mark nowhere in his Gospel presents a dramatic conversion on this scale (unlike Luke-Acts) and thus it would be highly illogical to assume that he is intending to cast the centurion's words in the light of a dramatic conversion. Johnson's study is careful and well presented, but he may claim too much. The central issue at hand is not historical. It

---

204. An overview of the roles, functions, and positions in the Roman army, see Brand, *Roman Military Law*; Grant, *Army of the Caesars*; Judson, *Caesar's Army*.

205. Johnson, "Is Mark 15 the Key," 11.

206. The range of meaning of "centurion" in the Roman world is illustrated by the surveys by D'Amato, *Roman Centurions*; Ross and Langford, *Roman Centurion*; Watson, *Roman Soldier*, 86–88.

207. Collins, *Mark*, 763–64.

208. Johnson, "Is Mark 15 the Key," 13.

may be improbable that the centurion switches allegiance to Jesus. But, it is also improbable that Israel's Messiah healed, exorcised demons, and worked wonder, and this is exactly what Mark is leading his reader to believe. It will be argued in chapter 5 that this is what Mark is requesting of his reader: to accept the pronouncement of the centurion as being not only truthful, but as a model to imitate. To summarize the interplay between historical probabilities and narrative dimension, Boring's thoughts are on point,

> The centurion's confession is a climactic christological statement of the Gospel, carefully composed, with every word important. It is to be understood at the level of Markan narrative, not at the level of historical reporting. The questions of what a 30 C.E. Roman officer might have said at the crucifixion of Jesus, and what he might have meant by that statement in the Markan narrative, or what tone of voice he might have used, are irrelevant to the Markan meaning.[209]

An additional point of clarification is in order surrounding the intersect of history and narrative. What is not in view here is the argument that what is preserved is necessarily the *ipssissma verba* (very words) of the historical individual that was on guard at the crucifixion, though this very well may be. The historical reliability and criterion by which questions of this nature are answered is beyond the scope of this study. What is most germane to the present line of argumentation is that as a character, functioning in Mark's developed and nuanced narrative, the centurion is being presented as one who sees and expresses something beyond what even he may intend.

The grammar of the verse is difficult to be confident about. This is due to "Son of God" lacking the article (υἱὸς θεοῦ). The possibilities range from "a son of a god" to "the Son of God." Stein, in his treatment on Mark, helpfully notes the different ways that English translations render the two words: "Son of God" adopted by RSV, NAB, NASB, NJB, NIV, TNIV, NLT, and ESV, while "a son of God" by REV and JB (with RSV and NRSV placing this reading in the footnotes).[210] The anarthrous rendering is not found in 1:11; 3:11; 9:7; or 14:61–62; these all have the article. Seven times in Mark's Gospel, the verb "to be" (εἰμί) and "son" (υἱός) are seen together. They are:

- Mark 1:11   (σὺ εἶ ὁ)
- Mark 3:11   (σὺ εἶ ὁ υἱὸς τοῦ θεοῦ)
- Mark 5:7   (υἱὲ τοῦ θεοῦ τοῦ ὑψίστου)

---

209. Boring, *Mark*, 434.
210. Stein, *Mark*, 718.

- Mark 9:7 (ἐστιν ὁ υἱός μου ὁ ἀγαρητός)
- Mark 14:61 (ὁ υἱὸς τοῦ εὐλογητοῦ)

Each of these is anarthrous with υἱὸς in the predicate. One is linked with a proper name (David) in 12:35 and thus can be considered definite. The only other occurrence that is anarthrous is in 15:39.

The centurion's confession mirrors the wording of Mark 1:1. It seems obvious that Mark 1:1 is definite. Mark's Christology is clearly such that he identifies Jesus as "the" Son of God, not as a Divine Mam. Since 15:39 mirrors the anarthrous 1:1 it makes sense to view it as identical to the incipit. Schweizer comments that this argument, "is confirmed by the recognition that the confession of Jesus as the Son of God determines the overall construction of this gospel."[211] Additionally, the anarthrous predicate nominative is often best translated as definite. This grammatical principal is well known and originally presented by Colwell.[212] Colwell argues that a definite predicate noun often takes the article when it occurs in a sentence with the verb "to be." There are a few exceptions to this rule, though it is generally accepted as valuable in most instances.

Johnson argues that since "Colwell's Rule" is not certain in some instances, and, since the centurion said "was" (ἦν) that he was most likely just communicating that "a man of divine origin has passed away."[213] Kim has addressed some of Johnson's assertions, and insists that the Roman background of the centurion, especially the function of the Imperial cult and the apotheosis of Augustus and the language that surrounded it, would lead to reader to, in essence, understand the centurion's confession as his own appropriation of the person of Jesus in the vernacular that he is familiar with.[214] Specifically, Kim argues that the Latin *Divi filius*, when brought directly to Greek, would most likely end up without the article (υἱὸς θεοῦ).[215] Suffice it to say, the grammar does leave some level of ambiguity in intention and meaning, but the mirroring of 15:29 and 1:1 seem to lend to it being

---

211. Schweizer, *Good News according to Mark*.

212. Colwell, "Definite Rule for the Use of the Article." Although the formula is far from absolute, it is generally accepted. Wallace argues against Brooks and Winberry, and points out that the article is not solely used for "definitizing." He offers three primary uses of the article: conceptualizing, identifying, and "definitizing." Wallace, *Greek Grammar*, 209; Contra Brooks and Winbery, *Morphology of New Testament Greek*, 73–80. Wallace argues that because the demonstrative (οὗτος) cannot stand in attributive position, 15:39 should be translated "Truly *this man* was God's Son." Wallace, *Greek Grammar*, 242.

213. Johnson, "Is Mark 15 the Key," 8.

214. Kim, "Anarthrous υἱὸς θεοῦ."

215. Ibid., 220–24.

understood as a christological confession that continues the theology of the rest of Mark, rather than one that contradicts it.

A number of perspectives on the exegetical and narrative dimensions of this passage are worth reviewing. First, Kingsbury, in commenting on this section, begins to lay his argument out by focusing attention on the lack of identification of Jesus as the "Son of Man" by the characters in the story. This, he argues, indicates that "Mark does not utilize the title 'Son of Man' to explain to the reader 'who Jesus is.'"[216] He presents the point that the trial and crucifixion of Jesus are linked together in Mark's narrative and thus together they reveal to the reader and the characters in the story who Jesus is. Kingsbury also points to the repetition of the verb "to see" (ὁράω) as being significant in the passage. In contrast to the reviling coming from the characters in 15:32, 36, the centurion's confession occurs when he "sees" the manner in which Jesus dies (15:39).[217] Kingsbury explains the import of the centurion's words as being used by Mark to indicate that the centurion had "converted" in some sense.[218] This, he argues, can be seen in the word "truly" (ἀληθῶς) in 15:39.[219] His thinking goes like this: the word "truly" indicates that he is making some sort of agreement with something that has been implied or stated before and the most likely thing that he is referring to is the mocking found in 15:18–20. In spite of all the exegetical and narratival work done by Kingsbury on this passage, his most significant contribution lies in a simple observation that has some dramatic implications for developing an assessment of the narrative flow of the Gospel. The observation is this: The centurion is the first human character in the Gospel who sees the truth about who Jesus is and calls him "the Son of God."[220] This observation will factor into the present study in chapter 5. But for now, attention will be given to the passage itself rather than the role it plays in the narrative.

Taylor's influential commentary of Mark served as one of the original insistences of the view that Mark intended the centurion's words as a christological confession that ran parallel with 1:1.[221] Gundry, in his commentary, makes a similar claim and views 1:1 and 15:39 as transforming the shameful death of a criminal into a revelation of the divine sonship of Jesus. He writes, "Mark does not preset a Christology of the Cross to foster

---

216. Kingsbury, *Christology of Mark's Gospel*, 123.

217. Ibid., 129.

218. Ibid., 131.

219. Ibid.

220. Ibid., 132.

221. Taylor, *Gospel according to St. Mark*, 597. This seems to be the viewpoint of a number of commentators. See: Boring, *Mark*, 434; Mann, *Mark*, 654; Stein, *Mark*, 718.

a theology of suffering, then, but the Christology of divine sonship to counteract the scandal of the cross."[222] Collins authored two articles on the title "Son of God" in Mark, one considering it from the Jewish readers' point of view[223] the other examining the way it would be interpreted by a Greaco-Roman audience[224] Both of these studies are eloquent and demonstrate a familiarity with the primary texts and Greaco-Roman literature that is quite impressive. The problem with these studies, however, is found in the approach. While the question about how Mark's narrative may be received is important, the manner in which Mark expected his implied reader (or indefinite reader) to understand the Gospel ought to be the primary matter under consideration. More in keeping with this line of thinking, in her commentary on the Gospel, she states plainly,

> If the statement [centurion's confession] is read as part of the Gospel of Mark as a whole, especially from the point of view of audiences knowledgeable about Jewish traditions from the period of Second Temple, the centurion can be understood as recognizing Jesus' messiahship.[225]

The small caveat that she offers above about the Gospel being read as a whole is important. This is the important qualifier to keep in mind. The Evangelist is not haphazard with his writing. Thus far it has been demonstrated that Mark took great care shaping and fleshing out his narrative so that it is both engaging and emotionally potent. This is the climatic christological event in the narrative that Mark is writing. One would anticipate that the same care and finesse that went into Mark's narrative up to this point would be found in this significant section as well. We would expect more drama, not less, in the climax.

The cross casts a shadow over the Gospel of Mark. In 8:34 Jesus teaches his disciples that the instrument of destruction is one of the hallmarks of discipleship. Myers's words concerning the emotional impact of the entire scene are worth noting:

> The cross: according to humanists of antiquity, an intolerably cruel form of capital punishment; according to Jesus' call to discipleship, the concrete consequence of the liberating practice of the kingdom; according to apocalyptic symbolic of Mark's story,

---

222. Gundry, *Mark*, 974.
223. Collins, "Mark and His Readers: The Son of God among Jews."
224. Collins, "Mark and His Readers: The Son of God among Greeks and Romans."
225. Collins, *Mark*, 767.

the mythic moment when the sun retreats, the powers are overthrown, and the worlds comes to an end.[226]

It is here, in this climactic, cosmic scene that the Mark's essential Christology is most clearly revealed. It is here that the "Son of God" is seen for who he is.

CONCLUSION

This chapter has taken the time to carefully assess the exegetical dimensions of each of the instances in which the title "Son of God" comes into play in the book of Mark. It has been argued that, in each instance, significant narratival elements, trends, and motifs are present. Additionally, a few preliminary observations were offered. First, the Old Testament is the foundation from which Mark is inviting his reader to understand, interpret, and relate to the title "Son of God." Second it was noted that it is a sonship of authority, hearkening his role as the king, or put another way, his role as the Messiah of Israel that is in view. Third, that it is related to the suffering of Jesus in such a way that the picture of Jesus' sonship is only understood in light of the crucifixion.

The next task at hand is to synthesize the data and note the narrative contours of the book as a whole. The two conversation partners, exegesis and literary considerations, must be invited to enmesh themselves together. In this union, a more profitable and balanced interpretive method is possible. Since the exegetical data has been laid out, the remainder of space and time in this Study will be devoted to stepping back and taking in the whole. From the onset, the intention of this study has been to offer a thesis that is both exegetically plausible and narratively defensible. One cannot miss the forest for the trees, so to speak, and so this chapter has taken a good look at the trees, taking in each and every one that comprises the forest. The task to accomplish now begins by stepping back and taking in the forest that these trees make up. Chapter 5 will examine the flow of the Gospel of Mark from a bird's eye perspective. It will be demonstrated that the important themes of secrecy and revelation are most aptly described as the motifs of allegiance, misunderstanding, and opposition. The Gospel of Mark will be evaluated with these three themes in view.

---

226. Myers, *Binding the Strong Man*, 383.

5

A Synchronic Approach to Son of God Theology in Mark

INTRODUCTION

At this point, a short review is in order. The study began with a look at the history of narrative criticism and its relationship to the traditional, historical, critical methods of investigation. It was argued that narrative criticism does not replace the other methods, but rather helps to serve as guideposts ensuring that the forest is not missed for the trees, so to speak. Next, it was argued that the most logical and plausible context from which one is to understand the title "Son of God" is the Old Testament Messianic eschatological hope. The implied reader is one who is familiar and reveres the work of God in history and Scripture. Even so, the narrator is deliberate in ensuring that his audience knows and understands that Jesus is the Messiah and that he stands in the tradition of God's revelation through the Old Testament. The implied reader is expected to understand Jesus in this way, and not in the vein of Greco-Roman Divine Mam. Next, an exegetical analysis was completed on all the texts that relate to Jesus' divine sonship in Mark. The reason that this is so crucial, it was explained, is that any hypothesis on the meaning or expected reaction to Mark's narrative must be in line with the text as it is. A grand hypothesis about the narratival dimension of Mark's text that is not inherently exegetical, rather than surface level, is open to the charge of subjectivism and, generally, not helpful. This chapter is one in which the exegetical data that was mined in chapter 4 is approached, teased, and filtered through a narrative critical framework. The "bones" of this framework are the tripartite relationship between "author," "text," and "reader." Having examined the "text" component from an exegetical standpoint, the remaining two of these, "author" and "reader," will require time and space to develop. Here, it will be demonstrated that when the narrative is approached from sensitivity to the themes of misunderstanding, opposition, and allegiance, meaningful insights regarding the rhetorical impact of Mark 15:39 come to light.

This chapter offers a synchronic approach to Mark's Son of God theology. Van Iersel explains this approach: "Commentators who adopt the synchronic approach regard the writer of Mark not as a redactor but as an author in his own right, and the Gospel of Mark as a coherent whole like any other literary text."[1] The chapter will examine the text and narrative flow from a perspective that is sensitive to the literary devices of the implied author. It will be argued that the "three pillars,"[2] help frame the narrative and serve to propel and build tension in the story world of Mark. These three pillars are the baptism, transfiguration, and crucifixion of Jesus in Mark.

To these, it seems wise to keep in view the significance of 1:1, Mark's incipit as an overarching umbrella, under which the narrative unfolds. Using these "pillars" as the significant narrative points in the story, the flow and contents of the Gospel will be analyzed from the motif of misunderstanding, opposition, and allegiance. Next, we will approach the narrative with reader response sensitivities in play. It will look at the implied author and how he develops and sets forward his point of view in the narrative world. This will be primarily done through an examination of 1:1–15. The point of view that is advocated for in this section is what the rest of the book continues to embrace. After this, the study will offer a walk-through of Mark's Gospel with the motifs of allegiance, misunderstanding, and opposition in mind. In the end, the view will be presented that, when the three pillars are examined and the motifs of misunderstanding, opposition, and allegiance are investigated, the centurion's confession in 15:39 serves as a christological high point in which a human character finally grasps the "revelation." It is only in the centurion's words that the motif of misunderstanding is resolved, and the motif of allegiance, in contradistinction to opposition, climaxes. This, it will be suggested, is the quintessential Markan Son of God

---

1. Van Iersel, *Mark*, 26.
2. Myers, *Binding the Strong Man*, 390–92.

Christology: To respond with allegiance to the person of Jesus in light of his suffering and death.

IMPLIED READER AND MARK'S POINT OF VIEW

How does this omniscient narrator anticipate his audience to respond to the narrative world and events that he offers them? Or, to put it another way, how would the implied reader be expected to respond to the text? To answer this question, again, the final text must serve as guide. The most logical manner in which to locate the implied reader is to look at the story the narrator has left. Obviously, there are an infinite number of possible readers, but the most probable one is the one that the text anticipates. For example, the implied audience of a silent film is obviously one that is not vision impaired. In the same way, it seems best to allow the text to guide our hypothesis as to the original readership.

For example, in Mark, the implied reader is likely not a Pharisee. Mark does little to cast the group in anything but a negative light (2:16, 18, 24; 3:6; 7:1, 3, 5; 8:11, 15; 10:2; 12:13). This group is held at a distance and portrayed in a negative light. They are flat characters in so far as they do not change or alter their patterns of behavior. From the beginning to the end they are opposing Jesus. If Mark was writing in the hopes of gaining the support from those in this group, he, no doubt, would have constructed his narrative in a vastly different manner than he does.

The implied reader is one who is interested in the revelation of Jesus. Powell lists three general points of agreement regarding the implied reader in Mark. They are:

1. [One who] receives the narrative in the manner they would be expected to receive it.
2. Knows everything that the reader of the story would be expected to know—but nothing else.
3. Believes everything the reader of this story is expected to believe—but nothing else.[3]

The difficulty in interpretation for modern scholars is that the reality in which they find themselves is vastly different from the world of the New Testament. Those who hold a high-Christology in the vein of Nicene tradition no doubt would agree with point (1) above, but struggle to approach the text with (2) and (3) functioning as interpretative markers because they

---

3. Powell, "Narrative Criticism," 24.

"know" and "believe" vastly more than the implied reader (a robust trinitarian theology). Likewise, a skeptical atheist would reject all three points because of a different set of presuppositions about Scripture, miracles, and the divinity of Jesus.

This is where the approach of narrative criticism comes into play. Yet, as has been argued in this study, if narrative criticism is not anchored to the historical critical approach, then subjectivity may be prone to develop unfettered. The question at hand is how would the expected audience respond to the unexpected events of the narrative in Mark? Or to simplify the question, what is the point of view being advocated by the implied author?

The term "implied author" is a textual concept (internal to the text). It is the author who can be discovered in the text and exists, primarily, in that realm. To be fair, the historical questions about the author of the Gospel (external to the text) are significant, but, for time being, attention will be given to the implied author of the narrative world that is present in Mark. The "implied author," which is often understood as the ideological perspective of the narrator, is defined by Waetjen as involving the following:

> The sum total of choices that a real author makes in telling a story: the repertoire selected to constitute the narrative, the strategies embedded in the text to foster the interaction between the reader and the text, the kind of narrator chosen to tell the story, the plot line to structure the narrative, and the characters to carry out the action.[4]

Regarding the identity or situation of the implied reader of Mark, a helpful observation must be made. In his reader-response commentary on Mark, John Paul Heil remarks,

> For the readers of audience, who already possess a fundamental knowledge of the story, the resurrection of Jesus is a past event. The audience, then, is situated between the resurrection and the "parousia" or second coming of Jesus (see Mark 13:24–27). More specifically, while the story of Jesus took place historically within the opening decades of the first century C.E., it is narrated to an implied reader located in the second half of the first century.[5]

However, the approach taken here is that of a synchronic study and, thus, as was explained in chapter 1, the finished text serves as vehicle of

---

4. Waetjen, *Reordering of Power*, xix.
5. Heil, *Gospel of Mark as a Model for Action*, 2–4.

communication rather than the *Sitz* of the community(s) to which Mark wrote.[6] Further, the view of an indefinite audience (as was discussed in chapter 2) makes the text less of something to be seen through to recreate a specific debate or conflict, but rather the text is the field in which we labor.[7]

There still remains a deep intrinsic value to questions that diachronic method asks. Literary critic Wolfgang Iser notes that readers are not passive in the experience, but play a significant role in the narrative world in that they complete what is lacking or, to follow van Iersel's paraphrase of Iser, "fill in the gaps that are always present in a literary texts."[8]

To summarize briefly, although there is value in the historical context of the original audience, what is being advocated here is primarily a synchronic approach to Mark's Christology. Thus, a reader who understands Mark the way in which he wrote to be understood is our starting point. This type of reader[9] is expected to adopt the point of view that the narrator of Mark advocates. The question that, thus, arises, then, is what view is it that the narrator presents?

IMPLIED AUTHOR: THE DEVELOPMENT OF A POINT OF VIEW

Although not extensive, there is a body of tradition about the historical author of the second Gospel.[10] These traditions are hotly debated and, for the present study, are not directly relevant. For the thesis that is being advocated here, attention will be primarily confined to the implied author we know through the text. This is not to say that the goal is uncovering authorial intent, *per se*, but that to understand the manner in which "Son of God" is expected to be received and understood, and what role the centurion's confession plays in it all, must not contradict what we see evidenced by the text through the implied author.

---

6. For a discussion on a diachronic or synchronic approach to the gospel of Mark, see Van Iersel, *Mark*, 14–29. Both his discussion and bibliography are helpful in this regard.

7. There can be no doubt that the relationship between implied reader and the intended reader is complex. Van Iersel, *Mark*, 22.

8. For reference, see Van Iersel, *Mark*, 18.

9. This is what some may refer to as "ideal reader." The concept of "ideal reader" is discussed by Fowler, *Let the Reader Understand*, 26–40. Here, he refers to the work done on this topic by literary scholars Jonathan Culle, Stanley Fish, Wolfgang Iser, and Steven Mailloux. See Fowler for sources.

10. A reappraisal of the value of the historical sources relating to the composition by Mark is presented by Hengel, *Studies in the Gospel of Mark*, 45–50.

The concept of point of view is closely tied to the "rhetoric" of the author. Wayne Booth explains rhetoric as the way the writer "tries, consciously or unconsciously, to impose his fictional world upon the reader."[11] In Mark, this is exactly what the reader experiences. Fowler explains it this way:

> [I]n Mark we never have to deal with a narrator's unreliability. To the contrary, we have reliability and authority in spades; . . . the implied reader puts forth a reliable, authoritative narrator, who puts forth a reliable authoritative protagonist named Jesus. If the rhetoric of the narrative is successful, then the *exousia* and *dynamis* attributed to Jesus by the narrator will implicitly garner *exousia* and *dyamis* for the narrator himself, and in turn for the implied reader.[12]

Resseguie is correct in noting that, in addition to the significance that an omniscient narrator has in creating a narrative to be trusted, the conceptual world which he creates is equally important.[13] More than just conveying that the narrator knows everything, and thus can be trusted, biblical narrative (especially the Gospels) creates an ideological point of view in which the "objective" point of view (of the omniscient narrator) and the "subjective" point of view (understood as ideological point of view) to get this point across.[14] In his treatment of point of view, Resseguie offers the headings "phraseological," "spatial-temporal," "psychological," and "ideological" point of view.[15] As he explains and defines each of these, it becomes evident that there exists in Mark a uniformed point of view that is presented.

So how does 1:1–15 invite the reader to understand the implied author's point of view? To answer that question, a close reading of this section and attention to the development of the author's point of view is in order.

The narrator begins his Gospel with startling words: "The beginning of the gospel of Jesus Christ Son of God" (1:1). This is not normal proclamation or drama of little consequence. Instead, it is the "beginning" or dawning of the good news. Right from the beginning, the author ensures that the reader is clear on the true identity of this "Jesus." He is Israel's Messiah and the Son of God. What this means, however, is yet to be seen. Yet, whatever occurs in the narrative world of Mark's Gospel, whatever twists and turns the story takes, the reader is assured of this one over-arching truth; what

---

11. Booth, *Rhetoric of Fiction*, xiii.
12. Fowler, *Let the Reader Understand*, 61.
13. Resseguie, *Narrative Criticism of the New Testament*, 168–69.
14. See ibid. for the difference between the "objective" and "subjective" understanding of point of view.
15. Ibid., 170–73.

they have before them (or, more likely being read to them) is the beginning of the gospel of Jesus Christ God's Son. It is as if the author is saying to his audience, "no matter what happens to Jesus, this narrative is good news! It has a happy ending!"

In addition to the pronouncement of Mark 1:1, the implied author links the good news of God's Son to the Jewish eschatological hope. He "tells" that the proper context for understanding Jesus' identity is the Old Testament (1:2–4). Additionally, he uses the primary character in his opening scene, John the Baptist, to bolster his authoritative claim that "good news" it about to come because Jesus (it is assumed) is going to "baptize with the Holy Spirit" (1:8). The implications of this are settled almost immediately in the next verses. Jesus is baptized by John in the Jordan and "immediately" he saw "heaven being torn open and the Spirit descending on him like a dove" (1:10). A voice from heaven proclaims: "You are my beloved Son; with you I am well pleased" (1:11). The voice is understood by the reader to be God himself.

Here, in only a few verses, the narrator has done some significant work in aligning the reader to his own point of view.[16] Since the voice from heaven addressed Jesus directly, Mark, in recording it and offering it to his readers, demonstrated his own omniscience of the events at hand. He is, in the classic sense, the omniscient narrator.[17] The narrator begins by "telling" (1:1) then "shows" (1:2–4 through prophetic and eschatological tradition that Jesus stands in) then has John "tell" (1:8), then, finally, heightens the drama and has God "tell" Jesus and, in extension, the reader, that Jesus is the Son of God. In this encounter, the omniscience of the narrator is transferred to the audience through the way of privileged information. No characters hear this pronouncement, but the narrator has made it available to the reader.

A number of spatial markers are used by the narrator in 1:1–11. First, the "wilderness" is mentioned. The place of testing and God's provision is now the place where Jesus enters the scene (and the place from which he will soon venture out in conflict with Satan; 1:9, 13). Additionally, the locale of "heaven" is introduced and affixes Jesus' uncontested validity as the Son of God (1:11). Since God himself endorses Jesus or, to put it another way, since God's point of view is one that adopts the narrator's (or *vice versa*), the reader's mind is settled; if the omniscient narrator, the Old Testament, John

---

16. The role of point of view in Mark is examined by Peterson, "Point of View in Mark." In the end, he argues that the narrative world of Mark is a significant literary creation and that interpretation of Mark must keep this in mind.

17. Resseguie, *Narrative Criticism of the New Testament*, 168; Powell, *What is Narrative Criticism*, 25–27.

the Baptist, and God himself understand Jesus to be the Son of God, then, "truly this man is the Son of God!" The point of view being presented by Mark is the point of view of his narrative as a whole. He works extensively to ensure that the model characters in the story adopt this view and seeks to influence his audience to do the same.

STRUCTURAL ANALYSIS OF MARK'S GOSPEL

Ched Myers' excellent examination of the book has served as a significant advancement in Markan studies relating to literary and socio-historical investigation. In his section on interpreting the second half of Mark, he offers an analysis of the apocalyptic moments in Mark. He explains,

> These moments have been placed like structural pillars at the beginning (Jesus' baptism), midpoint (Jesus' Transfiguration), and the end of the story. At the level of narrative, each moment is fundamental to the regeneration of plot.[18]

He then goes on to assess these events and note their similarities. He tables them as such:[19]

Baptism	Transfiguration	Crucifixion
Heavens rent and doves descends	Garments turn white; cloud descends	Sanctuary veil rent darkness spreads
Voice from heaven	Voice from cloud	Jesus' great voice
"You are my son, beloved"	"This is my son, beloved"	Truly this man was son of God
John the Baptist as Elijah	Jesus appears with Elijah	"Is he calling Elijah?"

christologically speaking, they undoubtedly serve as significant portions of Mark's Gospel. The timing of them in the narrative is also significant, since it includes events in the opening, midpoint, and conclusion. It is here that the motif of misunderstanding, opposition, and allegiance most clearly come into view. These pillars will be examined in light of these motifs. At this point, a definition of each of these themes is important. These definitions, however, are only possible to construct once the narrative dimension of the book have been examined in totality. They are unique to Mark, and find their genesis and develop in the world he constructs. They can be defined as such:

18. Myers, *Binding the Strong Man*, 390–92.
19. Ibid., 391.

1. *Misunderstanding*—To fail to grasp that which is central to the narrator's point of view. In failing to understand that Jesus is the Son of God, one often, because of the misunderstanding, finds oneself acting in opposition to Jesus.

2. *Opposition*—To resist (in actions and thoughts) the point of view of the omniscient narrator (and the character of God) and to adopt the "things of man" (Mark 8:33) as the central reality concerning Jesus, the Son of God and his crucifixion.

3. *Allegiance*—To embrace (in actions and thoughts) the point of view of the omniscient narrator (and the character of God) and to act in alignment with him specifically when it pertains to Jesus being the Son of God and his being crucified.[20]

How exactly these motifs are developed is the task of following section. It will be argued that when these themes are traced, they grow, and find their resolution and climax in the crucifixion scene, specifically in the words of the Roman centurion that Jesus, in light of his death, actually is the Son of God (15:39). At this point the themes will begin to be examined by noting the three christological "high points" in Mark.[21]

Allegiance, Opposition, and Misunderstanding Begin (Mark 1:11—9:1)

At this point in Mark's narrative, the reader has some important information about Jesus' identity. As mention above in chapter 4, the omniscient narrator presents a point of view and leads his reader to adopt the same perspective. The theme of misunderstanding has not yet been introduced. The reader, in some fashion, may assume that it is "clear sailing" from here on out since the Son of God has "come" into the scene (1:9). At the baptism, the reader is given an assessment of the claims that Mark has made about Jesus (that he is the Son of God; 1:1). The assessment that the reader is given is an unwavering endorsement; the voice from heaven proclaims, "this is my beloved Son" (1:11). The theme of allegiance, then, is introduced by Mark in Mark 1:1, and adopted by God in 1:11. This theme, broadly speaking, entails

---

20. Although discipleship plays a very significant role in Mark, understanding and finding a consensus has proven difficult for scholars. Due to this, the present study will take only a broad approach to the motif of allegiance rather than condense to include faith and repentance and the identification of a disciple. For a well-presented study on the theme of faith in Mark's Gospel, see Marshall, *Faith as a Theme in Mark's Narrative*.

21. Myers, *Binding the Strong Man*, 389.

the adoption of the perspective being presented by the omniscient narrator. He is a trustworthy narrator. It is implicitly communicated that to adopt his view on the life and ministry of Jesus is the "right view." So how does Mark ensure that his point of view is accepted by the implied reader? By using God himself as a "witness" to the claims of Mark 1:1. The question of point of view surrounding this first pillar in Mark is explained by Kingsbury:

> One thing Mark does not do: he does not deal with God in the same manner in which he deals with other characters of his story. . .Mark does not permit the reader to imagine that he has "unmediated access" either to heaven—God's abode (11:25)—or to his "mind."[22]

This does not mean, according to Kingsbury, that Mark is unintentional about demonstrating God's point of view. So how does Mark do this? Kingsbury explains that it occurs in two ways,

> Instead, Mark's procedure for incorporating God's evaluative point of view into his story is a dual one. Primarily, Mark colours his story with reference of quotations to the OT. In so doing, however, he shows that he is concerned, not just that God's evaluative point of view should be represented in his story, but that it should be afforded normative status. . . . For another thing, Mark, twice, has God enter the world story as an "actor" in order to address other characters directly, and both times God speaks words drawn from the OT.[23]

It is worth noting, that for the human characters in the story, 1:11 and God's evaluative point of view is entirely missed.[24] It is only to the reader that God's point of view of Jesus is revealed. This act serves to encourage the motif of allegiance to the readers. If the omniscient, trustworthy narrator adopts a point of view, and indicates through Old Testament quotations that it is a consistent point of view with Scripture, and has God appear in the narrative to bolster and reaffirm this point of view, there seems little doubt that the implied reader is invited to affirm and agree. Thus, the entire first scene, from Mark 1:1 to the "pillar" of the baptismal scene, is used by Mark to initiate the motif of allegiance in the narrative he is about to unfold. In so

---

22. Kingsbury, *Christology of Mark's Gospel*, 48.

23. Ibid.

24. Kingsbury, *Conflict in Mark*, 34, elsewhere explains that although this is missed to the characters in the story, to the implied reader, God's evaluation of Jesus is to be taken as "normative."

doing, he ensures that any reasonable reader—his implied reader—adopts the same point of view for which he is advocating.

The motif of allegiance—the adoption of the implied author's point of view—begins with the first scene, but does not go unchallenged. In the next few paragraphs, Mark introduces, and then develops, the motif of misunderstanding. What is interesting is that the first question about Jesus' identity ("What is this? A new teaching and with authority" 1:27), actually enhances and propels the claims of the narrator in 1:1. Mark uses the confusion of the crowd to unite the motif of misunderstanding and allegiance. After reading these words, the implied reader no doubt expects that the revelation will not be long in coming. Surely, all that it means for Jesus to be the Son of God may take a while for the crowds to grasp and, at this point, their question seems likely to be answered in short order. There is no animosity in these words, just a natural response to the revelation of the Son of God. Kingsbury explains, "Given the widespread activity and fame of Jesus, one is tempted to think that his identity would be a secret to no one. The opposite, however, is that case."[25] Despite what the implied reader has been made aware of, the characters in the story are presented as being unclear about who exactly Jesus is. This is the first glimpse of the theme of misunderstanding in Mark.[26]

As Jesus' ministry continues, his fame begins to spread (1:45; 2:2, 12, 15). Yet, even in this exciting time of revelation, there are signs of trouble brewing. The first hint at this occurs in 2:6–8. In these verses, Mark has the scribes offer the first negative assessment of Jesus' work and, thus, of his person. The charge that they level against Jesus because he heals and then forgives a man his sins is "blasphemy" (2:7). The rhetorical question that they ask in response to Jesus' actions and words is: "Who can forgive sins but God himself." The implied reader, who is already privy to Jesus' divine sonship, and understands that Jesus stands in Old Testament prophetic tradition, and has been endorsed by God, would likely reply: "Well the Son of God can forgive sins!" A trinitarian theology is not necessary to grant that Jesus has "authority" to do this. He is the Son of God (1:1) and his ministry is the "beginning of the gospel." The first time that "scribes" were mentioned was in Mark 1:22 where the crowd contrasts the authority of Jesus with scribes. This, although not explicitly a negative assessment of the entire group, does serve to point the reader forward to the numerous

---

25. Kingsbury, *Conflict in Mark*, 37.

26. In Mark there are a number of questions that directly pertain to the identity of Jesus. These are examined from a literary standpoint by Kingsbury, *Conflict in Mark*, 39–42.

times that the two parties—Jesus and the scribes (or religious leaders)—are not only contrasted by the crowds but are also engaging in direct conflict.[27]

The second time that the scribes are mentioned is in 2:6–8. Mark 2:6 has the scribes "questioning in their hearts." Mark has two options for character development: he can "show" his readers something about the characters, or he can "tell." He uses his position of omniscient narrator to delve into the hearts and thinking of the group and presents the readers with an overall negative assessment of the scribes. In fact, Mark is so deliberate here that he actually quotes, *verbatim*, what is occurring in the hearts of the scribes. He gives voice, in the form of a quotation, to what is going on inside the minds of the scribes. The inner dialogue is such that it arrives at charging Jesus with blasphemy. The trajectory of opposition begins in a rather subtle and internal fashion, but this soon begins to escalate until, in the end, Jesus is directly confronted by the religious leaders in a place of their choosing and under their leadership (14:53).[28] It is here that the motif of opposition can first be noted. The motif of opposition can be defined at that viewpoint a character exhibits that conflicts with the point of view being offered by the narrator. Going even further, to be on "God's side" one has to be on "Jesus' side," since the narrator is on Jesus' side!

Additionally, it is here in 2:6–10 that we see the motif of misunderstanding and wonderment continue to be refined. Mark records that the crowds, at this point, "glorify God"; Mark 2:12). They are giving their homage and allegiance to the character that authoritatively endorsed Jesus in 1:11. The narrator uses this little aside to "show" that the crowds, although not entirely clear about who Jesus is, are still open to being swayed, in some sense, to the desired point of view that Mark presents. They have not yet, clearly, arrived at a place of opposition or allegiance; they have yet to grasp the truth about Jesus' identity of which the reader is assured.

When Jesus calls Levi and enters his house, he is surrounded by "tax collectors and sinners" (2:13–17). Here, again, opposition ensues. The scribes "of the Pharisees" (γραμματεῖς τῶν Φαρισαίων) see that Jesus is sitting with the tax collectors and sinners and are not able to understand. They ask Jesus' disciples why this is so, but Jesus hears it and responds to them with a rebuke. Yet, again, the motif of opposition continues to grow. In short order, the proverbial lines in the sand are drawn and the opposition to Jesus becomes vehement.

---

27. A detailed assessment of the religious leaders in Mark is offered by Malbon, *In the Company of Jesus*, 131–65. In her chapter on the characterization of this group she primarily builds on the work by Cook, *Mark's Treatment of the Jewish Leaders*.

28. The role of these conflicts and their progression in directness and intensity is examined by Kingsbury, *Conflict in Mark*, 65–88.

In the next section, after being questioned about fasting and responding with a proverb about wineskins, and after being accused of breaking the Sabbath, the Pharisees seek to trap Jesus. In the opening verses of Mark 3, Jesus enters a synagogue on the Sabbath. Mark tells the reader that the Pharisees are "watching Jesus, to see whether he would heal on the Sabbath, so that they might accuse him" (3:2). Their opposition to Jesus has reached such a level that they are apparently only interested in accusing him.[29] In, yet, another instance, the narrator gives the reader privileged information about the motivations and intents of the religious leaders. They are presented as being in direct opposition to Jesus. They have moved, as it were, from misunderstanding and ambivalence to outright opposition. They have adopted the point of view that is contrary to the implied author and, thus are expected to be received by the reader as being on the "wrong side." But it is not merely dissatisfaction or annoyance that the Pharisees betray; it is murderous intent that they show. The Pharisees go out and "immediately" conspire with the Herodians to "destroy Jesus" (3:6). While Jesus "has come to destroy" (ἀπολέσαι) the evil spiritual beings that plague the people (1:24), the Pharisees are set on "destroying" (ἀπολέσωσιν) Jesus (3:6). The irony here is striking; what Jesus is doing against evil, the Pharisees are doing against the Son of God.

It appears that Mark is using the device in contrast to illustrate something significant here. In 3:1–6, the religious leaders, who one would accept as having God's point of view for their own, are seen to be acting in direct opposition to Jesus. They are blinded and, yet, the demonic beings understand and recognize Jesus for who he is (3:11). As soon as the pericope of the healing in the synagogue occurs, Mark has Jesus withdraw with his disciples and offers the aside that "whenever the unclean spirits saw him, they fell down before him and cried out, 'You are the Son of God'" (3:11). This narrative summary serves to contrast and draw attention to the level of opposition that the Pharisees are acting out. What the Pharisees miss, the unclean spirits confess. The parallels are worth noting as well: in 3:1–6, Jesus heals and the Pharisees want to destroy him; in 3:11 Jesus heals and the demons confess him Son of God.

In Mark's narrative, there exists a tension between the motifs of misunderstanding and opposition. For example, in 3:20, those who misunderstand (or fail to grasp) who Jesus is (in this case his "family") are susceptible to functioning like those in opposition. Mark's implicit point is that it is not simply direct, outright opposition that is dangerous and can alienate

---

29. The same word used for "accuse" is used elsewhere in Mark referencing the growing animosity from the Pharisees and religious leaders (see 15:3, 4).

oneself from the desired point of view, it can also be also be misunderstanding when it is allowed to develop unchecked. The accusation that they level at Jesus is "He is out of his mind." Clearly, they are not viewed as directly opposing Jesus, but they are still indirectly functioning as such. Here, we see an important nuance to the motif of misunderstanding: It is not enough to be close to the proper point of view; one can inadvertently act in opposition when they misunderstand who Jesus is.

The next time that the theme of opposition occurs, it is especially sharp. In 3:22–29 the charge leveled against Jesus is that "Beelzebub" possesses him and that he "casts our demons by the prince of demons." Jesus' response about "unpardonable sins" is cryptic, but the general thrust is clear; they are clearly standing in direct opposition. Even here, nuances in the text abound. The Pharisees claim that Jesus is casting out demons by the power of the prince of demons. In effect, they are claiming that Jesus is on the "other side" in opposition to God. Jesus, however, explains that, in reality, sins are forgiven, except the sin of blasphemy against the Holy Spirit. Jesus' point is that they are on the wrong side; they are against him and, since God is with him, they are against God. They leveled the charge of blasphemy against him in 2:7. Here, at least, it appears he is leveling the same charge at them (3:29).

Just after the reader is informed that a plot is afoot, and that the Pharisees and Herodians are conspiring against Jesus, Mark has the selection of the Twelve. At first read, knowing that two powerful groups are conspiring against Jesus, it seems a bit daunting. Although he is the "Son of God," the odds are not fair. Two groups against one individual. The reader, then, is pleased to see the tables being turned and Jesus gathering a group around him (3:13–19). Jesus "appoints" these individuals so that they can be "sent out and have authority to preach and cast out demons" (3:14). He is gathering a group around himself that are like him. Jesus teaches about the kingdom of God (1:14, 22) and so his disciples are called to "preach" (3:14). He casts out demons (1:24; 3:11) and so his disciples will do the same. The reader is glad to see Jesus having support, glad, that is, until the final name in the list is read: "Judas Iscariot, who betrayed him" (3:19). It is a surprise, narratively speaking, to the reader. This group is assumed to act in allegiance to Jesus, yet, one of their own, at some point in the narrative, will "betray" him and, apparently, act in direct opposition to Jesus.[30]

As the narrative progresses, the motif of opposition continues to be found. In 5:17 the people from the region of Gerasenes request that Jesus

---

30. The characterization of Judas in Mark is examined elsewhere by MacDonald, "Characterization of a False Disciple."

leave their region. They, much like Jesus' family in 3:20, 21, are not operating out of outright opposition, but indirectly, through their misunderstanding, are still siding with those in opposition.

The motif of misunderstanding and confusion, which can be defined by ambiguity or lack of clarity about Jesus' identity, comes to the forefront of the narrative in 6:1–6. The crowds express a high degree of confusion about who Jesus is. They know his parents, his occupation, his family, and, yet, they are unable to come to a clear grasp about who he is. In a number of instances, negative evaluations about peoples' understanding or response to Jesus are found in the text (6:6, 52; 7:5–7, 10, 18; 8:12, 17, 21). Some of these are authorial asides and some are found coming from Jesus.

Allegiance, Opposition, and Misunderstanding Become Outright (Mark 8:27—14:53)

Some resolution occurs at the midpoint of the narrative regarding the motif of misunderstanding. Jesus, at Caesarea Philippi, asks his disciples point blank: "Who do people say that I am?" (8:27–30). This is something that the implied reader has been waiting for. Up until this point, the opposition motif has come from the Pharisees, scribes, and Herodians. The disciples, like the crowds, and Jesus' family, have been subject to the motif of misunderstanding. Yet, as it has been demonstrated, the motif of misunderstanding is, for all intents and purposes, closely related to opposition. In some instances, individuals who operate and function out of this point of view end up relating to Jesus with opposition (cf. 3:20, 21; 5:17). So, at this point, the reader welcomes the direct question by Jesus. Finally, or so it seems, the truth that the reader knows so well will be grasped by the characters in the story. The answer that is given, although correct, is in some respects incomplete. Peter answers, "You are the Christ" (8:29). The first time that the word "Christ" is used in Mark is the incipit, 1:1. This, in 8:29, is the second time "Christ" is used. From a redaction critical point of view, the Synoptic parallels of this passage are intriguing. The parallels are Matt 16:13–16 and Luke 9:18–20. Matthew renders Peter's answer as:

- You are the Christ, the Son of the living God.
- ἀποκριθεὶς δὲ Σίμων Πέτρος εἶπεν· σὺ εἶ ὁ χριστὸς ὁ υἱὸς τοῦ θεοῦ τοῦ ζῶντος

Luke has it as:

- The Christ of God.

- τὸν χριστὸν τοῦ θεοῦ

This is not the only occurrence in which Mark's presentation of a narrative point does not make use of the title "Son of God" (in some form) where the Synoptics do. Another instance of this editorial hesitation is the account of Jesus walking on water (6:45–52). In Mark's account, Jesus walks on water, enters the boat, and the reader is told, "they were utterly astounded" (6:52). Matthew's account makes use of the title "Son of God" here as well (Matt 14:33):

- And those in the boat worshiped him, saying, "Truly you are the Son of God."
- λέγοντες·ἐάληθῶς θεοῦ υἱὸς εἶ

It is clear that the divine sonship of Jesus is significant in Mark; yet, as he builds his narrative and develops this significant theme, he does not simply insert the title over and over in a haphazard manner. Instead, in a more nuanced way, there are select times that he does use it and times that he does not, even when he has opportunity. In the passages above where he has the opportunity for a dramatic revelation that Jesus is the Son of God, he does not use the title. In fact, as has been noted in Mark, until the centurion in 15:39, no human character identifies Jesus correctly and completely. It is not until the "confession" of the centurion that Peter's confession is completed (when both "Christ" and "Son of God" are combined). In the passage of Peter's confession, the motif of allegiance is seen, but so, too, is the motif of misunderstanding because, although Peter answers correctly, he answers incompletely.

As soon as Peter makes his confession about Jesus being the Messiah, Mark returns to the motif of opposition again in dramatic fashion. In 8:32–33, Jesus tells his disciples that the opposition against him has reached such a fevered pitch that it will end in his demise. Jesus explains that he will be "rejected" and "killed" by the elders, chief priests, and scribes. This is the same group that has been carrying the theme of opposition throughout the narrative. Mark has already "tipped" the reader off that the scribes and Pharisees are plotting to kill Jesus. Up until this time, although Jesus faces opposition, the mood remains positive. After all, this is the story about the "good news" of Jesus. Jesus is Israel's Messiah, and God's Son; surely good things are in store. It is here, in the first of three predictions about his death that a darker mood begins to settle in on the story. Mark addresses questions that his audience may have by giving a voice to his implied reader through Peter's words and, in essence, rebukes Jesus. The reader knows that Jesus is the Son of God; how, then, can he be murdered? Peter is wondering the same thing and questions Jesus.

Jesus' response further demonstrates just how central the motifs of allegiance, opposition, and misunderstanding are for Mark. Jesus rebukes Peter in light of his rebuke, and says emphatically, "Get behind me, Satan. For you are not setting your mind on the things of God, but on the things of man" (8:33). Here, Mark, through Jesus' words, explains that the question about allegiance is more complex than one may have thought. Within Jesus' prediction is a cryptic point about his being raised (8:31). This seems to indicate that the story of "good news" is not bound up in just avoiding the death of the protagonist. Jesus goes even further and, in his rebuke of Peter, explains, to continue the metaphor, that to be on "God's side" or to operate out of allegiance may look different than originally thought. Amazingly, Peter's desire to protect or stop the murder of Jesus from occurring is taken for acting in opposition to God's agenda and sides him with the enemy, Satan! The theme of allegiance, then, is not found in thinking along the lines of the "things of men" but on the "things of God" who works in ways that, at this point in the narrative, no characters, and likely, no implied reader can yet understand. To be in allegiance to Jesus means to properly understand the impending death of Jesus from the point of view of God.[31]

The rhetorical value of Jesus' predictions of his death are worth mentioning. Danove, after a detailed linguistics and narrative examination of the characterization od the disciples as a group argues that the pattern of prediction then controversy (when the disciples resist Jesus' prediction) serves to give a voice to the readers own natural resistance to the death of the Son of God.[32]

After predicting his death, Jesus teaches on the nature of discipleship and the necessity of "denying himself" (8:34–38). Jesus' words here are worth quoting in full:

---

31. The rhetorical impact of the vacillation of the disciples and their struggles to follow Jesus is explained by Marshall. "Knowing that his audience would naturally identify with the disciples, and wishing to challenge them with the full demands and reality of Christian discipleship, Mark depicts following Jesus as a constant dialectic between success and failure." In Marshall, *Faith as a Theme in Mark's Narrative*, 211.

32. Danove, *Rhetoric of Characterization*, 126.

> For what does it profit a man to gain the whole world and forfeit his soul? For what can a man give in return for his soul? For whoever is ashamed of me and of my words in this adulterous and sinful generation, of him will the Son of Man also be ashamed when he comes in the glory of his Father with the holy angels. (Mark 8:36–37; ESV)

The argument that Jesus makes, quiet clearly, is that to be in allegiance to Jesus means being in opposition to this "adulterous and sinful generation." In fact, "gaining the world" means standing in opposition to Jesus or, rather, to have Jesus standing in opposition to them ("of him will the Son of Man be ashamed"; 8:28).

The second "pillar"[33] occurs shortly after Jesus' teaching on discipleship (8:34–38). Here again there are a number of commonalities with the baptism and crucifixion. There is the mention of "Elijah" (9:4), cosmic events in the heavens (9:7), and a voice that declares from heaven that Jesus is the "Son" (9:7). But before examining the second christological marker, it is worth reviewing the narrative flow from 1:1 to 9:2. Mark's incipit sets the stage. He reveals to the reader that Jesus is "Christ, Son of God" (1:1). This revelation is one that is given to the reader alone, and not to the characters in the story. In fact, this privileged information is not given to the human characters in the story at the baptismal scene. Mark has the scene being one where God addresses Jesus and in which the reader is given access. Throughout 1:1–11, the narrator does significant work to recruit the implied reader to his vantage point—to view Jesus as he does. He does this through scriptural allusions and citations from the Old Testament, having John the Baptist point forward and revere Jesus, and in casting the baptismal scene as one in which God, from heaven, further enforces the point of view that the omniscient narrator is propagating. As the narrative unfolds, the themes of allegiance, opposition, and misunderstanding slowly begin to develop. To have allegiance is understood to believe and act out in accordance with the point of view of the narrator. To be in opposition is to work against the narrator and, in extension, Jesus and God since they are in agreement with the author. The theme of misunderstanding is understood to be, simply stated, an incomplete or partially correct (or partially wrong) approximation of Jesus. It is demonstrated that, to operate out of the basis of misunderstanding, may mean siding with the opposition, as is the case with the rebuke of Peter in 8:33. Part of the narrative analysis demonstrated that the initial pillar, the baptismal scene, is the essential foundation for accepting the narrator's viewpoint as the authoritative and absolute view.

---

33. Myers, *Binding the Strong Man*, 390–91.

After all, if God himself agrees with what the narrator has communicated, how can he be wrong?

Now, the focus is cast on the second "pillar" in Mark, the transfiguration. Here, Jesus takes with him to the "mountain" the inner circle of his disciples. He takes with him those who are supposed to be in allegiance to him. While on the mountain, he is transfigured and a number of cosmic events ensue. Again, Elijah is mentioned, along with a supernatural event in the heavens ("clouds"), and a voice from heaven proclaims, "This is my beloved Son; listen to him" (9:7). In this scene, the character of God affirms to the reader what was revealed in Mark 1:1, and this is the second time that he does so. Allegiance, as a theme, is presented here in a number of ways. First of all, the presence and acquiescence of Elijah and Moses demonstrate that Jesus stands in agreement and in the tradition of the most revered characters in the Old Testament. Second, as was mentioned, God himself breaks in and authoritatively commends the authority of his Son to the disciples and the reader (9:7). The entire account is rich in eschatological and cosmic implications. It stands as one of the three most significant christological points in the narrative. Mark uses the words of God from heaven to only solidify and reinforce the point of view being set forward, but also to increase the authority of Jesus since God, himself, requires that the disciple (and reader) listen to Jesus (9:7).

Although Mark reserves the motif of opposition in the account of the transfiguration, the theme of misunderstanding does present itself. It can be seen in Peter's words and in Mark's editorial clarification that the motive behind Peter's question about building tents was, "For he did not know what to say, for they were terrified." This does not function as an outright rebuke like 8:33 did, but still is used my Mark to draw attention to the motif of misunderstanding once again, specifically the disciples.

After this second pillar of revelation, Jesus heals a boy with an unclean spirit (9:14–29). Jesus' unique authority and power are on display here since even the disciples could not cast this particular spirit out. Yet, in the wake of Jesus' act demonstrating unique power he turns to his disciples as they passed through Galilee and predicted, for the second time, that he would be betrayed, killed and raised (9:30, 31). This is the second time that Jesus has spoken about his death. For the reader, who has learned that to try to prevent Jesus from this course of action (or inaction) of being killed places one squarely in opposition to Jesus and in allegiance with Satan (8:33). This second instance gives room for pause. In response to this confusing plot development, the reader likely shares the viewpoint of the disciples: "they did not understand the saying, and were afraid to ask him" (9:32). At this point in the narrative, direct opposition has come from the religious leaders, demons, and, by way of editorial aside, Judas Iscariot. It is understood that, in some manner, these parties will conspire and will be involved in the event.

The motif of misunderstanding appears in a number of instances in the next few chapters. In 10:14 Jesus rebukes his disciples because they do not understand the value and place of the children. Again, in 10:17-31, Jesus interacts with the wealthy man who asks about "eternal life." After this, Jesus explains to his disciples that those who have wealth find it hard to enter the "kingdom of God" (10:23). The point being made is that to be in allegiance to Jesus and act out of that reality conflicts with ambition, greed, and injustice. This component of Jesus' teaching is also found in 9:33-37, 42-49; 10:32, 35-45.

After the interaction with the wealthy man, Jesus predicts his death for the third time. The third prediction is the most explicit and has the most details (10:32-34). In this instance, the motif of misunderstanding is not found after Jesus' statement, but before (10:32). Additionally, it occurs "going up to Jerusalem," and Jesus explains his death will occur in Jerusalem. In this final prediction, Mark does not present the disciple's opinion of the evaluation of Jesus' death or their response to the notion that Jesus will die. Jesus simply offers the prediction and it is followed by silence. It is as if Mark is giving a pause for the reader to develop and formulate their own response to this revelation. The implicit question may be: What motif will the reader adopt in response to Jesus' coming death? Will they act in opposition and misunderstanding and, like Peter, try to protest? Or will they "set their minds on things of God" (8:33)?

What Mark has done is build the case that the response to Jesus' death indicates where one stands on the spectrum of allegiance and opposition. Peter resisted the idea that Jesus would die, and was strongly rebuked (8:33), the disciples were afraid and "do not understand" (9:32). The question hangs, how will the implied reader respond? With allegiance or with opposition?

As the narrative progresses, the opposition continues to grow and become more public and visible. In 11:15-19 Jesus is presented as standing in opposition to the temple and, by extension, the religious leaders. The result of this is that "the chief priests and the scribes heard it and were seeking for a way to destroy him" (11:18). A few sentences later, in 11:27-33, the chief priests and scribes come to Jesus and ask directly, "By what authority are you doing these things?" (11:28). The reader, who has been following the narrative, understands what the religious leaders do not; Jesus' authority comes from his being the Son of God. After all, God from heaven decrees that the characters are to "listen to him" (9:7).

In the parable of the tenants, as was examined in chapter 4, the implications are significant: the religious leaders of Mark 11:27, are the wicked tenants; the "son" that is sent is Jesus; and the landowner is God. The motif of opposition is applied here to the religious leaders again and, in this instance, they are seen to be in opposition to, not only Jesus (since they kill the son), but also to God (the landowner). The result of opposition to Jesus and God is "destruction" (Mark 12:9). Jesus "destroys" demons (Mark 1:24); the Pharisees want to "destroy" Jesus (Mark 3:6; 11:18); the demonic forces attempt to "destroy" humanity (9:22); and yet, the landowner will "destroy" the evil tenants. The point made here is that to stand in opposition to Jesus means standing in opposition to God, which has dire consequences.

Immediately following this parable, the Pharisees and Herodians come and attempt to trap Jesus (12:13–17). In this episode, Mark's ability as a storyteller is especially pronounced. Each line is rich with literary dynamics, which lead the reader to a specific point—being the same point perceived by the characters in the account. This approach of creating opportunities for his reader to experience the same feelings and emotions as the characters in the story is one which he will return to again. The account begins with the perspective of the omniscient narrator being used to create tension and give the reader ample reason to resist the words and actions of the Pharisees and Herodians: "And they sent to him some of the Pharisees and some of the Herodians, to trap him in his talk" (12:13; ESV). The "they" of 12:13 are the religious leader about whom Jesus told the parable in 12:1–12. Here, Mark gives privileged information about the motives and intents of the group. By beginning this episode in such a way, he casts every word and every action that these characters take from here on out in a negative light. This is not new. The groups referred to as the Pharisees have been negatively portrayed by Mark in the parable (12:1–12), but lest the reader think that this is an outlier of sorts, he introduces the motives of these individuals to color everything they do in the account. The reader knows they are here to trap Jesus. What follows, then, is especially ironic since the words of the Pharisees and their actions are not in accordance. Resseguie notes, "Irony's effectiveness relies on exploitation of the distance between words and events and their contexts."[34] The irony is not apparent to the characters in the story, only to the reader. Although their question to Jesus is presented in respectful terms and sounds earnest, the reader knows the true intention of the Pharisees. The ruse is ridiculous to the reader, and, to the character Jesus. In 12:15 the omniscient narrator notes that Jesus "knew" their hypocrisy. Mark creates a solidarity and identity with Jesus by allowing him to manifest the response that the reader has to face. Just as the reader is aware of the deep hypocrisy of the Pharisees' words because of Mark's editorial insertion about

---

34. Resseguie, *Narrative Criticism of the New Testament*, 67.

motives and intents, so too does the character Jesus in Mark's account. The reader, then, is especially satisfied when the religious leaders are stumped by Jesus' brilliant response. The characters in the account "marvel" at Jesus' response (12:17). This is the same response Mark is leading his readers to have in response to the episode.

The motif of opposition is presented here again. Mark makes a point to demonstrate that it is not the words that a person or group speaks that indicates their allegiance or opposition to Jesus, it is their intentions and motives. For example, the Pharisees and Herodians call him, "Teacher," and one who "teaches the way of God" (12:14), yet their motives are to "destroy him" (3:6). The theme of allegiance is present only so far as it is the opposite of what is occurring. The point is that to be in allegiance to Jesus entails not only "saying" the right things about Jesus, but also having the right motives and intentions towards him.

The ruse continues in the account that follows (12:18–27). Instead of the Pharisees and Herodians, it is the Sadducees that approach Jesus in this instance. The events that transpire in this account are similar to one that preceded it. Mark gives the reader privileged information here again. He tells his audience, not about the intentions of the characters as he did with the Pharisees and Herodians (12:12–17), but, instead, tells his readers about the beliefs of the group antagonizing Jesus. He mentions that the Sadducees "say that there is not resurrection" (12:18). After an elaborate and complex question by the Sadducees about marriage, remarriage, death, and resurrection, Jesus responds,

> Is this not the reason you are wrong, because you know neither the Scriptures nor the power of God? For when they rise from the dead, they neither marry nor are given in marriage, but are like angels in heaven. And as for the dead being raised, have you not read in the book of Moses, in the passage about the bush, how God spoke to him, saying, "I am the God of Abraham, and the God of Isaac, and the God of Jacob"? He is not God of the dead, but of the living. You are quite wrong. (Mark 12:24–27; ESV)

Especially interesting to the reader are the words of 12:26–27. Jesus explains that the dead are raised because of scriptural precedence and common sense (God is the God of the living). This is a relief to the anxious reader because, at this point, three times Jesus has predicted his death and his "being raised" (8:31; 9:30–32; 10:32–34). Thus, it is comforting to know that, in spite of what Jesus seems confident will occur in Jerusalem, his claim that he will "rise again" has some manner of Old Testament precedence. In this instance, opposition to Jesus takes the form of a ruse, but also includes believing wrongly about God, the Scriptures, and Jesus being "raised."

An interesting break with the opposition motif is found in the next encounter. In rapid succession, these encounters come at the reader. First, the Pharisees and Herodians, then the Sadducees, next, it is a scribe who comes to Jesus to ask questions. This encounter takes a different route than the others. In this account (12:28–34), no motivation or intent is given for the scribe's encounter with Jesus. All the reader is told is that the scribe notices how well Jesus had answered the others and, so, decides to ask his own. The question, "what is the greatest commandment?" is one which Jesus answers from Old Testament Scripture (12:29–31). The scribe rephrases Jesus' answer back to him and captures the essence and point that Jesus is making. Mark records: "And when Jesus saw that he answered wisely, he said to him, 'You are not far from the kingdom of God.' And after that no one dared to ask him any more questions" (12:34). Up until this point in Mark's narrative, the group known as the "scribes" have been presented in quite a negative light (i.e., 2:6, 16; 3:22; 7:1, 5). Additionally, in the predictions of his death in Mark 8:31 and 10:33, the reader is told that the scribes would have a hand in Jesus' death. In this instance, where a scribe comes and, in some sense, is responded to positively by Jesus and given credit for his "wise" answer, the motif of opposition is altered, for a time. The theme is altered by Mark and demonstrates, among other things, that one can respond positively to Jesus even if one finds themselves as a member of a group that, generally speaking, opposes Jesus. The lack of insight into this character's thinking and emotions heightens the tension of the scene. The reader expects, no doubt, another confrontation, but is presented with something else: an ambiguous encounter which leaves the door open for one to respond positively to Jesus if they are an outside or against him[35] In this account, it is worth noting that allegiance is again understood to be acting and interacting with Jesus in agreement with who he claims he is, and how Mark presents him. The scribe's words, "You are right, Teacher," capture the spirit of this theme

---

35. See Myers's comments: "Mark carefully constructs this encounter around ambiguity. One the one hand, we expect a conflict story, for the antagonist is one of the scribal archopponents. We assume—based on the previous stories—that his flattery of Jesus ('Well done, teacher, you have answered forthrightly!' 12:32, see 12:14) must be insincere." Myers, *Binding the Strong Man*, 317.

(12:32). This will be seen to be the case throughout Mark and especially in 15:39.

Just as in 12:13–17, the narrator shows his readers that it is the inner thoughts and motives, and not the words or even actions, that one demonstrates that shows if one is in allegiance to Jesus, the character Jesus says the same in 12:38–40. Here, instead of the omniscient narrator doing the work to cast the Pharisees in opposition, it is Jesus, himself, who does so. Jesus tells the people to "Beware of the scribes, who like to walk around in long robes and like greetings in the marketplace" (12:39). Jesus gives the characters in the story (whose names are not defined) and, by extension, the readers, a glimpse into the thinking and heart of the religious leaders. These individuals, Jesus says, can be found in synagogues and places of honor at religious feasts, associate with the needy (widows) and are involved in long prayers; yet, they do it "for pretense" (12:39, 40). Here again, Jesus explains that the question of allegiance or opposition (to be in accordance with God's point of view or not) is not a matter of outward actions, but an inner consistency in which one's beliefs about God (and Jesus) and one's actions measure up. The cost of being found in the place of opposition to Jesus is explained as being in the place of "greater condemnation" (12:40). In this encounter, the character Jesus, enforces what the author, Mark has been leading his reader to see and adopt.

After a series of encounters where an individual's words and actions are not in accordance, Mark presents, through Jesus' lips, a character who is consistent. In 12:41–44 a widow gives two small copper coins. In so doing, Jesus explains, she gave everything she had to live on. Here, again, the question about one's standing in relation to Jesus, and the assessment that Mark implicitly offers about individuals, is not a matter of actions or words, but inner intent and matters of the heart. After all, it is not the issue of giving that sets the woman apart, because "many rich people put in large sums," but it was the humble act by the widow that gained recognition by Jesus.

The eschatological discourse in Mark 13 is the longest unbroken teaching from Jesus in the narrative. A detailed exegetical analysis of the chapter in its entirety is not possible at this point, but the importance for the study at hand are the two verses that begin the chapter. When they are in Jerusalem, the disciples turn to Jesus and remark about the stones in the temple building. The relationship between Jesus and the temple in Mark has been hotly debated.[36] Two particular authors, Sanders and Crossan, argue that the Jesus' interaction with the temple should be described as a symbolic act signifying destruction.[37] Most scholars, however, see the issue of cleansing as the core of Jesus' interaction.[38] In 13:2 Jesus responds to the disciple's comment about the temple with some cryptic words about the temple's destruction. Whether the view that "cleansing," in some sense, is implied, or that Jesus and the temple relate, primarily, around the theme of destruction, what can be seen in this passage is that Jesus stands in opposition to the temple. Just as in 11:15, the temple is functioning as a reality that Jesus views negatively.

In the next series of events, which occur in Jerusalem in the lead up to the Passover, Mark's use of contrast and irony are on display.[39] The first few lines in Mark 14 give a significant temporal marker that comes into play later in the narrative. Shortly before the "Passover" and the "Feast of Unleavened Bread," the chief priests and the scribes are seen plotting how to kill Jesus in such a manner that does not draw attention. Mark records in Mark 14:1 that they are seeking to kill him by "stealth" (δόλῳ). These underhanded intentions are realized shortly when Judas, one of the Twelve, agrees to betray Jesus. Mark notes (14:1) that the chief priests and the scribes are "seeking" (ἐζήτουν) to kill Jesus.[40]

As noted, the sequence of events is used by Mark to contrast the actions of individuals and their relationship to Jesus. First, Mark opens this section with the reality that the religious leaders are plotting to kill Jesus (14:1–2). Next, Jesus enters the house of Simon the leper and, as he is there, a woman enters and pours perfume on Jesus. This act is explained by Jesus as "anointing him" for his burial (14:3–6). In this passage, a contrast is presented between Jesus and Judas, and the Religious leaders and the unnamed

36. For a helpful assessment and overview of ten interpretations of Jesus' interaction with the temple, see Van Eck, *Galilee and Jerusalem*, 345–54.

37. Sanders, *Jesus and Judaism*, 74–77; Crossan, *Historical Jesus*, 357.

38. Van Eck, *Galilee and Jerusalem*, 347.

39. Some of the analysis and evaluation of Mark 14 is taken from MacDonald, "Characterization of a False Disciple."

40. The literarily significant manner in which Mark uses this word throughout his narrative is noted by Danove, *Rhetoric of Characterization*, 9–10. Danove argues that the word is used to negatively assess individuals in the story. For example, in 3:32; 8:11, 12; 11:18; 12:12; 14:1, 55 "seek" is used to negatively characterize individuals. The Pharisees and religious leaders are "seeking" to kill Jesus, and an evil generation "seeks" a sign. It is only in Mark 16:6 that the pattern is broken and it is used positively.

woman. In Mark's Gospel, the woman remains unnamed. This is important to the reader because it demonstrates that she is not a member of an elite social or religious group, but, rather simply, an unnamed disciple. Jesus calls her deed "a beautiful thing" (14:6). This woman, who has, so far as the reader is concerned, no past relationship or standing with Jesus comes and does an act that is deemed beautiful. The note about the financial cost of the perfume is also not without consequence. In her act, the nature of her actions, and her interaction with Jesus, she is presented as a contrast to Judas. Where she gives up financial gain to demonstrate her allegiance to Jesus, Judas demonstrates his opposition for monetary gain (14:11).

In contrast to the unnamed woman, Judas is one of the privileged "Twelve." The reader, at this point, is already aware that Judas is responsible for betraying Jesus (3:19). In fact, in Mark's Gospel, Judas is called the "betrayer" more than he is called "Judas."[41] While Judas enjoys a place of prominence, intimacy, and privilege, the woman in Bethany is, essentially, in the narrative world, a "nobody." Yet, despite Judas' advantageous place in relation to Jesus, he is seen as being in complete opposition to him. Later, when Jesus is talking about the soon to come betrayal, he says that, for the one who does this act of betrayal, it would "be better for that man if he had not been born" (14:21). Jesus is saying that existence, condemnation, and even the memory of this man is a negative thing. Contrast this with the unnamed woman, who will be remembered for all future generations (14:9). Judas, on the other hand, after his act of betrayal in the garden (14:45), disappears from the narrative world of Mark. For him, it is as if "he had never been born." The contrast can be tabled,

   A) Jesus reclining at a meal (14:3)

      B) Woman, in humility, gives gift of great value (14:3b)

         C) Jesus: "This act of hers will always be remembered" (14:9)

            D) Judas, out of selfishness, betrays for money (14:10, 11)

   A) Jesus reclining at a meal (14:18)

      B) Jesus, in humility, gives gift of great value (14:22–25)

         C) Jesus: "Better for this man to have never been born" (14:21)[42]

Judas, as a character in Mark's story, epitomizes all that the motif of opposition is about. Opposition can occur through outright conflict and aggression (as is the case, predominantly, with Jesus' interactions with the Pharisees), or, as has been demonstrated, it can occur when one's words

   41. MacDonald, "Characterization of a False Disciple," 123.
   42. Ibid., 127.

and actions do not align with the inner motives and intent towards Jesus. Judas is the extreme example of the latter. In his interaction with Jesus in the garden as he is betraying Jesus, this distinction is especially pronounced. He comes to Jesus and uses respectful language and gestures. He calls Jesus "Rabbi" and gives him a "kiss" (14:45). This act typifies all that Judas represents in the narrative. Symbols of honor are used to capture and dishonor Jesus. The irony in this scene is reminiscent of the irony in 12:13-17. The narrator makes use of his privileged position to reveal to the reader certain information about the intentions towards Jesus. Mark has done this with Judas in significant ways. From the first mention of Judas, (3:19) to the last, 14:44, Judas is presented as the "betrayer." The reader is able to see the gap in meaning between Judas' words and actions ("Rabbi," and a kiss) and his murderous intentions. This reaffirms the argument that, to be in allegiance to Jesus, means more than just not doing certain outright acts of defiance or betrayal. It means being consistent in actions, words, and intentions towards Jesus. Here, Judas says and does the "right" things, but his intentions demonstrate which side he is on.

The motif of misunderstanding appears only in passing in these passages. In 14:26-31 Jesus foretells Peter's denial. The theme of misunderstanding is present here in relation to Jesus' persona agenda of dying and being raised. After three instances in which Jesus tells his disciples about his death and his being raised to life, Peter is still unable to understand the cosmic plan that is afoot. Jesus anchors the truth that he will be abandoned in Old Testament Scripture: "strike the shepherd and the sheep will scatter" (14:27). Peter argues that this will not be the case and that he will never deny Jesus. In this encounter, a level of misunderstanding can be noticed in Peter's failure to appropriately respond to Jesus' claims. Peter is cast in this light, and the reader waits for the time when such will come to pass. This assessment of Peter (and James and John) is also found in the garden at Gethsemane. In this instance, the disciples seem unable to grasp the significance of this time for Jesus and, so, are presented as falling asleep a number of times (14:37-42).

Allegiance, Opposition, and Misunderstanding Reach Their Pinnacle (Mark 14:43—15:41)

After being arrested, Jesus is brought before the council and interrogated (14:53-65). In this encounter, the theme of opposition that climaxed in the evil actions of Judas continues to maintain a high degree of importance in the narrative. Here is Jesus, whom the reader knows is the Son of God and who stands as the eschatological hope of the Old Testament. He is in Jerusalem, surrounded by the religious leaders of the day. They, as a group, confront him openly and directly. Yet, in doing so, they are not interested in the truth, which as has been noted, for Mark, is more significant than actions or words. The author tells the reader that the chief priests, elders, and scribes are seeking to find testimony against Jesus, and go so far as to allow "false witnesses" to be counted (14:56). As was the case in 12:13–27, the interactions that the leaders have with Jesus are a farce. Here, they are not interested in questioning Jesus to find the truth (cf. "scribe" in 12:28–34); they are here to condemn him. Eventually, Jesus is asked directly if he is the "Son of the Blessed" (14:61). He answers in the affirmative and they charge him with "blasphemy" (14:64). What is ironic in this instance is that the truth about Jesus' divine sonship is finally revealed to a character in the story and, when faced with responding to this truth with either allegiance or opposition, the religious leaders embrace outright opposition. Jesus is then shamefully treated, but, he is treated this way only after the condemnation is given by the characters. In protecting this sequence, we see that the characters are acting consistently with their beliefs about Jesus. They are consistently acting and believing in opposition to Jesus. In 14:65 Jesus is beaten and the soldiers call out for him to "prophesy" who is hitting him. Even this is ironic since Jesus, in Mark's Gospel, consistently predicts events and knows people intimately. What was one of the greatest demonstrations of Jesus' power and authority is, here, used as a form of mockery.

Next, Mark records that the words of Jesus in 14:26–31 are fulfilled; Peter denies Jesus (14:66–72). The development of Peter as a character in Mark's narrative world is something into which Mark invests a significant amount of energy. Peter is named first in the calling of the Twelve (3:19), and is singled out along with James and John as participants in Jesus' inner circle (5:37). Both of these demonstrate that Peter is functioning individually, as a character's adopting of the allegiance motif, yet, as a member of the Twelve, he also is closely aligned with the motif of misunderstanding. As was examined, Peter's words in 8:27, and his response to Jesus' prediction of his death, indicate that he is, after all of his privileged access and opportunity, actually firmly in line with those who misunderstand the true identity of Jesus. This misunderstanding leads to acting in opposition to the agenda of Jesus. Mark has shown the reader that one can fail to understand who Jesus is, and, yet, even though the individual does not exhibit outright animosity, they are still functioning out of a perspective of opposition. In commenting on this scene, Malbon remarks:

> Not everyone is able to be a follower. And no followers, whether disciples or the crowd, find following easy. There is a profound irony in Peter's following (14:54, *akoloutheō*) Jesus at a distance into the courtyard of the high priest, for while the house of the high priest is the scene of Jesus' trial, the courtyard is the scene of Peter's denial.[43]

Discipleship is hard, even for those on the "inside." Yet, in 14:66–72, Mark introduces a redemptive element into the misunderstanding motif. Peter acts in opposition to Jesus by denying him, but his response to his actions is one of sorrow, and all hope is not lost for Peter. Later, in 16:7, Peter is mentioned by the man in the white robe at Jesus' tomb. While both Peter and Judas act in opposition, the reader sees that Peter, although he was operating primarily out of misunderstanding, is eventually, in some sense, "restored," or in the least, given hope for such a reversal. The final word on the character, Peter, is hope. Judas, on the other hand, does not appear in the narrative again. Jesus' damning words, about it being better for Judas to "never have been born," rings out and is conclusive. The final word on Judas is one of judgment. All this is used by Mark to show that the intents and motives towards Jesus are the primary reality that matter. One can act in opposition, but still be given hope if a change occurs. At the same time, one can act in allegiance, yet, in their motives and inner dialogue, be adversaries to Jesus.

Crucifixion Scene (Mark 15:1—16:8)

The situation for the protagonist of Mark's narrative continues to decline. Jesus is brought before Pilot, tried, and delivered to be crucified. In this sequence of events, Pilot embraces the role of one who misunderstands Jesus, and to begin with, is not entirely antagonist to Jesus, yet, by embracing his misunderstanding, he inevitably begins functioning as one who opposes Jesus. Pilot, Mark writes, knew what the intentions of the religious leaders were, that they were doing these things out of "envy" (15:10). Mark even goes so far as to express that Pilot was not entirely sure what the transgression was that Jesus actually committed (15:13: "Why, what evil has he done?"). In the end, he acquiesces and, in a desire to satisfy the crowds, goes over to the realm of opposition and sentences Jesus to death.

In 13—15:18 the narrator casts the religious establishment in Israel as acting in direct opposition to Jesus. In 15:16-20 the Roman authorities are casted as in opposition to Jesus. Up until this point, the Roman officials,

---

43. Malbon, *In the Company of Jesus*, 78.

delegates, and population have not played a significant role in the narrative. They have not been framed as entirely in allegiance or opposition. Unlike Jesus' interactions with the scribes and religious leaders, which, without a doubt, have some ambiguity and some positive points, Roman officials are given little attention. In 15:16–20 the soldiers lead Jesus away, cloth him in purple, twist a crown made of thorns and place it on his head, and begin to mock him. The level of opposition, which at this point has reached fevered pitch, is startling to the reader. Next, Mark tells the reader that after taking Jesus out, they bring him to Golgotha and crucify him.

At this definitive destination, the narrative world that Mark has created is rife with tension. What began as "the good news about Jesus Christ, God's Son" has now led to the point where that same Son of God is being executed. He is alone, abandoned, shamed, and hanging on a cross. The expectation of the triumph of the Son of God has been squelched, and those advocating for opposition seem to be gaining the upper hand. While on the cross, the two robbers and people passing by continue the mocking begun earlier. One of the criticisms that is leveled at Jesus, is that he stood in opposition to the temple, even claiming that he would "destroy it," and, yet, seems unable to save himself from his situation (15:29). The mocking continues, this time coming from the chief priests and leaders (15:30). Eventually, at the "ninth hour" (15:34), Jesus calls out, is offered wine, expires and breathes his last breath (15:37).

For the reader, who is puzzling out how Jesus' death can be hailed as the "good news," a series of significant events occur in the wake of Jesus' death. First of all, the curtain veil is torn. Second, a centurion who is standing near the cross, sees Jesus die and exclaims that "this truly was the Son of God" (15:39).[44]

The reader recognizes that this is the first time in the Gospel of Mark that any human character has vocalized the truth that Jesus is the Son of God. It has been argued that, in Mark, the theme of misunderstanding is not primarily about Jesus' Messianic identity, but rather, it is about his divine sonship. This is the one reality that the characters in the story are unable to grasp in full. It has been affirmed by the narrator (1:1; 3:11), admitted by the evil spiritual forces (1:24; 5:7), decreed by God (1:11; 9:7), hinted at by Jesus (12:1–12; 13:32; 14:46), and, finally, is now recognized by a very unlikely human character—a Roman centurion.

This is the third and final "pillar" in Mark's narrative.[45] Just as both the baptism and transfiguration featured cosmic events, the mention of Elijah,

---

44. The significance of the veil being torn was reviewed in chapter 4.
45. Myers, *Binding the Strong Man*, 391.

something happening in the heavens, and the reference to Jesus as the Son, so does this event. It has been argued that the theme of misunderstanding in Mark's Gospel relates more to Jesus' divine sonship than it does his Messiahship. Secondly, it has been argued that the motif of secrecy or misunderstanding functions along a revelatory context. Assuming these two points are convincingly demonstrated, it must be noted that in Mark 15:39, the secret, so to speak, is finally out and it is revealed that Jesus the Son of God.

The Rhetoric of Defamiliarization

The narratival impact of having a highly unlikely individual agree with the narrator (and God) that Jesus is God's Son is significant. But how do the themes of opposition, allegiance, and misunderstanding relate to the centurion's confession? How do these motifs come into play at this christological and narratively important scene?

As was discussed in chapter 4, the words that the centurion said can be taken a number of ways. What the historical character actually said, and, more importantly, what he meant by his words, are not the questions that are under investigation. Rather, what Mark intended his audience to think and believe is in view. How Mark anticipated his reader would understand the centurion's words is the issue at hand. To answer that, one must examine the way in which the allegiance theme comes to a climax in the centurion's word.

To begin with, the theme of allegiance is present in this account and in many ways reaches its climax. The centurion stands at the scene of ultimate opposition to Jesus. He, representing the authorities, oversees a brutal act of injustice. Yet, in one quick moment, Mark recasts the centurion from one who oppose Jesus to one who offers allegiance. Regardless of what the centurion means by his words, Mark uses him to demonstrate some significant truths about what it means to act in allegiance to Jesus. The reader remembers Jesus rebukes Peter for his failure to understand the theological significance of his coming death and for trying to circumvent its occurring. Here, on the other hand, a character stands directly in front of the event that causes Peter so much consternation, and, yet, is able to see clearly who Jesus is. One who epitomizes opposition "converts" to one who aligns his evaluation of Jesus with what the narrator has espoused as the correct view.

The centurion offers his assessment of Jesus when, according to Mark, he "saw that in this way he breathed his last" (15:39). The spatial marker is significant. It is not Jesus' teaching in the synagogue, nor his healing in the towns and cities that changes the centurion's perspective. It is the manner in which he expires on the cross. In this transformation of perspective, Mark has taken the centurion from a "stock" character to a "round" one. Mark has taken a faceless nameless character who, by the nature of his employment, stands in opposition, and moved him to align his thinking to the "right side." This is exactly what Peter failed to do.

Additionally, the centurion is a member of a character group in Mark; he is a Roman soldier. Soldiers appeared early in the narrative in 15:16–20. As a minor character group, they function as adversaries to Jesus. The more significant character group, the disciples, is not the one that ultimately arrives at the understanding about Jesus' true identity, though they come close. It is a member of the Roman army. Out of the minor antagonist character group of the soldiers, a character emerges who sees spiritual reality in a clear way. The narrator presents an "unlikely convert." As was discussed in chapter 4, some have argued that the reader of Mark would not be able to handle a Roman centurion acting in such a way or saying such a thing. That, however, is exactly the point that Mark is making. Further, it was the truth hinted at in all of Mark's characterization of outsiders who exhibits some manner of positive interactions with Jesus.

For example, it is not only the centurion who moves from outsider to insider in Mark. There are other examples of this. In 7:24–29 Jesus heals the daughter of a Syrophoenician woman. He questions her, and Jesus takes her response as correct; and, so she, an outsider to ethnic Israel, is welcomed into Jesus' ministry of healing and hope. In 9:28–41 an unknown exorcist, who is unnamed and lacking a back-story, is taken from an outsider (in the disciple's perspective) to an insider (by virtue of his being "for us"). Likewise, in Mark, a number of people are expected to be on the "inside" act in direct opposition to Jesus and, thus, isolate themselves from alignment with Jesus. Furthermore, Jesus himself functions as an outsider in Mark. He is confronted and opposed by the authorities of both Jerusalem and Rome.[46] Van Eck understands Mark as presenting three competing kingdoms: Rome, temple elite, and God's.[47] He explains that while two of these kingdoms were clear in what types of people were "outsiders," God's kingdom enacted in Christ as patron, proclaiming the one gospel, is marked by the acceptance

---

46. Jesus as outsider in Mark is explained by Kingsbury, *Conflict in Mark*, 56.
47. Van Eck, "Mission, Identity and Ethics in Mark," 6.

of the outsider to the level on kinship.[48] His case is convincing and captures well the openness of the new kingdom made visible by Jesus. Here then, in a centurion, an outsider (to the implied reader) moves to become an insider.

The crucifixion scene is also rather ironic. On one hand, Mark presents the religious leaders who stand before Jesus and directly question him. Even though they have unfettered access to Jesus and ask him outright about his identity (14:53–64), they are unable to see the truth. On the other hand, Mark presents the centurion, who simply sees the manner in which Jesus expires and responds by affirming the central christological epithet that Mark is advocating. What every human character and character group fail to perceive in Mark, a Roman solider finally understands. Additionally, where Peter declares, "I do not know *this man* of whom you speak" (14:71) the centurion declares, "Truly, *this man* was God's Son" (15:39). Discipleship is difficult, but loyalty must play a central role.[49]

What then, is the effect of all this? How does the narrative structure of the book and the themes of opposition, allegiance, and misunderstanding develop, morph, and grow and then climax at the scene in 15:21–39? Resseguie argues that one of the ways in which this plays itself out in a narrative can be determined is by examining the process of defamiliarization in a given text.[50] Resseguie points to the work by Wolfgang Iser in which he explains the two terms, "defamiliarization" and "estrangement."[51] Elsewhere, Iser explains,

> This process is steered by two main structural components within the text: first, a repertoire of familiar literary patterns and recurrent literary themes, together with allusions to familiar social and historical contexts; second, techniques or strategies used to set the familiar against the unfamiliar. . . . This defamiliarization of what the reader thought he recognized is bound to create a tension that will intensify his expectations as well as his distrust of those expectations.[52]

Defamiliarization occurs when the normal, anticipated, and expected does not take place, but, instead, something startling occurs that was not what the reader foresaw would take place. This occurs frequently in the New Testament. The privileged, powerful, and religious leaders are often seen to be at odds with God's point of view; while the outsiders, children, women,

48. Ibid., 8.
49. Van Eck, "Mission, Identity and Ethics in Mark," 7.
50. Resseguie, *Narrative Criticism of the New Testament*, 33–35.
51. Ibid., 33, n. 41.
52. Iser, *Act of Reading*, 65.

Gentiles, sinners, and the unclean are cast favorably, and affirmed, in some sense, by the reader. How then does defamiliarization occur in this passage? Mark shapes his narrative in one direction, and then introduces an outlier, something unexpected. It can be expressed this way, as Mark presents a negative direction in his narrative flow:

1. The spatial setting is one of shame and rejection
2. Jesus is rejected by religious leaders and his own disciples
3. Jesus is physically and verbally abused
4. The Roman soldiers are complicit and malicious in the abuse
5. Crowd and passers-by mock and deride Jesus
6. Jesus is misunderstood by those standing by
7. Jesus dies

Then, in response to all this, what the readers finds is not a continuation of the pattern, but a startling reversal. Following all of this, a centurion correctly identifies Jesus as the Son of God. Resseguie explains the use of defamiliarization in narrative:

> Defamiliarization works best when textual disruptions cause the reader to slow down and take notice, or when norms and value firmly held by an implied audience are developed and then dashed.[53]

Resseguie then goes on to quote George Young who explains defamiliarization as "the point of commonality between the first century reader and the twentieth century reader."[54] Applying this point means acknowledging that the words of the centurion are as startling for the implied reader as it is for the modern reader. This is demonstrated anecdotally by the amount of literature that the centurion's words have garnered in recent academic research.

Mark also provides, at first, indication of the nature of the words that the passers-by and roman soldiers are saying, but, in the account of the centurion, little information is given about motives or intentions. For example, in 15:20, the reader is told that the soldiers are mocking Jesus—that their words are intended not as proclamations of allegiance. Again, in 15:29, "Those who passed by hurled insults at him" (ἐβλασφήμουν). The chief priests are said to be "mocking" Jesus with their words, as are those

---

53. Resseguie, *Narrative Criticism of the New Testament*, 38.
54. Young, *Subversive Symmetry*, 37; Resseguie, *Narrative Criticism of the New Testament*, 38.

who were crucified with him. In these instances, the author gives insight into the motivation behind the words. For the centurion in 15:39, the author does not provide this information. It is left ambiguous. In fact, almost every word or line spoken by a character in the Passion narrative can "hardly be trusted."[55] So, what, then, is the motivation behind the manner in which the narrator cast the centurion and his words? The centurion's confession is a significant revelatory event in Mark. It is the first and only time that a human character verbalizes what the reader has known all along about Jesus' divine sonship. The twin question is: How does Mark use this event and to what end? What is the author's aim in shaping his narrative in such a way?

First, it would appear that one evident aim of Mark is to demonstrate that discipleship is not reserved for "insiders" only, but, rather, is available to those who align themselves with God's point of view and evaluation of Jesus as the Messiah and Son of God. As has been noted, those who function under the motif of opposition come from all levels of society, and from various religious backgrounds. In contradistinction to this is that those who exhibit allegiance are diverse as well. The way forward in discipleship is open for all and not confined to any one religious or ethnic group, nor is it, as is the case for the centurion, that to be a member of a group that categorically exhibits opposition prevents one from personally identifying with Jesus in allegiance. From a reader response viewpoint, this serves as an insight into just how dramatic a transformation of viewpoint of Jesus one can undergo. If the centurion can change his view, one who belongs to the most hostile groups imaginable to Jesus—a group that functions in outright opposition—then, surely any reader can be afforded the same opportunity. Danove's comments are correct and worth noting since they capture the essence of the narrative invitation:

> Thus, the characterization of the Christ encourages rejection of the authorial audience's erroneous beliefs about both the Son of Man and the Christ and acceptance of the narrative audience's newly cultivated beliefs which alone ensure that one is positively aligned with the parousaic Son of Man, who, coming in/with the clouds (13:26/14:62), will send angels to gather the elect (13:27) and will sit at the right hand of power (14:62).[56]

In addition to this, Marshall in his study on the theme of faith in Mark's Gospel, goes so far as to see the narrator as presenting the centurion as experiencing and exhibiting some form of faith in the work of Christ.[57] This,

---

55. Fowler, *Let the Reader Understand*, 157.
56. Danove, *Rhetoric of Characterization*, 89.
57. Marshall, *Faith as a Theme in Mark's Narrative*, 207.

however, is beyond the scope of the present study. Suffice it to note that in the centurion Mark has presented in broad strokes a pattern of one who embraces the theme of allegiance to the narrator's point of view, which is in essence, allegiance to Jesus. In a similar vein, Collins adds, "Those members of the audience of Mark familiar with the Imperial cult would understand that the centurions recognized Jesus as the true ruler of the world rather than the emperor."[58]

The second manner in which the centurion's character functions in the narrative, is to demonstrate that it is only in Jesus' death that his sonship is clearly understood. When the centurion sees the manner in which Jesus dies, he is then able to articulate the truth that the reader has known from the beginning—that Jesus is God's Son. What is clear to the reader has finally become clear to the characters in the narrative world.[59]

The position, title, and placement of this character and his subsequent transition from opposition to allegiance provide maximum emotional impact for the reader. As was noted in chapter 3, in a number of instances, Roman Caesars were given the epithet "Son of God" and here, one who is loyal to Rome switches allegiance from Caesar to Jesus.

CONCLUSION: OPPOSITION, MISUNDERSTANDING, AND ALLEGIANCE RESOLVED

This chapter has given its attention to an in-depth examination of the narrative contours of Mark. It is built significantly atop the exegetical data presented in chapter 4, which looked at each instance that "Son of God" was mentioned or referred to in the Gospel and assessed them individually. chapter 5, through the themes of opposition, misunderstanding, and allegiance evaluated the narrative Mark presents and demonstrated that these themes reach their climax in the passion narrative. Here, at the moment of Jesus' death, the opposition reaches its great pinnacle—all earth and supernatural forces seem to conspire against and abuse Jesus. Yet, it is also in the scene of opposition that we see one, who by all accounts, ought

---

58. Collins, "Mark and His Readers," 98.

59. That the "Messianic secret" is over at the crucifixion is not unique to this study. It is a dominant interpretation in Markan scholarship. See, for example, Schweizer, *Good News according to Mark*, 355–59; Kelber, *Kingdom in Mark*, 81; Kingsbury, *Christology of Mark's Gospel*, 132–33; Marcus, *Way of the Lord*, 58. For a reappraisal and alternative approach, see Shiner. "The ambiguous pronouncement of the centurion and the shrouding of meaning in Mark," who argues that in the centurion's words the secrecy (or misunderstanding) theme continues because the character misidentifies Jesus with something from his Roman religion.

to have embraced the motif of opposition, switch positions and vocalize what, for the implied reader, amount to the central christological title and the truth that remained hidden from those who followed the motif of misunderstanding. In the centurion's words "Truly this was God's Son" (15:39), the theme of allegiance is explained and the theme of misunderstanding is resolved. Thus, two options for the reader remains: opposition or allegiance to Jesus, the Son of God.

Mark has accomplished all this by creating a coherent testimony about Jesus' identity. The witnesses that he presents culminate in a forceful case that invites the reader to adopt his point of view. The testimonies are:

1. The omniscient narrator (Level 1—as omniscient narrator, he controls the world which he creates).

2. God himself (Level 2—God as God functions as the highest level of authority of any characters in the narrative world).

3. Jesus himself (Level 3—Jesus, as the Son of God, embraces this point of view of his identity).

4. Cosmic evil spiritual forces (Level 4—although evil, these forces undoubtedly possess a high level of spiritual insight and ability. They shrink back in fear and affirm that Jesus is the Son of God).

5. And, finally, the characters in the story (Level 5—the one closest to the death of Jesus, and one who stood in direct opposition, affirms that Jesus truly is the Son of God).

What the omniscient narrator offers in 1:1 (that Jesus is the Son of God), is reinforced by God in 1:11 and 9:7. Kingsbury succinctly notes, "Since God in Mark's story is the supreme ruler of the universe and all history, the reader recognizes that God's understanding of Jesus is normative."[60] The narrator presents Jesus as embracing this as well (12:1–9) and, in addition to Jesus' acceptance of his divine sonship, he seeks Old Testament justification for his actions and authority.[61] The evil spirits reiterate that Jesus is the Son of God (3:11; 5:7), and finally, by a Roman centurion (15:39). With the themes of allegiance, opposition, and misunderstanding, Mark leads his readers to the conclusion that only in Jesus death can he be understood for who he is: the Son of God. But, in addition to doing this sequentially, he also presented his case by demonstrating a progression in the level of authority of his "witnesses." This is the exact reason why hypothetical approaches

---

60. Kingsbury, *Conflict in Mark*, 34.

61. Myers, *Binding the Strong Man*, 97–99. Some examples of this appeal to the Old Testament by Jesus that Myers notes, include 2:24—3:1; 10:2–19; 11:7; 12:24–27.

to how a reader may or may not respond to a text is so problematic. For example, Collins' article, "Mark and His Readers: The Son of God among the Greeks and Romans," although engaging, suffers from this issue. Her approach about how a reader "might" respond seems less important and even less legitimate than the manner in which the implied reader and the narrative are structured. A person may respond to a text in a number of ways. Her thesis would stand, essentially, if a person read the mythology that she points to, and failed to listen to the Gospel in its totality, and if they read it divorced from a community of those proclaiming the Apostles Teachings. Surely more benefit comes from a thorough engagement with the text that we have. This is what she does, to her credit, in a second, similar article, "Mark and his Readers, the Son of God among the Jews."

In summation, by virtue of his development and the nuances with which he presents the themes of allegiance, opposition, and misunderstanding, and, in light of the levels of authority of his witnesses, all of which affirm that Jesus is the Son of God, Mark rests his case. His initial statement in 1:1, "The beginning of the gospel of Jesus Christ, the Son of God" is now completed. Mark, in approaching his theme from these two perspectives (developmentally through motifs and with the levels of authoritative witnesses) invites his reader to side with "right" point of view; with himself, God, Jesus, all spiritual forces that Jesus is the Son of God. The second, implicit initiation in this and model the actions of the centurion who switched allegiance from Caesar son of god, to Jesus, the true Son of God, the culmination of Israel's history, who is known and revealed only in his crucifixion for the many (14:24) and the alarming revelation that "He is risen. He is not here" (16:6).

6

Concluding Thoughts and Reflections

METHODOLOGICAL REVIEW

Much ground has been covered and a review of our study to this point is in order. This final chapter will begin by providing a summary of the arguments that have been set forward thus far. In addition to this, a distillation of the central and primary thesis that is being advocated will be offered. In this, original research will be highlighted. Finally, this chapter will offer some additional line of inquiry for future study. To begin with, then, is the summary of the journey thus far.

The first chapter introduced the topic at hand: "Jesus Christ the Son of God" according to Mark's Gospel. A short history of interpretive approaches to the Gospels was set forward. In this, form, reaction, social-scientific, and New Criticism was presented and the adoption of certain tenants of these approaches was highlighted. Chapter 1 also offered a condensed history and appraisal of Wrede's Messianic secret. Here it was argued, in contradistinction to Wrede, that the motif of secrecy pertains more to the divine sonship of Jesus rather than his Messiahship. Further, it was argued that the motif centers more on the twin theme of revelation and misunderstanding than predestination or something other. The methodological approach of the thesis was explained as being one in which the finished text that we possess serves as the central guide for interpretation. Thus, from the onset, the desire was clear: to have a study that presents a thesis which is both possible and probable. This, it was explained, can occur only when the tripartite grid of author, text, and reader are examined both historically and literarily. Chapter 1 also previewed the road which lay ahead and offered a brief introduction to where the following Chapters would lead the reader. In the end, the central thesis was stated and explained as being: When the interpreter of Mark examines the motif of divine sonship from the tripartite perspective of author, text, and reader, it becomes clear that Mark has crafted his narrative in such a way that the revelation of Jesus' person occurs at the centurion's confession at 15:39. This, however, is only part of the thesis. The second line of the central thesis is that when the themes of allegiance, misunderstanding, and opposition are noted, it too points the interpreter to the climax in 15:39. With the centurion's words, the "secret" (which is more misunderstanding) is out: Jesus is the Son of God. The effect of all this is to ensure that the reader is left with two possibilities: act in allegiance to Jesus (which means to adopt the author's point of view) or to act in opposition to Jesus (which means to reject the author's point of view). This will be more fully explained when chapter 5 is summarized.

Since a narratival approach to the Gospel is the methodological foundation from which the study proceeds, a short history of this discipline is presented in chapter 2. In this chapter, after noting the development and refinement of this approach, the conversation turned to questions about the legitimacy of a narrative approach to Mark's Gospel. This question was answered by first noting the literary relationship between the Synoptics. After this, attention was given to questions of audience. The point being set forward in this section was that a narrow audience or specific community as the addressees is not the most fitting. Instead, following Bauckham, it was argued that a general or indefinite audience is not only historically possible, but more in keeping with a desire to focus on the finished text we have rather than a community that gave the Gospel birth, of whose identity we cannot be certain. After addressing the question of audience, the next point discussed was the genre of Mark. Obviously, the genre of a literary work affects the manner in which the reader responds to and interacts with the text. After noting some scholarly answers to the question of genre, the arguments of Richard Burridge were accepted that the genre which best describes Mark is *bioi*.

After establishing the audience and taking a broad view of both, the next issue addressed is: from what historical context is "Jesus the Son of God" best understood? Since the concept of an individual being referred to as the son of god was somewhat common in antiquity, how is the reader to approach Jesus in Mark? It was noted in chapter 3 that, although a number of theories about which historical contexts offer answers to this question, the most fitting answer is found in Mark itself. After examining the manner in which divine sonship is introduced and explained in the Dead Sea Scrolls, Old Testament, the answer is clear: the context which Jesus the Son of God should be understood as stemming from was the Old Testament and the eschatological hope of a royal Messiah figure who is deemed God's Son.

Chapter 4 presented the exegetical data in Mark surrounding Jesus' divine sonship. Each instance which the title is used, implied, or referenced was examined. The purpose of this was to ensure that whatever narratival judgments on the text were made, they would avoid be subjective and, thusly must fit with what is discovered from a historical critical exegetical method. Special attention in this chapter was given to Mark's incipit and the textual uncertainty that surrounds 1:1. It was argued that the internal evidence supports its inclusion, while the external evidence is split. To be sure, chapter 4 did present some assessments and interpretation of Mark that feature a narrative essence, but it primarily approached the Gospel from an exegetical standpoint.

Chapter 5 combines the narrative critical approach that was examined in chapter 2 with the exegetical data presented in chapter 4. In this chapter, the broad contours of the book were examined. A number of points were noted. First of all, it was made clear that Mark has a definite point of view that he is seeking to communicate. The central point for which he is advocating is that Jesus is the Son of God. Mark does this through presenting his point of view at the onset, and then recruiting various authorities in the text to bolster his view point. First, he recruits Old Testament Scripture (and John) as baring witness to Jesus' divine sonship. Next, he has God, himself, speak form heaven and affirm for all who are listening (which just so happens to be only Jesus and the reader of Mark) that Jesus is his Son. Throughout the narrative, Mark demonstrates that the demonic forces of evil reiterate his point that Jesus is the Son. Finally, through implicit, veiled reference, Mark has the character Jesus affirm this viewpoint as well. In doing this, Mark makes it very difficult to reject his initial assessment of Jesus' divine sonship, for to do so is to go against a host of witnesses that are esteemed and authoritative.

Chapter 5 also went to lengths in explaining and examining the themes of misunderstanding, allegiance, and opposition. These three all relate to Mark's point of view. To misunderstand, it was argued, means that one fails to grasp who Jesus is as the Son of God. In this failure, Mark makes it clear that it is very easy for someone to end up acting in opposition. In the end, the theme of misunderstanding on the part of the characters in his narrative world is resolved when the centurion (the only human character in the story to do so) verbalizes the central truth that Mark's point of view centers on:

Jesus is the Son of God. Thus, it was concluded, Mark presents his readers with two options: Adopt his point of view about Jesus being the Son of God, or act in opposition and ignore Mark's words, the host of authoritative witnesses he gathers, and reject the view that Jesus is the Son of God.

SUMMARY OF POINT OF VIEW IN MARK AND THE RHETORIC OF ALLEGIANCE TO JESUS SON OF GOD

In Mark, a unified and intentional point of view is presented. The reader is made aware of this from the beginning (1:1). The omniscient narrator who controls the narrative world and functions as the supreme authority presents Jesus as the Son of God.

1. Mark is a coherent story and *bioi* and can be interpreted narratively.
2. Mark has a definite point of view he presents. He recruits characters in the story to bolster his claim that Jesus is the Son of God.
3. Mark must be interpreted in such a way that attention is given to author, text, and audience. An interpreter cannot fail to engage anyone of these in his or her approach to the text.
4. There are three central motifs that relate to the responses to the declaration by Mark that Jesus is the Son of God. They are misunderstanding, allegiance, and opposition.
5. When text is approached with these three motifs in view, a clear rhetorical thrust is offered by Mark: Since he explains who Jesus is and since "word is out" (centurion vocalizes the truth), there are two options which the reader can choose: allegiance or opposition.
6. To act in allegiance is to adopt Mark's point of view. To act in opposition is to reject Mark's point of view about Jesus the Son of God.

Central to all of this, is Mark's point of view. It was argued that Mark states his point of view plainly (1:1) and recruits additional witness to Jesus' divine sonship. They were labeled with "levels" indicating their rhetorical impact on the audience. The testimonies are:

1. The omniscient narrator (Level 1—as omniscient narrator, he controls the world which he creates).
2. God himself (Level 2—God as God functions as the highest level of authority of any characters in the narrative world).

CONCLUDING THOUGHTS AND REFLECTIONS 179

3. Jesus himself (Level 3—Jesus, as the Son of God, embraces this point of view of his identity).

4. Cosmic evil spiritual forces (Level 4—although evil, these forces undoubtedly possess a high level of spiritual insight and ability. They shrink back in fear and affirm that Jesus is the Son of God).

5. And, finally, the characters in the story (Level 5—the one closest to the death of Jesus, and the one who stood in direct opposition, affirm that Jesus truly is the Son of God).

Chapter 5 presented that the most significant point of Mark's rhetoric occurs in 15:39. This, it was explained, occurred through the process of what is called defamiliarization. This process occurs when readers are lead to anticipate one thing, only to have the opposite occur. This is exactly what happens at the crucifixion scene. The readers already know that the human characters either misunderstand or oppose Jesus, and the centurion before the cross is likely expected to also respond negatively to Jesus. But the opposite occurred. The crucifixion scene (the ultimate scene of opposition) was explained as following a pattern:

1. The spatial setting is one of shame and rejection
2. Jesus is rejected by religious leaders and his own disciples
3. Jesus is physically and verbally abused
4. The Roman soldiers are complicit and malicious in the abuse
5. Crowd and passers-by mock and deride Jesus
6. Jesus is misunderstood by those standing by
7. Jesus dies

Although a pattern is established by Mark, he deviates here and presents a dramatic reversal that leaves the reader stunned. Someone finally gets it, and it is a centurion! This implicit invitation for the implied, indefinite reader, is to model the centurion's reversal and respond in allegiance to the Son of God.

ORIGINAL CONTRIBUTION

To begin, there are two minor contributions, methodologically speaking, that this study advances. First, although a number of books focusing on Mark from a narrative critical perspective have been penned, these are primarily concerned with the "how." The question that narrative critics often ask is, "How is the author saying it." This study offered fresh insights by not only asking that question, but in also asking "what." How does Mark present what he does about Jesus the Son of God? The marriage of narrative criticism, and legitimacy of narrative criticism combined with actually engaging the task of synchronic interpretation are seldom presented in the same volume.

In addition to these two minor notes, the most notable original contribution is the application of the theme of misunderstanding to Jesus' divine sonship and the investigation of the themes of allegiance and opposition. The rhetorical significance of these two themes and the way they function throughout the narrative and reach their climax in the crucifixion scene are legitimate new approaches. The development of these themes from Mark and the manner in which defamiliarization occurs at the crucifixion scene is significant. Add to this the rhetorical impact of the various "witnesses" that Mark's points to for the better understanding of his literary and didactic aims.

AREAS OF FUTURE STUDY

In addition to the methodological and synchronic insights that this study presented, a number of additional avenues of research are worth taking further and investigating in their own right. One area in which future study would be useful, is the application of these themes to women in Mark. Women, undoubtedly, play a minor yet significant role in Mark. How do the women characters interact with the themes of allegiance and opposition? Perhaps examining the manner in which they, by their gender may have functioned as outsiders from a social-scientific perspective in first century Jewish life, still function significantly in the narrative will prove fruitful. The appearance of the man in white and the conversation the women have with him at the tomb (16:1–8) is significant and most definitely another illustration of defamiliarization—it is not Peter or John to whom the proclamation of the resurrection is given, it is the women.

If the rhetoric and thematic contours of Mark have been fruitful ground for study in understanding the Christology of the narrator, how does this compare with Matthew, Luke, and John? For example, how do the infancy narrative of Jesus factor into the comprehensive christological presentation that Luke and Matthew make? What role do the genealogies play in developing the concept of sonship in these respective Gospels? Alternatively, comparing the rhetoric of Mark's Son of God theology with the apostolic teaching presented in books such as Romans, Corinthians, Philippians, and others is worth pursuing. Mark indicates that it is only in the death of Jesus for the many that Jesus' identity can be understood. If this is correct, as this study has presented, how does this correlate to Pauline and Petrine articulations of the identity of Jesus? For example, an exegetical treatment of Acts 8:1–4; 17:2–3; 26:22–33; Rom 8:31–34; and Phil 2:5–11 with the rhetoric and Christology found in Mark may prove a fruitful line of inquiry.

In recruiting "witnesses" the omniscient narrator presents an argument that is difficult to refute. If he, the Old Testament, God himself, Jesus, and hosts of cosmic forces understand Jesus to be the Son of God, how can anyone argue? Taking the time to examine the rhetoric, the role of omniscient narrator, and the recruitment of "witnesses" to bolster a viewpoint would likely yield significant results in literary assessments of the New Testament.

One final area that was beyond the scope of this study but nevertheless may be worthwhile to examine, is the manner in which the themes of misunderstanding, allegiance, and opposition present themselves when Mark has Galilee and Jerusalem in view. Van Eck's work on the opposition between these two locales may provide additional insights into the motif of opposition in Mark's depiction of the story of Jesus.[1]

FINAL REMARKS

The aim of this study has been to examine not simply what Mark says about Jesus the Son of God, but *how* he says it. The motifs that he develops of misunderstanding, opposition, and allegiance present the reader, both ancient and modern, with a choice. Mark's perspective, his point of view, is clear: Jesus is the Son of God who stands in fulfillment of Israel's history. This was the fundamental view of Jesus that Mark leads his readers to accept. In addition to this, just as 1:1 casts an interpretive shadow over the rest of the work, coloring how the reader understands and navigate the literary world created by Mark, so too does the brief resurrection account at the end of Mark offer its hues and shades to the book when it is read with the end in mind. The reader is offered some aid in interrupting the death of the Son of God, because in the end, a spiritual authority, confesses that the story is not yet complete—there is more to learn because "he is risen."

In presenting a series of authoritative witnesses that affirm his perspective, and by resolving the motif of misunderstanding through the words

---

1. Van Eck, *Galilee and Jerusalem*.

of a very unlikely convert, Mark urges his reader to make a choice. Will the reader respond with opposition and refuse to acknowledge Jesus as the true Son of God, or will the reader respond with allegiance and after reading (or hearing) the Gospel declare with the centurion: "Truly this man was the Son of God." So powerful is Mark's argumentation and rhetoric, that the ethical and personal implications of such allegiance have been the Church's concern for 2000 years. Even today, the invitation of Mark continues to be proclaimed as the Church, her adherents, leaders, and pastors urge those who currently stand in opposition to Jesus to offer him their allegiance.

Appendix

Exodus 23:20	"Behold I send my messenger before you."
Malachi 3:1	"Who will prepare your way."
Isaiah 40:3	"The voice of one calling out in the wilderness: 'Prepare the way of the Lord; make straight his paths.'"

Mark	Topic	Psalm
15:24	division of garment	22:18
15:29	mockery, wagging head	22:7
15:30–31	Save yourself!	22:8
15:32	reviling	22:6
15:34	cry of dereliction	22:1
15:36	gave him vinegar to drink	69:1
15:40	looking on at a distance	38:11

Baptism	Transfiguration	Crucifixion
Heavens rent and doves descends	Garments turn white; cloud descends	Sanctuary veil rent darkness spreads
Voice from heaven	Voice from cloud	Jesus' great voice
"You are my son, beloved"	"This is my son, beloved"	Truly this man was son of God
John the Baptist as Elijah	Jesus appears with Elijah	"Is he calling Elijah?"

Bibliography

Ahearne-Kroll, Stephen. *The Psalms of Lament in Mark's Passion: Jesus' Davidic Suffering*. Camdridge: Cambridge University Press, 2007.
Aland, Kurt, and Barbara Aland, eds. *The UBS Greek New Testament: A Reader's Edition*. New York: American Bible Society, 2005.
Alexander, Loveday. "What Is a Gospel?" In *The Cambridge Companion to the Gospels*, edited by Stephen C. Barton, 13–33. Cambridge Companions to Religion. Cambridge: Cambridge University Press, 2006.
Alter, Robert. *The Art of Biblical Narrative*. New York: Basic Books, 2011.
Anderson, Hugh. "Old Testament in Mark's Gospel." In *The Use of the Old Testament in the New and Other Essays*, edited by Efird James, 280–306. Durham: Duke University Press, 1972.
Anderson, Janice Capel, and Stephen D. Moore, eds. *Mark and Method: New Approaches in Biblical Studies*. Minneapolis, MN: Fortress, 2008.
Arbeitman, Yoël. "The Suffix of Iscariot." *Journal of Biblical Literature* 99 (1980) 122–24.
Aune, David. "The Problem of the Genre of the Gospels: A Critique of C. H. Talbert's 'What Is a Gospel?'" In *Gospel Perspectives*. Vol. 2, *Studies of History and Tradition in the Four Gospels*, edited by R. T. France and David Wenham, 9–60. Eugene, OR: Wipf & Stock, 2003.
Baird, J. Arthur. *A Comparative Analysis of the Gospel Genre: The Synoptic Mode and Its Uniqueness*. Lewiston, NY: Edwin Mellen, 1992.
Barker, Margaret. "Beyond the Veil of the Temple: The High Priestly Origins of the Apocalypses." *Scottish Journal of Theology* 51 (1998) 1–21.
Barr, James. "Abba Isn't Daddy." *Journal of Theological Studies* 39 (1988) 28–47.
Bartlett, David L. *Exorcism Stories in the Gospel of Mark*. New Haven: Yale University Press, 1972.
Barton, Stephen C., ed. *The Cambridge Companion to the Gospels*. Cambridge Companions to Religion. Cambridge: Cambridge University Press, 2006.
Bateman, Herbert W. "Defining the Titles 'Christ' and 'Son of God' in Mark's Narrative Presentation of Jesus." *Journal of the Evangelical Theological Society* 50 (2007) 537–59.
Bauckham, Richard. *The Gospels for All Christians*. Edinburgh, UK: T. & T. Clark, 1997.
———. *Jesus and the Eyewitnesses: The Gospels as Eyewitness Testimony*. Grand Rapids, MI: Eerdmans, 2006.
———. "The Son of Man: 'A Man in My Position' or 'Someone.'" *Journal for the Study of the New Testament* 23 (1985) 23–33.

Bauer, David. *The Structure of Matthew's Gospel: A Study in Literary Design*. London: Bloomsbury, 2015.
Bauer, D. R. "Son of God." In *Dictionary of Jesus and the Gospels*. Edited by Joel B. Green, Scot McKnight, and I. Howard Marshall, 773. Downers Grove, IL: InterVarsity, 1992.
Bayer, Hans F. *A Theology of Mark: The Dynamic between Christology and Authentic Discipleship*. Phillipsburg, NJ: P & R, 2012.
Beale, G. K. *Handbook on the New Testament Use of the Old Testament: Exegesis and Interpretation*. Grand Rapids, MI: Baker, 2012.
Beard, Mary, John North, and Simon Price. *Religions of Rome*. Vol. 2, *A Sourcebook*. Cambridge: Cambridge University Press, 1998.
Beardslee, William A. *Literary Criticism of the New Testament*. Philadelphia: Fortress, 1970.
Beasley-Murray, George. *Jesus and the Last Days*. Peabody, MA: Hendrickson, 1990.
Beavis, Mary Ann. *Mark's Audience: The Literary and Social Setting of Mark 4.11-12*. Journal for the Study of the New Testament 33. Sheffield, UK: JSOT, 1989.
Belo, Fernando. *A Materialist Reading of the Gospel of Mark*. Maryknoll, NY: Orbis, 1981.
Bertram, G. "Hypsistos." In *TDNT*, edited by Gerhard Kittel, 602-20. Grand Rapids, MI: Eerdmans, 1964.
Best, Ernest E. *Mark: The Gospel as Story*. Studies of the New Testament and Its World. Edinburgh, UK: T. & T. Clark, 1983.
Bingen, Jean. *Hellenistic Egypt: Monarchy, Society, Economy, Culture*. Los Angeles, CA: University of California Press, 2007.
Bird, Michael F. *Jesus Is the Christ: The Messianic Testimony of the Gospels*. Downers Grove, IL: InterVarsity, 2013.
Black, C. Clifton. *The Disciples according to Mark: Markan Redaction in Current Debate*. Grand Rapids, MI: Eerdmans, 2012.
Black, David Alan, and David S. Dockery, eds. *Interpreting the New Testament: Essays on Methods and Issues*. Nashville: B. & H. Academic, 2001.
Blevins, James L. *The Messianic Secret in Markan Research, 1901-1976*. Washington, DC: University Press of America, 1983.
Bock, Darrell L. "Form Criticism." In *New Testament Criticism & Interpretation*, 173-96. Grand Rapids, MI: Zondervan, 1991.
Bolt, Peter. *Jesus' Defeat of Death: Persuading Mark's Early Readers*. Cambridge: Cambridge University Press, 2003.
Bolt, Peter G. *The Cross from a Distance: Atonement in Mark's Gospel*. Downers Grove, IL: InterVarsity, 2004.
Booth, Wayne C. *The Rhetoric of Fiction*. Chicago: University of Chicago Press, 1983.
Boring, M. Eugene. *Mark: A Commentary*. Louisville, KY: Westminster John Knox, 2006.
Bornkamm, Guenther, Gerhard Barth, and Heinz Joachim Held. *Tradition and Interpretation in Matthew*. London: SCM, 2014.
Bourquin, Yvan. *La Confession Du Centurion: Le Fils de Dieu En Croix Selon L'évangile de Marc*. Aubonne, Switzerland: Du Moulin, 1996.
Bousset, Wilhelm. *Kyrios Christos: A History of the Belief in Christ from the Beginnings of Christianity to Irenaeus*. Nashville: Abingdon, 1970.
Boyd, Gregory A. *Cynic Sage Or Son of God?* Grand Rapids, MI: Baker Academic, 1995.

Brand, C. E. *Roman Military Law*. Austin: University of Texas Press, 2011.
Bratcher, Robert G. "A Note on υιος υεου (Mark Xv. 39)." *Expository Times* 68 (1956).
Bratcher, Robert G., and Eugene A. Nida. *A Handbook on the Gospel of Mark*. London: United Bible Societies, 1993.
Broadhead, Edwin Keith. "Narrativity and Naiveté: Critical Reflections on Literary Analysis of the Gospels." *Perspectives in Religious Studies* 35 (2008) 9–24.
———. *Prophet, Son, Messiah: Narrative Form and Function in Mark 14–16*. Journal for the Study of the New Testament 97. Sheffield, UK: JSOT, 1994.
———. *Teaching With Authority: Miracles and Christology in the Gospel of Mark*. Journal for the Study of the New Testament. Supplement Series 74. Sheffield, UK: JSOT, 1992.
Brooks, James A., and Carlton L. Winbery. *A Morphology of New Testament Greek: A Review and Reference Grammar*. Lanham, MD: University Press of America, 1994.
Brown, Raymond E. *A Crucified Christ in Holy Week: Essays on the Four Gospel Passion Narratives*. Collegeville, MN: Liturgical, 1992.
———. *The Death of the Messiah: From Gethsemane to the Grave*. New York: Doubleday, 1994.
———. *Introduction to the New Testament Christology*. New York: Paulist, 1994.
———. *An Introduction to the New Testament*. New York: Doubleday, 1997.
Broyles, Craig C. "Psalm 72's Contribution to the Messianic Ideal." In *Eschatology, Messianism, and the Dead Sea Scrolls*, edited by Craig A. Evans and Peter W. Flint. Grand Rapids, MI: Eerdmans, 1997.
Bruce, F. F. *Paul: Apostle of the Heart Set Free*. Grand Rapids, MI: Eerdmans, 2000.
Bryan, Christopher. *The Resurrection of the Messiah*. New York: Oxford University Press, 2011.
Bultmann, Rudolf. *The History of the Synoptic Tradition*. Translated by John Marsh. Oxford: Blackwell, 1963.
———. *Theology of the New Testament*. Translated by Kendrick Grobel. New York, NY: Scribner, 1951.
Bultmann, Rudolph. *Jesus Christ and Mythology*. Upper Saddle River, NJ: Prentice Hall, 1981.
Burnett, F. W. "M." *Dictionary of Jesus and the Gospels*, edited by Joel B. Green, Scot McKnight, and I. Howard Marshall, 511–12. Downers Grove, IL: InterVarsity, 1992.
Burridge, Richard A. "The Graeco-Roman Context of Early Christian Literature." *Journal of Theological Studies* 50 (1999) 271–73.
———. "The New Testament in Its Literary Environment." *Journal for the Study of the New Testament* 36 (1989) 122–24.
———. *What Are the Gospels?: A Comparison with Graeco-Roman Biography*. Society for New Testament Studies, Monograph Series 70. Cambridge: Cambridge University Press, 1992.
Byrskog, Samuel. "A Century with the Sitz Im Leben: From Form-Critical Setting to Gospel Community and Beyond." *Zeitschrift Für Die Neutestamentliche Wissenschaft Und Die Kunde Der älteren Kirche* 98 (2007) 1–27.
Camery-Hoggatt, Jerry. *Irony in Mark's Gospel: Text and Subtext*. Cambridge: Cambridge University Press, 2005.

Campbell, William S. "Engagement, Disengagement and Obstruction: Jesus' Defense Strategies in Mark's Trial and Execution Scenes (14.53–64; 15.1–39)." *Journal for the Study of the New Testament* 26 (2004) 283–300.

Carotta, Francesco. *Jesus Was Caesar: On the Julian Origin of Christianity*. Poland: Aspekt, 2005.

Carson, D. A, and Douglas J. Moo. *An Introduction to the New Testament*. Grand Rapids, MI: Zondervan, 2005.

Carson, D. A, and John D. Woodbridge. *Scripture and Truth*. Grand Rapids, MI: Baker Academic, 1992.

Charlesworth, James H., Hermann Lichtenberger, and Gerbern S. Oegema. *Qumran-Messianism: Studies on the Messianic Expectations in the Dead Sea Scrolls*. Tübingen, Germany: Mohr Siebeck, 1998.

Charlesworth, Martin Percival. "Some Observations on Ruler-Cult Especially in Rome." *Harvard Theological Review* 28 (1935) 5–44.

Chronis, Harry. "The Torn Veil: Cultus and Christology in Mark 15:37–39." *Journal of Biblical Literature* 101 (1982) 97–114.

Ciampa, Roy E., and Brian S. Rosner. *The First Letter to the Corinthians*. Grand Rapids, MI: Eerdmans, 2010.

Collins, Adela Yarbro. *Is Mark's Gospel a Life of Jesus: The Question of Genre*. Milwaukee: Marquette University Press, 1990.

———. *Mark: A Commentary*. Hermeneia. Minneapolis, MN: Fortress, 2007.

———. "Mark and His Readers: The Son of God among Greeks and Romans." *Harvard Theological Review* 93 (2000) 85–100.

———. "Mark and His Readers: The Son of God among Jews." *Harvard Theological Review* 92 (1999) 393–408.

Collins, Adela Yarbro, and John J. Collins. *King and Messiah as Son of God: Divine, Human, and Angelic Messianic Figures in Biblical and Related Literature*. Grand Rapids, MI: Eerdmans, 2008.

Collins, John J. "The Background of the 'Son of God' Text." *Bulletin for Biblical Research* 7 (1997) 51–61.

———. "Jesus, Messianism and the Dead Sea Scrolls." In *Qumran-Messianism: Studies on the Messianic Expectations in the Dead Sea Scrolls*. Tübingen, Germany: Mohr Siebeck, 1998.

———. *The Scepter and the Star: Messianism in Light of the Dead Sea Scrolls*. Grand Rapids, MI: Eerdmans, 2010.

Colwell, Ernest Cadman. "A Definite Rule for the Use of the Article in the Greek New Testament." *Journal of Biblical Literature* 52 (1933) 12–21.

Cook, Michael J. *Mark's Treatment of the Jewish Leaders*. Leiden, Netherlands: E. J. Brill, 1978.

Crossan, John Dominic. *The Historical Jesus: The Life of a Mediterranean Jewish Peasant*. San Francisco: Harper, 1991.

———. *In Parables: The Challenge of the Historical Jesus*. Sonoma, CA: Polebridge, 1992.

———. *Jesus: A Revolutionary Biography*. San Francisco: Harper, 1994.

Croy, Clayton. "Where the Gospel Text Begins: A Non-Theological Interpretation of Mark 1:1." *Novum Testamentum* 43 (2001) 105–27.

Cunningham, Phillip. *Mark: The Good News Preached*. New York: Paulist, 2002.

D'Amato, Raffaele. *Roman Centurions 31 BC–AD 500: The Classical and Late Empire*. Oxford: Osprey, 2012.

Danove, Paul L. *Linguistics and Exegesis in the Gospel of Mark: Application of a Case Frame Analysis and Lexicon*. Sheffield, UK: Sheffield Academic, 2004.

———. "The Narrative Rhetoric of Mark's Ambiguous Characterization of the Disciples." *Journal for the Study of the New Testament* 70 (1998) 21–38.

———. *The Rhetoric of Characterization of God, Jesus, and Jesus' Disciples in the Gospel of Mark*. London: T. & T. Clark, 2005.

Dart, John. "Judas Is a 'Demon' in New Read of Gospel." *Christian Century* 124 (2007) 12–13.

Davidsen, Ole. *The Narrative Jesus: A Semiotic Reading of Mark's Gospel*. Aarhus, Denmark: Aarhus University Press, 1993.

Davies, W. D., and Dale C. Allison. *A Critical and Exegetical Commentary on the Gospel according to Saint Matthew*. Edinburgh: T. & T. Clark, 1991.

Davis, Philip G. "Mark's Christological Paradox." *Journal for the Study of the New Testament* 35 (1989) 3–18.

Day, John. *King and Messiah in Israel and the Ancient Near East: Proceedings of the Oxford Old Testament Seminar*. London: T. & T. Clark, 2013.

Dewey, Joanna. *Disciples of the Way: Mark on Discipleship*. Women's Division, Board of Global Ministries, United Methodist Church, 1976.

———. *The Oral Ethos of the Early Church: Speaking, Writing, and the Gospel of Mark*. Eugene, OR: Wipf & Stock, 2013.

Dibelius, Martin. *From Tradition to Gospel*. The Scribner Library SL124. New York: Scribner, 1965.

———. *From Tradition to Gospel*. Cambridge: James Clarke & Co., 1971.

Donahue, John R. "Jesus as Parable in the Gospel of Mark." *Interpretation* 32 (1978) 369–86.

Dreyer, Boris. "Heroes, Cults, and Divinity." In *Alexander the Great: A New History*. West Sussex, UK: Blackwell, 2009.

Dreyer, Yolanda. "Names of Jesus in Mark's Story." *In Die Skriflig* 35 (2001) 389–403.

———. "Son-of-God Traditions in the Synoptic Gospels: Ferdinand Hahn's Diachronic Perspective." *HTS Theological Studies* 57 (2001) 506–30.

Dungan, David. *A History of the Synoptic Problem: The Canon, the Text, the Composition, and the Interpretation of the Gospels*. The Anchor Bible Reference Library. New York: Doubleday, 1999.

Dunn, James D. G. *Jesus, Paul, and the Gospels*. Grand Rapids, MI: Eerdmans, 2011.

———. *Jesus Remembered*. Grand Rapids, MI: Eerdmans, 2003.

———. "The Messianic Secret in Mark." *Tyndale Bulletin* 21 (1970) 92–117.

———. *New Testament Theology: An Introduction*. Louisville, KY: Abingdon, 2009.

———. *The Oral Gospel Tradition*. Grand Rapids, MI: Eerdmans, 2013.

———. *The Theology of Paul the Apostle*. Grand Rapids, MI: Eerdmans, 2006.

Dwyer, Timothy. *The Motif of Wonder in the Gospel of Mark*. Sheffield, UK: Sheffield Academic, 1996.

Eaton, John H. *Kingship and the Psalms*. The Biblical Seminar. Sheffield, UK: JSOT, 1986.

Edwards, James R. *The Gospel according to Mark*. Grand Rapids, MI: Eerdmans, 2001.

Ehrman, Bart. "The Text of Mark in the Hands of the Orthodox." *Lutheran Quarterly* 5 (1991) 143–56.

Elliott, John H. *What Is Social Scientific Criticism?* Minneapolis, MN: Fortress, 1993.
Elliott, Neil, and Mark Reasoner. *Documents and Images for the Study of Paul.* Minneapolis, MN: Fortress, 2011.
Erskine, Andrew. *A Companion to the Hellenistic World.* Aarhus, Denmark: Wiley-Blackwell, 2005.
Evans, Craig A. *Ancient Texts or New Testament Studies: A Guide to the Background Literature.* Peabody, MA: Hendrickson, 2005.
———. "Are the Son of God Texts at Qumran Messianic?" In *Qumran-Messianism: Studies on the Messianic Expectations in the Dead Sea Scrolls*, edited by James H. Charlesworth, Hermann Lichtenberger, and Gerbern S. Oegema, 135–53. Tübingen, Germany: Mohr Siebeck, 1998.
———. "Jesus and the Dead Sea Scrolls from Qumran Cave 4." In *Eschatology, Messianism and the Dea Sea Scrolls*, edited by Craig A. Evans and Peter W. Flint, 91–100. Grand Rapids, MI: Eerdmans, 1997.
———. *Mark 8:27–16:20.* Word Biblical Commentary. Nashville: Thomas Nelson, 2001.
———. "Mark's Incipit and the Priene Calendar Inscription: From Jewish Gospel to Greco-Roman Gospel." *Journal of Greco-Roman Christianity and Judaism* (2000) 69–81.
———. "Source, Form and Redaction Criticism." In *Approaches to New Testament Study*, edited by Stanley E. Porter and David Tombs, 17–45. Sheffield, UK: Sheffield Academic, 1995.
Evans, Craig A., and John J. Collins. *Christian Beginnings and the Dead Sea Scrolls.* Grand Rapids, MI: Baker Academic, 2006.
Evans, Craig A., and Peter W. Flint. *Eschatology, Messianism, and the Dead Sea Scrolls.* Grand Rapids, MI: Eerdmans, 1997.
Farmer, William R. *Synopticon: The Verbal Agreement between the Greek Texts of Matthew, Mark and Luke Contextually Exhibited.* London: Cambridge University Press, 1969.
Farmer, William Reuben. "Jesus and the Gospels: A Form-Critical and Theological Essay." *Perkins Journal* 28 (1975) 1–62.
Fee, Gordon D. *The First Epistle to the Corinthians.* Grand Rapids, MI: Eerdmans, 1987.
Fitzmyer, Joseph A. "4Q246: The 'Son of God' Document from Qumran." *Biblica* 74 (1994) 153–74.
———. *The Dead Sea Scrolls and Christian Origins.* Grand Rapids, MI: Eerdmans, 2000.
———. *The One Who Is to Come.* Grand Rapids, MI: Eerdmans, 2007.
———. *Romans.* New Haven: Yale University Press, 1993.
Fokkelman, J. P. *Reading Biblical Narrative: An Introductory Guide.* Louisville, KY: Westminster John Knox, 1999.
Forster, E. M. *Aspects of the Novel.* London: Penguin, 1927.
Fowler, Alastair. *Kinds of Literature: An Introduction to the Theory of Genres and Modes.* Oxford: Clarendon, 1985.
Fowler, Robert M. "Irony and the Messianic Secret in the Gospel of Mark." *Proceedings: Eastern Lakes Biblical Society and Midwest Society of Biblical Literature* 1 (1981) 26–36.
———. *Let the Reader Understand: Reader-Response Criticism and the Gospel of Mark.* Minneapolis, MN: Fortress, 1991.

France, R. T. *The Gospel of Mark*. Grand Rapids, MI: Eerdmans, 2002.
France, R. T., and David Wenham, eds. *Gospel Perspectives*. Vol. 2, *Studies of History and Tradition in the Four Gospels*. Eugene, OR: Wipf & Stock, 2003.
Freedman, David Noel. *The Anchor Bible Dictionary*. New York: Doubleday, 1992.
Fullmer, Paul. *Resurrection in Mark's Literary-Historical Perspective*. 1st ed. London: T. & T. Clark, 2007.
Gamel, Brian K. "Salvation in a Sentence: Mark 15:39 as Markan Soteriology." *Journal of Theological Interpretation* 6 (2012) 65–77.
Gathercole, Simon J. *The Preexistent Son: Recovering the Christologies of Matthew, Mark, and Luke*. Grand Rapids, MI: Eerdmans, 2006.
Giles, K. "'L' Tradition." In *Dictionary of Jesus and the Gospels*, edited by Joel B. Green, Scot McKnight, and I. Howard Marshall, 431–32. Downers Grove, IL: InterVarsity, 1992.
Gnilka, Joachim. *Jesus of Nazareth: Message and History*. Peabody, MA: Hendrickson, 1997.
Goetz, S. C., and C. L. Blomberg. "The Burden of Proof." *Journal for the Study of the New Testament* 11 (1981) 39–63.
Goodacre, Mark. *The Case against Q: Studies in Markan Priority and the Synoptic Problem*. Harrisburg, PA: Trinity Press International, 2002.
———. *The Synoptic Problem: A Way Through the Maze*. London: T. & T. Clark, 2005.
Gradel, Ittai. *Emperor Worship and Roman Religion*. New York: Oxford University Press, 2004.
Grant, Michael. *Army of the Caesars*. New York: MacMillan, 1974.
Grant, Michael. *From Alexander to Cleopatra*. London: Weidenfeld and Nicolson, 1982.
Grant, Frederick Clifton. "Where Form Criticism and Textual Criticism Overlap." *Journal of Biblical Literature* 59 (1940) 11–21.
Green, Joel B., Scot McKnight, and I. Howard Marshall. *Dictionary of Jesus and the Gospels*. Downers Grove, IL: InterVarsity, 1992.
Griesbach, J. J. *Synopsis Evangeliroum Matthei, Marci, et Lucae Una Cum Iis Joannis Pericopis: Quae Historian Passionis et Resurrectionis Jesus Christi Complectuntur*. Halle Saxonum, Germany: J. J. Curtii Haeredes, 1797.
Guelich, Robert. "Mark." In *Dictionary of Jesus and the Gospels*, edited by Joel B. Green, Scot McKnight, and I. Howard Marshall, 512. Downers Grove, IL: InterVarsity, 1992.
———. *Mark 1–8:26*. Word Biblical Commentary. Nashville: Thomas Nelson, 1989.
Gundry, Robert Horton. *Mark: A Commentary on His Apology for the Cross*. Grand Rapids, MI: Eerdmans, 2000.
Hans, Schmidt. *Eucharisterion. Studien zur religion und literature des Alten und Neuen Testaments. Hermann Gunkel*. Charleston, SC: BiblioBazaar, 2009.
Harner, Philip B. "Qualitative Anarthrous Predicate Nouns: Mark 15:39 and John 1:1." *Journal of Biblical Literature* 92 (1973) 75–87.
Harris, Stephen, and Gloria Platzner. *Classical Mythology: Images and Insights*. Colombus, OH: McGraw-Hill Education, 1995.
Heckel, Waldemar, and Lawrence A. Tritle. *Alexander the Great: A New History*. Chichester, UK: Wiley-Blackwell, 2009.
Heil, John Paul. *The Gospel of Mark as a Model for Action: A Reader-Response Commentary*. New York: Paulist, 1992.

Hendrickx, Herman. *Passion Narratives of the Synoptic Gospels*. Edinburgh, UK: Chapman, 1984.

Hengel, Martin. *Crucifixion in the Ancient World and the Golly of the Message of the Cross*. Minneapolis, MN: Augsburg Fortress, 1977.

———. *The Son of God: The Origin of Christology and the History of Jewish-Hellenistic Religion*. Philadelphia: Fortress, 1977.

———. *Studies in the Gospel of Mark*. Philadelphia: Fortress, 1985.

Hoffmann, Paul, Norbert Brox, and Wilhelm Pesch, eds. *Orientierung an Jesus. Zur theologie der Synoptiker. Für Josef Schmid*. Freiburg; Basel; Wien: Herder, 1973.

Hoffmeier, James K. "Son of God: From Pharaoh to Israel's Kings to Jesus." *Bible Review* 13 (1997) 44–49.

Hölbl, Günther. *A History of the Ptolemaic Empire*. New York: Routledge, 2000.

Holladay, Carl R. *Theios Aner in Hellenistic Judaism: A Critique of the Use of This Category in New Testament Christology*. Atlanta: Society of Biblical Literature, 1977.

Holtzmann, Heinrich Julius. *Die synoptischen Evangelien: ihr Ursprung und geschichtlicher Charakter*. Leipzig: W. Engelmann, 1863.

Hooker, Morna D. "The Expression 'Son of Man' and the Development of Christology: A History of Interpretation." *Journal of Theological Studies* 64 (2013) 651–52.

———. "Good News about Jesus Christ, the Son of God." In *Mark As Story: Retrospect and Prospect*, edited by Kelly R. Iverson and Christopher W. Skinner, 165–80. Atlanta: Society of Biblical Literature, 2011.

Hooker, Morna Dorothy. *Gospel according to St. Mark*. London: A. & C. Black, 1991.

Hultgren, Stephen. *Narrative Elements in the Double Tradition: A Study of Their Place within the Framework of the Gospel Narrative*. Berlin: Walter de Gruyter, 2001.

Huntress, E. "'Son of God' in Jewish Writings Prior to the Christian Era." *Journal of Biblical Literature* 54 (1935) 117–23.

Hurtado, Larry W., and Paul Owen. *"Who Is This Son of Man?" The Latest Scholarship on a Puzzling Expression of the Historical Jesus*. Library of New Testament Studies. London: T. & T. Clark, 2011.

Iser, Wolfgang. *The Act of Reading: A Theory of Aesthetic Response*. Baltimore: Johns Hopkins University Press, 1980.

———. "The Reading Process: A Phenomenological Approach." In *Reader-Response Criticism: From Formalism to Post-Structuralism*, edited by Jane P. Tompkins, 279–99. Baltimore: Johns Hopkins University Press, 1980.

Iverson, Kelly R. "A Centurion's 'Confession': A Performance-Critical Analysis of Mark 15:39." *Journal of Biblical Literature* 130 (2011) 329–50.

Iverson, Kelly R., and Christopher W. Skinner. *Mark as Story: Retrospect and Prospect*. Society of Biblical Literature, 2011.

Jackson, Howard M. "The Death of Jesus in Mark and the Miracle from the Cross." *New Testament Studies* 33 (1987) 16–37.

Jacoby, Felix. *Die Fragmente Der Griechischen Historiker Continued*. Leiden, Netherlands: Brill Academic, 1998.

Jeremias, Joachim. *Prayers of Jesus*. Norwich, UK: SCM, 1967.

Johnson, Earl S. "Is Mark 15:39 the Key to Mark's Christology." *Journal for the Study of the New Testament* 31 (1987) 3–22.

Johnson, Luke Timothy. *The Real Jesus: The Misguided Quest for the Historical Jesus and the Truth of the Traditional Gospels*. New York: HarperOne, 1997.

Judson, Harry Pratt. *Caesar's Army: The Evolution, Composition, Tactics, Equipment and Battles of the Roman Army*. London: Leonaur, 2011.
Keck, Leander E. "The Introduction to Mark's Gospel." *New Testament Studies* 12 (July 1966) 352–70.
Keener, Craig S. *The Gospel of Matthew: A Socio-Rhetorical Commentary*. Grand Rapids, MI: Eerdmans, 2009.
Kelber, Werner H. *Kingdom in Mark: A New Place and a New Time*. Philadelphia: Augsburg Fortress, 1974.
Kelber, Werner H. "Mark 14:32–42: Gethsemane: Passion Christology and Discipleship Failure." *Zeitschrift Für Die Neutestamentliche Wissenschaft Und Die Kunde Der älteren Kirche* 63 (1972) 166–87.
―――. *The Oral and the Written Gospel*. Philadelphia: Fortress, 1983.
Kelly, Carl. "The Messiah: Whose Son Is He? Another Look at the Son of David and Son of God Titles in Matthew." *Trinity Seminary Review* 26 (2005) 17–28.
Kennedy, George A. *New Testament Interpretation through Rhetorical Criticism*. Chapel Hill: University of North Carolina Press, 1984.
Kim, Seyoon. *The "Son of Man" as the Son of God*. Wissenschaftliche Untersuchungen zum Neuen Testament 30. Tübingen, Germany: J. C. B. Mohr, 1983.
Kim, Tae Hun. "The Anarthrous υἱὸς θεοῦ in Mark 15,39 and the Roman Imperial Cult." *Biblica* 79 (1998) 221–41.
Kingsbury, Jack Dean. *The Christology of Mark's Gospel*. Minneapolis, MN: Fortress, 1983.
―――. *Conflict in Mark: Jesus, Authorities, Disciples*. Minneapolis, MN: Fortress, 1989.
―――. "The Figure of Jesus in Matthew's Story: A Literary-Critical Probe." *Journal for the Study of the New Testament* 6 (1984) 3–36.
―――. "Review of 'Critical and Exegetical Commentary on the Gospel according to Saint Matthew.'" *Journal of Biblical Literature* 110 (1991) 344–46.
Klassen, William. *Judas: Betrayer or Friend of Jesus?* Minneapolis, MN: Fortress, 1996.
Kline, Leslie. "Redaction Criticism of the Gospels." *Restoration Quarterly* 10 (1967) 177–84.
Kloppenborg, John S. *The Tenants in the Vineyard: Ideology, Economics, and Agrarian Conflict in Jewish Palestine*. Tübingen, Germany: Mohr Siebeck, 2006.
Köstenberger, Andreas J., and Scott R. Swain. *Father, Son and Spirit: The Trinity and John's Gospel*. Downers Grove, IL: InterVarsity, 2008.
Kozar, Joseph Vlcek. "Bad Boy Bad Boy What Are You Going to Do When They Come for You?: Matthew's Scenes of Judas' Betrayal of Jesus and Judas' Suicide." *Proceedings: Eastern Lakes Biblical Society and Midwest Society of Biblical Literature* 20 (2000) 1–15.
Kramer, Werner R. *Christ, Lord, Son of God*. Naperville, IL: A. R. Allenson, 1966.
Kreitzer, Larry Joseph. "Apotheosis of the Roman Emperor." *Biblical Archaeologist* 53 4 (1990) 211–17.
Kummel, Werner G. *Theology of the New Testament*. London: SCM, 1976.
Kuntz, J. Kenneth. "God and Earthly Power: An Old Testament Political Theology: Genesis-Kings." *Catholic Biblical Quarterly* 72 (2010) 353–54.
Lachmann, Karl. "De Ordine Narrationum Im Evangeliis Synoptics." *Theologische Studien und Kritiken* 8 (1835) 570–90.
Ladd, George Eldon. *A Theology of the New Testament*. Grand Rapids, MI: Eerdmans, 1993.

Lane, William L. *The Gospel of Mark*. Grand Rapids, MI: Eerdmans, 1974.
Larson, Jennifer L. *Greek Reroine Cults*. Madison, WI: University of Wisconsin Press, 1995.
Leim, Joshua E. "In the Glory of His Father: Intertextuality and the Apocalyptic Son of Man in the Gospel of Mark." *Journal of Theological Interpretation* 7 (2013) 213–32.
Levin, Yigal. "Jesus, 'Son of God' and 'Son of David': The 'Adoption' of Jesus into the Davidic Line." *Journal for the Study of the New Testament* 28 (2006) 415–42.
Licona, Michael. *The Resurrection of Jesus: A New Historiographical Approach*. Downers Grove, IL: InterVarsity, 2010.
Longenecker, Richard N., and Merrill C. Tenney, eds. *New Dimensions in New Testament Study*. Grand Rapids, MI: Zondervan, 1974.
Longman, Tremper, III. "Form Criticism, Recent Developments in Genre Theory, and the Evangelical." *Westminster Theological Journal* 47 (1985) 46–67.
Louw, J. P., and Eugene A. Nida. *Greek-English Lexicon of the New Testament: Based on Semantic Domains*. Swindon, UK: United Bible Societies, 1989.
Luz, Ulrich. "Das Geheimnismotiv Und Die Markinische Christologie." *Zeitschrift Für Die Neutestamentliche Wissenschaft Und Die Kunde Der älteren Kirche* 56 (1965) 9–30.
MacDonald, Deven K. "The Characterization of a False Disciple: Judas Iscariot in Mark's Gospel." *McMaster Journal of Theology and Ministry* 15 (2014) 119–35.
———. *The Son of God in Mark: With Special Reference to 15:39*. Acadia, Nova Scotia: Acadia University Press, 2011.
Mack, Burton L. *A Myth of Innocence*. Minneapolis, MN: Augsburg Fortress, 1998.
———. *Who Wrote the New Testament?: The Making of the Christian Myth*. New York: HarperOne, 2013.
Malbon, Elizabeth Struthers. *Hearing Mark: A Listener's Guide*. Harrisburg, PA: Trinity International, 2002.
———. *In the Company of Jesus: Characters in Mark's Gospel*. Louisville, KY: Westminster John Knox, 2000.
———. *Mark's Jesus: Characterization as Narrative Christology*. Waco, TX: Baylor University Press, 2009.
Malina, Bruce J., and Richard L. Rohrbaugh. *Social-Science Commentary on the Synoptic Gospels*. Minneapolis, MN: Fortress, 2003.
Mann, C. S. *Mark: A New Translation with Introduction and Commentary*. New York: Doubleday, 1986.
Marcus, Joel. *Mark 1–8*. Anchor Bible Commentary. New Haven, CT: Yale University Press, 2002.
———. *Mark 8–16*. Anchor Bible Commentary. New Haven, CT: Yale University Press, 2009.
———. *The Way of the Lord: Christological Exegesis of the Old Testament in the Gospel of Mark*. Louisville, KY: Westminster John Knox, 1992.
Marshall, Christopher D. *Faith as a Theme in Mark's Narrative*. Cambridge: Cambridge University Press, 1989.
Marxsen, Willi. *Mark the Evangelist: Studies on the Redaction History of the Gospel*. Nashville: Abingdon, 1969.
Matera, Frank J. "'He Saved Others; He Cannot Save Himself': A Literary Critical Perspective on Markan Miracles." *Interpretation* 47 (1993) 15–26.

———. *Passion Narratives and Gospel Theologies: Interpreting the Synoptics through Their Passion Stories*. New York: Paulist, 1986.
McGinley, Laurence J. "Form-Criticism of the Synoptic Healing Narratives." *Theological Studies* (1942) 203–30.
McGrath, James F. *John's Apologetic Christology: Legitimation and Development in Johannine Christology*. Society for New Testament Studies, Monograph Series 111. Cambridge: Cambridge University Press, 2004.
McKnight, Edgar V. "Form and Redaction Criticism." In *New Testament and Its Modern Interpreters*, 149–74. Philadelphia: Fortress, 1989.
McKnight, Edgar V. *What is Form Criticism?* Eugene, OR: Wipf & Stock, 1969.
McKnight, Edgar V., and Elizabeth S. Malbon, eds. *The New Literary Criticism and the New Testament*. Valley Forge, PA: Trinity Press International, 1994.
McLaren, James S. "Jews and the Imperial Cult: From Augustus to Domitian." *Journal for the Study of the New Testament* 27 (2005) 257–78.
Meagher, John Carney. "Die Form—Und Redaktionsungeschickliche Methoden: The Principle of Clumsiness and the Gospel of Mark." *Journal of the American Academy of Religion* 43 (1975) 459–72.
Meye, R. P. *Jesus and the Twelve: Discipleship and Revelation in Mark's Gospel*. Grand Rapids, MI: Eerdmans, 1968.
Mikalson, Jon D. *Ancient Greek Religion*. 2nd ed. Chichester, UK: Wiley-Blackwell, 2009.
Moloney, Francis J. "Constructing Jesus and the Son of Man." *Catholic Biblical Quarterly* 75 (2013) 719–38.
Momligliano, Arnaldo. "How Roman Emperors Became Gods." *The American Scholar* 55 (1986) 181–93.
Moo, Douglas J. *The Old Testament in the Gospel Passion Narratives*. Eugene, OR: Wipf & Stock, 2008.
Moritz, Thorsten. "Mark." *Theological Interpretation of the New Testament*, edited by Kevin J. Vanhoozer, Daniel J. Treier, and N. T. Wright, 39–49. Grand Rapids, MI: Baker Academic, 2008.
Moule, C. F. D. "On Defining the Messianic Secret in Mark." In *Jesus Und Paulus: Festschrift Für George Kümmel*, edited by E. E. Ellis and E. Grässer, 239–52. Göttingen, Germany: Vandenhoeck & Reprecht, 1975.
———. *The Origin of Christology*. Cambridge: Cambridge University Press, 1978.
Mowery, Robert L. "Son of God in Roman Imperial Titles and Matthew." *Biblica* 83 (2002) 100–110.
Myers, Ched. *Binding the Strong Man: A Political Reading of Mark's Story of Jesus*. Maryknoll, NY: Orbis, 2008.
Neill, Stephen, and N. T. Wright. *The Interpretation of the New Testament, 1861–1986*. New York: Oxford University Press, 1988.
Neusner, Jacob. *Why No Gospels in Talmudic Judaism?* Atlanta: Scholars Press, 1988.
Nock, A. D. "The Place of Religion: Rome in the Early Empire." In vol. 1 of *The Cambridge Ancient History*, edited by Stanley Arthur Cook, F. E. Adcock, and M. P. Charlesworth. Cambridge: Cambridge University Press, 1952.
Nolland, John. *Luke 1:1—9:20*. Word Biblical Commentary. Nashville: Thomas Nelson, 1989.
Novum Testamentum Graece (NA28). Nestle-Aland, 28th rev. ed. Stuttgart: German Bible Society, 2015.

Paffenroth, Kim. *Judas: Images of the Lost Disciple.* Louisville, KY: Westminster John Knox, 2001.

Parker, H. M. D. *Roman Legions.* Cambridge: W. Heffer and Sons, 1958.

Parry, Donald W., and Stephen D. Ricks. *Current Research and Technological Developments on the Dead Sea Scrolls: Conference on the Texts from the Judean Desert.* Leiden, Netherlands: Brill Academic, 1996.

Peabody, David Barrett. *Mark as Composer.* New Gospel Studies. Macon, GA: Mercer University Press, 1987.

Pennington, Jonathan T. *Reading the Gospels Wisely: A Narrative and Theological Introduction.* Grand Rapids, MI: Baker Academic, 2012.

Peppard, Michael. "The Eagle and the Dove: Roman Imperial Sonship and the Baptism of Jesus (Mark 1.9–11)." *New Testament Studies* 56 (2010) 431–51.

Perrin, Norman. "The Christology of Mark: A Study in Methodology." *The Journal of Religion* 51 (1971) 173–87.

———. "The Son of Man in the Synoptic Tradition." *Biblical Research* 13 (1968) 3–25.

———. *What Is Redaction Criticism?* Philadelphia: Fortress, 1981.

Petersen, Norman R. *Literary Criticism for New Testament Critics.* Eugene, OR: Wipf & Stock, 2008.

———. "Point of View in Mark." *Semeia* 12 (1978) 97–121.

Pleket, H. W. "An Aspect of the Emperor Cult: Imperial Mysteries." *The Harvard Theological Review* 58 (1965) 331–47.

Porter, Stanley. *Scrolls and the Scriptures: Qumran Fifty Years After.* New York: Continuum, 1997.

Porter, Stanley E. *The Messiah in the Old and New Testaments.* Grand Rapids, MI: Eerdmans, 2007.

Porter, Stanley E., and Dennis L. Stamps. *Rhetorical Criticism and the Bible.* Sheffield, UK: Sheffield Academic, 2002.

Porter, Stanley E., and David Tombs, eds. *Approaches to New Testament Study.* Sheffield, UK: Sheffield Academic, 1995.

Powell, Mark Allan. "Narrative Criticism: The Emergence of a Prominent Reading Strategy." In *Mark as Story: Retrospect and Prospect,* edited by Kelly R. Iverson and Christopher W. Skinner. Atlanta: Society of Biblical Literature, 2011.

———. *What Is Narrative Criticism?* Minneapolis, MN: Fortress, 1990.

Price, S. R. F. *Rituals and Power: The Roman Imperial Cult in Asia Minor.* Cambridge: Cambridge University Press, 1985.

Pryke, E. J. *Redactional Style in the Marcan Gospel: A Study of Syntax and Vocabulary as Guides to Redaction in Mark.* Cambridge: Cambridge University Press, 1978.

Rahlfs, Alfred, and Robert Hanhart, eds. *Septuaginta.* Peabody, MA: Deutsche Bibelgesellschaft, 2007.

Räisänen, Heikki. *Das "Messiasgeheimnis" Im Markusevnagelium.* Helsinki, Finland: Länsi-Suomi, 1976. http://www.antikvaari.fi/naytatuote.asp?id=1207114.

Resseguie, James. *Narrative Criticism of the New Testament: An Introduction.* Grand Rapids, MI: Baker Academic, 2005.

Rhoads, David. *Reading Mark: Engaging the Gospel.* Minneapolis, MN: Fortress, 2004.

Rhoads, David M., Joanna Dewey, and Donald M. Michie. *Mark as Story: An Introduction to the Narrative of a Gospel.* Minneapolis, MN: Fortress, 1999.

Richards, J. R. *Jesus, Son of God and Son of Man: A Marcan Study.* Cardiff, UK: Church in Wales Publications, 1974.

Riesner, Rainer. "Jesus as Preacher and Teacher." In *Jesus and the Oral Gospel Tradition*. London: T. & T. Clark, 2004.
Ross, Allen P. *A Commentary on the Psalms*. Kregel Exegetical Library. Grand Rapids, MI: Kregel Academic, 2011.
Ross, Stewart, and Alan Langford. *A Roman Centurion*. Vero Beach, FL: Rourke Enterprises, 1987.
Rüpke, Jörg. *A Companion to Roman Religion*. Hoboken, NJ: Wiley-Blackwell, 2007.
Ryken, Leland. *The New Testament in Literary Criticism*. New York: Frederick Ungar, 1981.
Sanders, E. P. *Jesus and Judaism*. Fortress, 1985.
———. *Paul*. New York: Oxford University Press, 1991.
———. *The Tendencies of the Synoptic Tradition*. Society for New Testament Studies, Monograph Series 9. Cambridge: Cambridge University Press, 1969.
Schmidt, Karl Ludwig. *Der Rahmen der Geschichte Jesu: literarkritische Untersuchungen zur ältesten Jesusüberlieferung*. Darmstadt, Germany: Wissenschaftliche Buchgesellschaft, 1964.
Schnackenburg, Rudolf. "'Das Evangelium' Im Versta¨ndnis Des Altesten Evangelisten." In *Orientierung an Jesus: Zur Theologie Der Synoptike*, edited by P. Hoffman, 309–24. Freiburg: Herder, 1973.
Schoeps, Hans. *Paul: The Theology of the Apostle in the Light of Jewish Religious History*. Philadelphia, PA: Westminster, 1961.
Schreiner, Thomas R. *New Testament Theology: Magnifying God in Christ*. Grand Rapids, MI: Baker Academic, 2008.
Schweitzer, Albert. *The Quest of the Historical Jesus*. Edited by John Bowden. Subsequent edition. Minneapolis, MN: Augsburg Fortress, 2001.
———. *Von Reimarus Zu Wrede. Eine Geschichte der Leben-Jesu-Forschung*. Tübingen, Germany: J. C. B. Mohr, 1906.
Schweizer, Eduard. *The Good News according to Mark*. Louisville, KY: Westminster John Knox, 1970.
Shiner, Whitney. "The Ambiguous Pronouncement of the Centurion and the Shrouding of Meaning in Mark." *Journal for the Study of the New Testament* 78 (2000) 3–22.
Shuler, Philip. "The Synoptic Gospels and the Problem of Genre." *Open Access Dissertations and Theses*, 1976. http://digitalcommons.mcmaster.ca/opendissertations/3045.
Shuler, Philip L. *A Genre for the Gospels: The Biographical Character of Matthew*. Minneapolis, MN: Fortress, 1982.
Skarsaune, Oskar. "From the Jewish Messiah to the Creeds of the Church." *Evangelical Review of Theology* 32 (2008) 224–37.
Smith, Julien. "The Construction of Identity in Mark 7:24–30: The Syrophoenician Woman and the Problem of Ethnicity." *Biblical Interpretation* 20 (2012) 458–81.
Snodgrass, K. "Recent Research on the Parable of the Wicked Tenants: An Assessment." *Bulletin for Biblical Research* 8 (n.d.) 187–216.
Soulen, Richard N., and R. Kendall Soulen. *Handbook of Biblical Criticism*. Louisville, KY: Westminster John Knox, 2001.
Stambaugh, John E., and David G. Rice. *Sources for the Study of Greek Religion*. Atlanta, GA: Society of Biblical Literature, 2000.
Stamps, Dennis L., and Stanley E. Porter. *The Rhetorical Interpretation of Scripture: Essays from the 1996 Malibu Conference*. Sheffield, UK: Sheffield Academic, 1999.

Stein, Robert H. *Mark*. Grand Rapids, MI: Baker Academic, 2008.

———. *The Method and Message of Jesus' Teachings*. Louisville, KY: Westminster John Knox, 1994.

———. *The Method and Message of Jesus' Teachings*. Rev. ed. Louisville, KY: Westminster John Knox, 1994.

———. *Studying the Synoptic Gospels: Origin and Interpretation*. Grand Rapids, MI: Baker Academic, 2001.

Strauss, Mark L. *Four Portraits, One Jesus: A Survey of Jesus and the Gospels*. Grand Rapids, MI: Zondervan, 2007.

Streeter, B. H. *The Four Gospels: A Study of Origins*. London: MacMillan, 1926.

Sweet, Louis Matthew. *Roman Emperor Worship*. Boston: Richard G. Badger, 1919.

Talbert, Charles H. *What Is a Gospel? The Genre of the Canonical Gospels*. Macon, GA: Mercer University Press, 1985.

Tannehill, Robert C. "The Gospel of Mark as Narrative Christology." *Semeia* 16 (1975) 57–95.

Tarn, W. W. *Hellenistic Civilization*. London: E. Arnold & Co., 1927.

Taylor, Joan E. "The Name 'Iskarioth' (Iscariot)." *Journal of Biblical Literature* 129 (2010) 367–83.

Taylor, Lily Ross. *The Divinity of the Roman Emperor*. Middletown, CT: American Philological Association, 1931.

Taylor, Vincent. *Formation of the Gospel Tradition*. London: MacMillan, 1933.

———. *The Gospel according to St. Mark*. London: MacMillan, 1966.

Telford, W. R. *The Theology of the Gospel of Mark*. Cambridge: Cambridge University Press, 1999.

Terrien, Samuel L. *The Psalms: Strophic Structure and Theological Commentary*. Eerdmans Critical Commentary. Grand Rapids, MI: Eerdmans, 2003.

Thatcher, Tom. "Jesus, Judas, and Peter: Character by Contrast in the Fourth Gospel." *Bibliotheca Sacra* 153 (1996) 435–48.

"The Gospel according to St. Mark by Rudolf Schnackenburg." LibraryThing. http://www.librarything.com/work/4190735.

The Gospels for All Christians: Rethinking the Gospel Audiences. Grand Rapids, MI: Eerdmans, 1998.

Theiselton, Anthony C. *The First Epistle to the Corinthians*. Grand Rapids, MI: Eerdmans, 2013.

Thielman, Frank. *Theology of New Testament*. Grand Rapids, MI: Zondervan, 2005.

Tuckett, C. M., ed. *Messianic Secret*. Philadelphia, PA: SPCK, 1983.

Ulansey, David. "Heavens Torn Open: Mark's Powerful Metaphor Explained." *Bible Review* 7 (1991) 32–37.

———. "The Heavenly Veil Torn: Mark's Cosmic Inclusio." *Journal of Biblical Literature* 110 (1991) 123–25.

Van Eck, Ernest. "Eschatology and Kingdom in Mark." In *Eschatology of the New Testament and Some Related Documents*, 64–90. Tübingen, Germany: Mohr Siebeck, 2011.

———. *Galilee and Jerusalem in Mark's Story of Jesus: A Narratological and Social Scientific Reading*. HTS Supplementum 7. Pretoria, South Africa: University of Pretoria, 1995.

———. "Mission, Identity and Ethics in Mark: Jesus, the Patron for Outsiders." *HTS Theological Studies* 69 (2013).

———. "A Sitz for the Gospel of Mark? A Critical Reaction to Bauckham's Theory on the Universality of the Gospels." *HTS Theological Studies* 56 4 (2000) 968–1003.
———. "The Tenants in the Vineyard (GThom 65/Mark 12:1–12) A Realistic and Social-Scientific Reading." *HTS Theological Studies* 63 (2007) 909–36.
Van Eck, Ernest, and Andries G. Van Aarde. "A Narratological Analysis of Mark 12:1–12: The Plot of the Gospel of Mark in a Nutshell." *HTS Theological Studies* 45 (1989) 778–800.
Vanhoozer, Kevin J., Daniel J. Treier, and N. T. Wright. *Theological Interpretation of the New Testament: A Book-By-Book Survey*. Grand Rapids, MI: Baker Academic, 2008.
Van Iersel, B. M. *Mark: A Reader-Response Commentary*. Journal for the Study of the New Testament. Supplement Series 164. Sheffield, UK: Sheffield Academic, 1998.
Van Iersel, B. M., and A. J. M. Linmans. "The Storm on the Lake, Mk 4:35–41 and Mt 8:18–27 in the Light of Form-Criticism, 'Redaktionsgeschichte' and Structural Analysis." In vol. 2 of *Miscellanea Neotestamentica*, edited by T. Baarda, A. F. J. Klijn, and W. C. van Unnik, 17–48. Leiden, Netherlands: Brill Academic, 1978.
Votaw, Clyde Weber. "The Gospels and Contemporary Biographies." *The American Journal of Theology* 19 (1915) 45–73.
Waetjen, Herman C. *A Reordering of Power: A Sociopolitical Reading of Mark's Gospel*. Minneapolis, MN: Fortress, 1989.
Wallace, Daniel. *Greek Grammar beyond Basics*. Grand Rapids, MI: Zondervan, 1997.
Walsh, Jerome T. *Style and Structure in Biblical Hebrew Narrative*. Collegeville, MI: Liturgical, 2001.
Wansbrough, Henry. *Jesus and the Oral Gospel Tradition*. Journal for the Study of the New Testament. Supplement Series 64. Sheffield, UK: JSOT, 1991.
Wasserman, Tommy. "The 'Son of God' Was In the Beginning (Mark 1:1)." *The Journal of Theological Studies* 62 (2011) 20–50.
Watson, Duane Frederick, ed. *Persuasive Artistry Studies in New Testament: Studies in New Testament Rhetoric in Honor of George A. Kennedy*. Sheffield, UK: Sheffield Academic, 1991.
Watson, Francis. "The Social Function of Mark's Secrecy Theme." *Journal for the Study of the New Testament* 24 (1985) 49–69.
Watson, G. R. *The Roman Soldier: Aspects of Greek and Roman Life*. London: Thames & Hudson Ltd., 1969.
Watts, Rikki E. *Isaiah's New Exodus in Mark*. Grand Rapids, MI: Baker Academic, 2001.
———. "Mark." Edited by D. A. Carson and G. K. Beale. *Commentary on the New Testament Use of the Old Testament*. Grand Rapids, MI: Baker Academic, 2007.
Weeden, Theodore J. "The Heresy that Necessitated Mark's Gospel." *Zeitschrift Für Die Neutestamentliche Wissenschaft Und Kunde Der Älteren Kirche* 59 (1968) 145–58.
Weinstock, Stefan. *Divus Julius*. Oxford: Clarendon, 1971.
Weisse, Christian Hermann. *Die evangelische geschichte, kritisch und philosophisch bearbeitet*. Leipzig, Germany: Breitkopf und Hartel, 1838.
Wenham, John. *Redating Matthew, Mark and Luke: A Fresh Assault on the Synoptic Problem*. Downers Grove, IL: InterVarsity, 1992.
Wills, Lawrence M. *The Quest of the Historical Gospel: Mark, John and the Origins of the Gospel Genre*. London: Routledge, 1997.
Winn, Adam. *The Purpose of Mark's Gospel: An Early Christian Response to Roman Imperial Propaganda*. Tübingen, Germany: Mohr Siebeck, 2008.

Wise, Michael Owen. *The First Messiah: Investigating the Savior before Jesus.* San Francisco, CA: Harper, 2007.

Witherington, Ben. *The Gospel of Mark: A Socio-Rhetorical Commentary.* Grand Rapids, MI: Eerdmans, 2001.

Wolters, Al. "The Messiah in the Qumran Documents." In *The Messiah in the Old and New Testaments,* edited by Stanley E. Porter, 75–89. Grand Rapids, MI: Eerdmans, 2007.

Worthington, Ian. *Alexander the Great: A Reader.* London: Routledge, 2003.

Wrede, William. *Das Messiasgeheimnis in Den Evangelien: Zugleich Ein Beitrag Zum Verständnis Des Markusevangeliums.* Gottingen, 1901.

———. *The Messianic Secret.* Cambridge: James Clarke & Co., 1971.

Wright, N. T. *Jesus and the Victory of God.* Minneapolis, MN: Fortress, 1996.

———. *The Resurrection of the Son of God.* Minneapolis, MN: Fortress, 2003.

Wright, William M., IV. "Greco-Roman Character Typing and the Presentation of Judas in the Fourth Gospel." *Catholic Biblical Quarterly* 71 (2009) 544–59.

Young, George W. *Subversive Symmetry: Exploring the Fantastic in Mark 6:45–56.* Leiden, Netherlands: Brill Academic, 1999.

Zetterholm, Magnus, ed. *The Messiah: In Early Judaism and Christianity.* Minneapolis, MN: Fortress, 2007.

Ancient Documents Index

OLD TESTAMENT/ HEBREW BIBLE

Genesis

1:28	102
2:19–20	102
3:14–20	102
6:1–4	103
6:2	52
14:18	107
14:19	107
14:20	107
14:22	107
22:2	76, 99
22:12	76, 99
22:16	76

Exodus

2:11	95
3:1	101
4:22	76, 102, 103
23:20	89, 90
24:16	117
27:16	130

Numbers

21:4–9	101

Deuteronomy

3:25	52
8:15	101

Judges

18:31	95

2 Samuel

4:10	88
7:14	52, 53
7	78
18:20–22	88

1 Kings

1:42	88
17:18	105
19:1–8	102
19:4–6	101

2 Kings

1:8	94

1 Chronicles

17:13–14	53
22:10	53

Ezra

2:28	53
7	53
13	53
14	53

Job

1:6	52

Psalms

2	52–53, 78
2:2	52
2:7	52, 98–99
22:1	129
22:6	129
22:7	129
22:8	129
22:18	129
38:11	129
40:9	88
45	52
68:11	88
69:1	129
89:26–27	52
96:2	88
110	127
118:22–23	119

Isaiah

5:1–7	118
5:1	119
11:1	121
11:4	53
40:3	89–90, 98
41:27	88
42:1	99
52:7	88
56:3	107
63	102

Jeremiah

6:26	76
8:42	76
9:38	76
20:15	88
23:5	121
31:33	95
33:15	121

Daniel

3:35	52
7	53
7:13–14	127

Hosea

11:1	52, 72

Joel

3:1	95

Amos

8:10	76

Zechariah

3:8	121
6:12	121
13:4	94

Malachi

2:7	90
2:10	76
3:1	89–90
4:5	94

APOCRYPHA

2 Esdras

	121

4 Esdras

2:8	53

Psalms of Solomon

17:21	121

Wisdom of Solomon

2:13	53
2:16	53
2:18	53

Sirach

4:10	53

NEW TESTAMENT

Matthew

1:18–25	74
2:15	72
3:13–17	74
4:1	27
4:1–11	74
8:26	27
8:27	27
11:25–27	72, 78
11:27	73
12:46—13:58	24
14:28–31	11
14:33	152
16:6	151
16:16	72
16:13–23	72
16:22–23	74
16:32—20:34	24
19:13–15	25
19:20	27
26:39–42	74
27:28	129

Mark

1:1–15	81, 89, 138, 142
1:1	10, 13, 19, 81, 83–86, 88–90, 93, 97–98, 109–10, 115, 128, 133, 138, 142–43, 145–47, 151, 154, 166, 173
1:2	74, 90–91, 93, 95, 99, 110
1:3	91, 93, 98, 101, 109
1:4	94, 101, 114, 143
1:7–8	94
1:8	96, 97, 103, 143
1:8	109
1:9	95
1:10	94, 96, 143
1:11–13	1, 81, 94–100, 103, 106, 109, 111, 119, 131, 143, 145–46, 148
1:12–13	74, 81
1:12	96
1:13	101–2, 143
1:14	81, 114, 150
1:15	81
1:16–20	81, 103, 111
1:21–28	81, 106, 111
1:22	74, 103, 105, 111, 147, 150
1:23	14, 106
1:24	1, 14, 103–4, 128, 149, 150, 157, 166
1:25	104
1:27	8, 13–14, 105, 147
1:28	8, 13–14, 110, 147
1:29	104
1:32	8, 14
1:34	14, 110
1:38	104
1:34	106
1:40–45	81
1:41	110
1:45	147
1:49	77
2:1–12	74, 81, 110
2:2	8, 13–14, 147
2:6	148, 159
2:7	110, 147, 148
2:8	109
2:10	127
2:12	8, 13–14, 147, 148, 109, 139, 159
2:16	109, 139, 159
2:18	139
2:19	109
2:15–17	81, 104
2:19–20	113
2:22–26	74
2:24	139
2:28	127

Mark *(continued)*

3:1–6	74, 149
3:2	81, 149
3:5	113
3:6	81, 113, 139, 149, 157–58
3:7	8, 13
3:11	1, 100, 105–7, 111, 128, 131, 149–50, 166, 173
3:12	7, 109
3:13	74
3:17–22	33
3:18	77
3:19	120, 150, 162–64
3:20–21	113, 149, 151
3:22	113, 159
3:23–28	106
3:24	109
3:27	106
3:29	150
3:31–35	113
4:1	8, 13
4:11	7
4:13	113
4:34	7, 113
4:40	113
4:41	27
4:45–41	82
5:1–20	112
5:5	106–7
5:7	1, 104, 106, 107–8, 128, 132, 166, 173
5:13	107
5:21–43	112
5:25	77
5:33	106
5:27	164
5:42	33
6:1–6	151
6:6	113, 151
6:13	106
6:14–15	114
6:15	114
6:16	114
6:30–44	112
6:52	151–52
6:53–56	112
7:1	139, 159
7:3	139
7:5–7	151
7:5	139, 159
7:10	151
7:11	33
7:17–23	7
7:18	113, 151
7:25	106
7:31–37	74, 112
7:31	113
8:1–10	112
8:11	139
8:12	151
8:15	139
8:17	151
8:21	151
8:22–26	74, 113
8:22	113
8:23	113
8:26	113
8:27–30	24, 114–15
8:27	82, 151–63
8:28	114, 154
8:29	10, 114, 151
8:31	7, 75, 115–16, 120, 127, 130, 153, 159
8:33	115, 153–56
8:34	115, 135
8:38	123, 154
9:1	83
9:2–10	116–18
9:4	154
9:5	117
9:6	117
9:7	1, 19, 99, 116, 119, 128, 132–33, 154–56, 166, 173
9:9	11, 75, 127
9:12	127
9:14–29	106
9:22	157
9:28	7, 168
9:30–37	82, 156
9:31	7, 127, 130
9:38	106
9:41	10, 115
9:42–49	156
10:2	139
10:13–16	25
10:14	156

10:17–31	156	14:32–42	123–24
10:32–34	7, 82, 156	14:36	1, 33, 122–25, 128
10:33	127, 159	14:43–51	82, 123
10:45	104	14:44	163
10:45–52	33, 113, 127	14:53—15:15	82
11:1–11	82	14:53	125
11:9	120	14:54–55	125
11:12–17	82, 156	14:61	10, 115, 125, 128
11:18	156–157	14:62	128
11:25	122, 146	14:71	169
11:27	77, 120, 157	15:2	130
11:28	118–19, 156	15:10	165
11:30	119	15:13	165
11:33	119	15:16–20	165–168
12:1–11	69, 118–20, 157, 173	15:18–20	134
12:1	1, 120, 128	15:18	130
12:2	1, 128	15:19	129
12:6	99	15:20	129
12:7	118	15:22	33
12:12	118	15:29	13, 129, 131, 133, 166, 170
12:13–17	157, 160, 163–64	15:30	166
12:13	120, 139, 157	15:31	130
12:14	158	15:32	10, 115
12:18–27	158	15:38–39	82
12:28–34	159, 164	15:38	96
12:28	120	15:39	1, 13, 19, 85, 128–36, 138, 145, 152, 166–69, 171, 173
12:32	160		
12:34	160	15:40	129
12:35	10, 115, 120, 128, 132	16:1–4	82
12:41–44	160	16:6	82
13:2	13, 161	16:7	165
13:3	7	16:8	82
13:14	122		
13:21–22	115	Luke	
13:21	10		
13:25	122	1:5—2:52	75
13:26	171	1:8–25	75
13:27	122, 171	1:26–35	74–75
13:32	1, 121–23, 128, 166	1:27	75
14:1–2	123, 161	1:32	75
14:3–9	123, 161	1:35	75
14:10–11	123, 162	1:69	75
14:12–26	82	2:4	75
14:18	162	2:11	75
14:21	127	2:49	75
14:22–25	123, 162	3:31	75
14:27–31	82, 123, 162, 164	3:38	75
14:30	75	4:1	27

Luke (continued)

4:3	75
4:9	75
4:16–30	75
4:25–27	75
4:31–41	76
4:41	75
5:1–11	11
5:12–16	76
7:1–10	76
7:40	75
7:48	76
8:19–56	24
8:25	27
8:26–29	76
8:40–56	76
8:49	75
9:18–20	24, 72, 151
9:35	75
9:37–43	76
9:38	75
10:21–22	72, 78
10:25	75
11:45	75
12:13	75
18:15–43	24
18:15–17	25
18:18	75
18:21	27
18:38–39	75
19:39	75
20:21	75
20:28	75
20:39	75
21:7	75
22:11	75

John

1:14	76
1:18	76
3:16	76, 99
5:25	76
10:36	76
11:4	76
11:27	76–77
15:23–24	77
19:7	76
20:31	76–77
21:1–8	11
21:7	11

Acts

1	13
1:2	13
1:9–12	11
1:10	13
2:36	7
9:20	68

Romans

1:1	88
1:3–4	70
1:3	68
1:4	7, 68
1:9	68, 88
1:15–16	88
2:16	88
5:10	69–70
5:12–21	103
8:3	68–70
8:29	68
8:32	68–70
10:16	88
11:28	88
15:16	88
15:19–20	88
16:25	88

1 Corinthians

1:2	31
1:7	88
1:9	68
4:15	88
9:5	31
9:12	88
9:14	88
9:16	88
9:18	88
9:23	88
15:1	70, 88
15:3–5	88
15:28	68, 70

16:3	31	2.5.11	59
		2.7.2	59

2 Corinthians

Arrian, *Anab*

1:19	70		
8:9	70–71	4.11	60
		VII.23.2	53

Galatians

Athenaeus, *Deipn.*

1:15	68		
1:16	70	XII.537–38	60
2:20	69		
4:4–5	69	

Dio Cassius, *Hist. rom*

Philippians

		LIX.2,4	66
2:6–11	7, 70		

Homer, *Il*

1 Thessalonians

		14.319	57
1:9–10	70		
2:14	31	

Ovid, *Metam.*

5.149–99	58
5.1–238	58

2 Peter

1: 17–21	11

Philo, *Eternity*

XL	66

DEAD SEA SCROLLS

Philo, *Moses*

4QpGen	55		
4Q174	55	2:128	130
4Q246	54–56		
4Q252	55	

Plutarch, *Alex*

3.5–9	59
2	60

GRECO-ROMAN WRITINGS

Strabo, *Geogr*

17.1.43	59

Apollodorus

2.4.1	59

www.ingramcontent.com/pod-product-compliance
Lightning Source LLC
Chambersburg PA
CBHW070255230426
43664CB00014B/2541